The Deming Guide to Quality and Competitive Position

Howard S. Gitlow

*Professor of Statistics and Management,
School of Business Administration,
University of Miami
Consultant in Deming Methods*

Shelly J. Gitlow

*Vice President and Management Consultant,
Miami Consulting Group, Inc.*

PRENTICE-HALL, INC.
Englewood Cliffs, New Jersey 07632

n Data

etitive

1. Deming, W. Edwards (William Edwards),
1900–   —Contributions in management.   2. Management.
3. Quality of products.   I. Gitlow Shelly J.,
1950–   II. Title.
HD38.D439G58 1987   658   86–18762
ISBN   0-13-198441-1

Editorial/production supervision and
  interior design: Richard Woods
Cover design: Lundgren Graphics Ltd.
Manufacturing buyer: Carol Bystrom

Printed in the United States of America

20 19 18 17 16 15 14 13 12

ISBN   0-13-198441-1   025

PRENTICE-HALL INTERNATIONAL (UK) LIMITED, *London*
PRENTICE-HALL OF AUSTRALIA PTY. LIMITED, *Sydney*
PRENTICE-HALL CANADA INC., *Toronto*
PRENTICE-HALL HISPANOAMERICANA, S.A., *Mexico*
PRENTICE-HALL OF INDIA PRIVATE LIMITED, *New Delhi*
PRENTICE-HALL OF JAPAN, INC., *Tokyo*
PRENTICE-HALL OF SOUTHEAST ASIA PTE. LTD., *Singapore*
EDITORA PRENTICE-HALL DO BRASIL, LTDA., *Rio de Janeiro*

*To our grandparents, parents,
and Ali—the next generation*

Contents

Foreword

Many people are ready to renounce the fallacies of the style of management that has grown up and taken root in the Western world, and to learn ways that will improve our export position and provide jobs and more jobs. Study of daily reports on production, sales, inventory, complaints of customers, costs of warranty, and annual reports on people, are not the kind of management that will halt the decline of our balance of trade. Business on price tag, with short-term contracts, is the wrong way. The fallacy of zero defects and the supposition that it will suffice to meet specifications cause severe loss.

There are better ways, and they are no secret. Japanese top management learned better beginning in 1950.

The Gitlows' book explains their understanding of the Deming method, which must replace legacies of the past. This book will be helpful to readers who wish to understand the need for change, and what must change.

W. Edwards Deming
Washington

ACKNOWLEDGMENTS

The authors gratefully acknowledge Dr. W. Edwards Deming, whose philosophy and guidance have had a profound impact on our lives.

We thank William W. Scherkenbach (Director of Statistical Methods, Ford Motor Company), W. J. Fabrycky (Virginia Polytechnic Institute and State University), and Joseph H. Mize (Garrett Turbine Engine Company).

Introduction

THE PARABLE OF THE CREAMIANS AND APAJEENS

Once upon a time there was a group of people who lived on an idyllic island. They were known as the Creamians, which loosely translates as "lucky ones." The Creamians prospered; the trees on their island were bountiful; their surrounding waters were abundant with fish. They were easily able to feed their population and also to export their products to a neighboring island that was not so plentiful. The inhabitants of the second island were known as the Apajeens or "those who must work smarter."

One day when the chief of the Creamians went to negotiate with the chief of the Apajeens, he realized that the Apajeen people were decreasing their order for Creamian products. He wondered why. The Apajeen chief told him that his people were "working smarter" and soon would not need any help from the Creamians. The Creamian chief was impressed and amazed. He wondered how this could be, considering that the Apajeen island had none of the natural resources that Creamia had. Actually, as he recalled, Apajee was barren when it was settled. The Creamian chief did not understand this "working smarter" routine, so he departed Apajee assuming that next time the Apajeens' order would have to be larger.

For days the Creamian chief pondered this notion of "working smarter," because secretly the chief had always worried about his own island and his people. He knew that some day his island's easy abundance would run out, and then what? Several times he had tried to organize his people to try and teach them how to plant and how to navigate. Each time the response was the same. "We don't need to learn these things; we are lucky and have trees and waters that are bountiful." Each time the chief accepted this answer because he didn't know what else he could say.

However, this "working smarter" idea kept nagging at the chief. He finally called his people together and again said that he wanted to teach them how to plant and navigate. Again they replied, "We don't need to

2

learn these things; we are lucky." This time the chief said, "The Apajeens are 'working smarter' and they don't need so many of our products anymore." For several minutes there was silence. Many of the Creamians looked at each other, but they didn't understand the chief's point. The chief explained, "I think we need to learn how to 'work smarter' in case our trees and waters no longer provide for us." The Creamians laughed hysterically. They even joked that maybe the chief had lost his mind or was spending too much time with those crazy Apajeens. So the chief finally dismissed his people and tried to forget the "working smarter" issue.

The next time the Creamian chief went to Apajee he was told the Apajeens did not need anything anymore. As a matter of fact, they had begun to export their products to the people of other islands. The Apajeen chief reported that he had even heard that Apajee was now considered more prosperous than Creamia by other islanders. The Creamian chief was happy for the Apajeens, but he despaired for his own people. He could see that the Apajeen people were happy and had a great deal of pride in their work. They shared and worked together to achieve their goals. His people, on the other hand, were bored and only did what had to get done each day. They fought with each other over their resources and had no common purpose.

As the Creamian chief was leaving Apajee, the Apajeen chief called out, "Oh, by the way, we hear that a terrible storm is about to strike our islands." On his way home, the chief noticed that the normally calm waters were very rough and that the wind was very powerful. He thought that the Apajeen chief was right and that he should warn his people, so they could prepare for the storm. When the chief arrived at Creamia, he told his people of the coming storm. They prepared as best they could, but after the storm their island was barren, their boats were sunk, and several islanders had died.

When calm returned, those islanders who remained tried to find some fish to eat. Unfortunately, the waters surrounding their island were no longer alive with fish. The Creamians asked the chief what they could do, and he said he didn't know what they were going to do, but he was going to Apajee where he hoped they would accept him and he could learn to "work smarter." The people laughed and said that Apajee was probably just as barren as their island now. The chief agreed with them but he began building a raft out of driftwood anyway.

THE PLIGHT OF AMERICAN INDUSTRY TODAY

In retrospect, that Creamian chief was quite a clever guy. He realized that he was entering a new era and that he had to adapt to it by learning new ways. He knew that he had to change his philosophy and his overall way of thinking about people and how they should work.

It's a tragic fact of American life today that American management has not been as clever as that old Creamian chief. Many leaders of U.S. industry have not had the foresight to recognize that we have entered a new economic age and that a different philosophy and corporate culture are needed.

The story of the Creamians and Apajeens dramatizes the plight of a people whose natural resources were abundant. They prospered, almost in spite of themselves, without ever learning how to work together and achieve common goals. This was contrasted with a group of people who, with no natural resources, were able to work together to produce and achieve common goals and eventually surpass the group with all the resources.

This scenario is all too familiar to us. American industry, once the most productive in the world, has now taken a back seat to Japanese industry and cannot produce quality goods and compete in the marketplace. Why? American management is adrift at sea without a rudder or a sail. It doesn't know how to get back on course. It may not even realize that it is off course. U.S. industry doesn't know how to regain its competitive position. What's the solution? American management must realize that we are all in a new economic age, one dominated by the production of quality goods and services at a low price rather than mass production of lower-quality products. If American managers are to steer their corporate ships, they need to transform their style of management. In this new economic age, the old management rules no longer apply. It is time for corporate America to swallow some hard medicine. It must recognize that it is sick and must seek treatment or perhaps become terminally ill and die, while other countries grow stronger and prosper.

Examples of the problems of American industry bombard us daily. We read about Japanese competition destroying the U.S. car industry, labor-management problems creating strikes, bankruptcies in the airline industry, massive lay-offs, and the concern over the quality of American goods. But more important, we accept poor quality as a way of life. We work in companies, service organizations, and governments that we know are not producing quality goods and services. This creates stress for us as managers and as workers because we know we could be doing better. This stress leads to problems on the job and personal problems such as drug and alcohol abuse or family strife. In other words, the effect of poor management is creeping into our lives and is pervasive in our culture.

If we still haven't convinced you that we have a problem, perhaps pondering the following questions will lead you to our contention that we are in deep trouble:

1. How many presidents (top administrators) has your company had in the last ten years?

    If your answer is more than one, there is cause for concern because your organization probably has not maintained a constancy of purpose. Think about the changes that have occurred each time a new chief executive took over. Chances are that the goals and day-to-day life of the organization have changed. This has impacted tremendously on management, employees, customers, vendors, and investors. It has left everyone wondering what the "new" corporation is all about and having to adapt to the new culture.

2. Does your organization have a mission statement that is known and lived by all its employees?

    If your answer is No, there is cause for concern because there probably is no consistency of goals among employees and departments. There is probably a great deal of confusion regarding policy and priorities on a continuing basis. This is not a healthy environment for productive work.

3. a. What is your organization doing to drive out fear?
   b. What is your organization doing to break down barriers between departments?

    If your answer is "Nothing" or "We don't have those problems," you are in serious trouble. Denying these problems will not make them disappear; they will only get worse and may become debilitating to your company. A comprehensive, ongoing effort must be made, starting at the top management level, to deal with these problems.

4. Do employees in your company have pride of workmanship?

    If your answer is "No, not anymore," we would ask, "What is being done to restore it?" If your answer is *yes*, you may be too far removed from the day-to-day problems and resulting negative feelings experienced by the worker. Employees are not inherently lazy and lacking in pride. They want to do a good job, but they can only do as good a job as their system allows.

We trust that you are now more aware of some of the problems that we face in corporate America. We all are part of these problems. Managers who manage in the absence of a philosophy, employees who are disenchanted, union officials who are unwilling to work with management— we all contribute to the problems; we are all a part of the problems. But, the good news is that we are all a part of the solution, too. The solution necessitates massive changes on the part of America's top managers, middle managers, workers, and unions. We must be willing to embark on a journey that will lead us to a new philosophy of management, one that will provide guidelines and a framework for action that will be consistent with the new philosophy. We invite you to join us on our "journey to quality."

HOW WE CAN GET BACK ON COURSE

Now that we have pointed out to you that we have a problem, you're wondering what you can do about it. Probably part of the reason you didn't want to acknowledge the problem in the first place was a fear of not being able to do anything about it; and let's face it, there are very few things that are worse than an unsolvable problem.

However, there is a navigational chart available to you that will get you back on course and guide you to your ultimate destination. Learning and living the management style of W. Edwards Deming will provide you with a holistic approach for management in which the organization is viewed as an integrated entity. It is a philosophical perspective from which a manager conducts the organization's business on a long-term basis, a perspective that also provides guidance for day-to-day action. This philosophy is driven by the force of quality and focuses on the never-ending improvement of all processes to improve quality. Dr. Deming's philosophy plans for the achievement of a desired goal (e.g., increase profits, increase customer satisfaction, increase employment, etc.), but it does not specify the goal to be achieved.

When Dr. Deming's philosophy is accepted and lived, you can improve the processes of your system, which will necessitate less rework and will produce more quality goods for less cost. Your unit cost will decrease, and you will gain greater price flexibility. With higher quality and greater price flexibility, you can capture the market. When you capture the market, your demand goes up, your profit goes up, and you create new and more secure jobs. You will have funds for improvement, research and development, and employees. You're probably reading this very skeptically and thinking, "Oh, this is another of those 'quick-fix' technique books that work well for a short period of time but don't hold up over the long haul." That couldn't be further from the truth. Unless you're interested in a long-term commitment to learning, growth, and change, you shouldn't attempt to adhere to the Deming philosophy.

Dr. Deming's philosophy is not problem solving, participative management, quality circles, just-in-time inventory, statistical quality control, lifetime employment, automation/robotics, or any other *technique* that can be learned in a one-day seminar or ingested in a two-hour reading. It is a total view and way of organizational life that must be learned, relearned, and refined over time in a supportive environment. Then and only then can the tremendous benefits be reaped by the organization and by those in the system.

WHO IS W. EDWARDS DEMING?

W. Edwards Deming is an internationally renowned consultant who is best known for his work in Japan, which revolutionized Japanese quality and productivity. Dr. Deming's philosophy and methods were largely responsible for the success of Japanese industry today.

In 1950, Dr. Deming was invited by the Union of Japanese Scientists and Engineers to speak to their leading industrialists who were concerned about breaking into foreign markets and about Japan's reputation for poor quality goods. Dr. Deming convinced them, despite their reservations, that Japanese quality could be the best in the world *if* they instituted his methods. The industrialists took Deming's philosophy to heart, and the rest is history.

Each year Japanese industry awards the coveted Deming prize to the company among them that has achieved the greatest gain in quality. The award ceremony is broadcast on national television; recipients have included Nissan, Toyota, Hitachi, and Nippon Steel. In 1985, Texas Instruments became the first U.S. company to win the Deming prize. Dr. Deming holds the Second Order Medal of the Sacred Treasure, which was bestowed on him by Emperor Hirohito, for contributions to Japan's economy.

The adoption of Dr. Deming's methods is finally spreading in the United States. Until recently, Dr. Deming has not received the attention in the United States that he has in Japan. Now, companies such as the Nashua Corporation, the Ford Motor Company, and the Pontiac Division of General Motors are listening to Dr. Deming and are trying to change their corporate cultures to reap the benefits.

Dr. Deming's clients have included railways, telephone companies, consumer researchers, hospitals, law firms, government agencies, and university research organizations. He has written extensively on statistics and is a professor emeritus at New York University Graduate School of Business Administration.

THE EXTENDED PROCESS

Organizations consist of manpower, methods, materials, and machines. These components make up the system and its process, within the organization. However, under the Deming philosophy, the company's process expands to include suppliers, customers, investors, and the community. This is known as the *extended process*. It starts with the needs of the consumer being communicated to the organization. The consumer is the most important element of the extended process because customer statisfaction is the ultimate goal. Unfortunately, purveyors of goods and services seem to have forgotten that. How many times have you waited in a store while a clerk talks on the telephone and ignores you? How many times have you had to spend your own time rectifying mistakes made by others which impact on the way you do business? Organizations are not paying attention to customers' needs. Under the Deming philosophy, firms perform consumer research to conceive and design their products. However, this research doesn't stop there. It is an ongoing process that determines how the products are performing and what new specifications would improve the customers' satisfaction.

At the other end of the extended process are the firm's suppliers. In order for the firm to produce quality products, it not only has to surpass the customers' specifications but it also has to communicate these needs to its suppliers. Suppliers then have to demonstrate that they are committed to providing materials that will enable the firm to surpass the customers' needs.

QUALITY

What this all leads up to is the capstone of the Deming philososphy—*quality*—which is achieved through the never-ending improvement of the extended process, for which management is responsible. There are three types of quality that managers must understand if they want to improve the extended process. These are: (1) quality of design/redesign, (2) quality of conformance, and (3) quality of performance. Quality of design begins with consumer research, sales analysis, and service call analysis, and leads to the determination of a prototype that meets the consumer's needs. In considering consumer's needs, it is critical that firms look years ahead to determine what will help customers in the future. Next, specifications are constructed for the prototype and are disseminated throughout the firm and back to the suppliers. Quality of conformance is the extent to which a firm and its suppliers are able to surpass the design specifications required to meet customers' needs. Quality of performance is the determination through research and sales/service call analysis of how the firm's products or services are actually performing in the marketplace. Quality of performance leads to quality of redesign, and so the cycle of never-ending improvement continues.

COMMON AND SPECIAL VARIATION

A process in a firm is like any other type of process—it varies. Consider a natural process or system such as your own appetite. Some days you are hungrier than you typically are, and some days you eat less than you usually do, and perhaps at different times. Your system varies from day to day, to some degree. This is *common variation*. However, if you go on a diet or become ill, you might drastically alter your eating habits for a time. This would be a *special variation* because it would have been caused by a change in the system. If you hadn't gone on a diet or become ill, your system would have continued on its former path of *common variation*.

Understanding the difference between common and special variation in a system is a critical element of the Deming philosophy. Management must realize that unless a change is made in the system (which only management can make), the system's process capability will remain the same. This capability will include the common variation that is inherent in any system. Workers should not be held accountable for or be penalized for common variation; it is beyond their control. Common variation could be caused by such things as poor lighting, lack of ongoing training, or poor product design. Special variation could be caused by new materials, a broken die, or a new operator. Workers can become involved in creating and utilizing statistical methods so that common and special variation can be differentiated and process improvements can be implemented. Since variation produces more defective and less uniform products, it is crucial that managers understand how to reduce and control variation. Understanding and controlling variation can lead to the total achievement of quality.

Managers must understand that there is no easy way to change the current situation. There can be no quick results because what is needed is a continuing cycle of improved methods of manufacturing, testing, consumer research, product redesign, etc. This view extends to include the company's vendors, customers, and investors. All must play a role in the continuing improvement of quality.

MANAGEMENT'S AND WORKER'S RESPONSIBILITIES

Managers have a monumental task before them. They must take responsibility for the process and must constantly seek to improve it. They have to stop blaming each other, the workers in the system, the suppliers, and the customers. Dr. Deming's philosophy necessitates a fundamental change in how organizations are viewed by the people who manage them and by those who work in them. This change will be a lot more palatable for the workers because, generally, workers are aware of many of the organization's problems and know that they are not the cause of the problems. Managers, on the other hand, must own up to their responsibility and must realize that the systems that they created and perpetuate cause approximately 85 percent of the problems. *NOTHING* can be done about these problems unless there is a change in the system. However, workers have a responsibility in the process, aside from performing their jobs. Their responsibility is to communicate to management the information they have regarding the system. Under the Deming philosophy this is possible because workers and management learn to speak the same language, *the language of statistics and process control.*

A true cooperative spirit flourishes in this type of environment. Team work is a prerequisite for the firm to function and to constantly improve the process. The corporate culture changes so that the workers are no longer afraid to point out problems in the system. Management is actively involved in the never-ending improvement of the process with the workers, and workers are afforded secure and economically rewarding jobs for their efforts. Management creates an atmosphere that encourages pride of workmanship and a belief in the process of never-ending improvement. This will eventually lead to higher quality, reduced costs, and greater profitability. However, those goals can only be reached by a slow, steady, real change in the organizational environment.

Management must make a total commitment to the change and must be willing to endure and deal with the workers' skepticism and doubts, as well as their own. These doubts have been built up over several years, in some cases, lifetimes, and are not easily dispelled. Total commitment and real change, over a period of time, will be evident to the employees, and they will start to trust the new atmosphere. Management will be tested many times. If the testing is handled properly, both management and workers will emerge with a strengthened commitment and a renewed sense of purpose.

THE FOURTEEN POINTS

Dr. Deming's methods incorporate the use of statistical tools and a monumental change in the corporate culture. Both are important to the successful implementation of his philosophy. Dr. Deming has outlined his methods for achieving quality and productivity in his "14 points for management."[1] The "14 points" together provide a framework for action and

---

[1] See W. Edwards Deming, *Quality, Productivity, and Competitive Position* (Cambridge, Mass.: M.I.T., Center for Advanced Engineering Study, 1982).

give management the basis on which to formulate a plan in the absence of experience with a particular issue. The acceptance and understanding of the "14 points" will lead to a commitment by management to change its thinking and behavior. To understand the "14 points," they must be viewed in the context of the new perspective presented rather than from the current viewpoint of American management. Many points are not intuitively obvious, and they appear radical to some.

This book will examine each of these points in depth and will provide practical examples and ideas on how to implement them. Although the points are presented separately and can create improvement individually, it is the synergistic implementation of all of the points that will transform an organization. We have a long and difficult journey before us, but with Dr. Deming as our navigator, we shall attempt to steer the ship back on its course toward quality.

1

Developing the Organization's Goals and Philosophy

CREATE CONSTANCY OF PURPOSE TOWARD IMPROVEMENT OF PRODUCT AND SERVICE WITH A PLAN TO BECOME COMPETITIVE, STAY IN BUSINESS, AND PROVIDE JOBS.

DISCUSSION OF POINT ONE

Old Short-Term View

American managers are stuck in day-to-day problems and crises of survival. They have become firefighters, dashing to solve the current most pressing problem. They are so embedded in this method of functioning that some do not even realize they can operate in another way. American management has traditionally been involved with the short run. Indicators of this are the daily production reports, quarterly dividends, quarterly performance appraisals, and job-hopping of management. All of these practices contribute to the overall problem we face: There is no long-term perspective and commitment in American organizations today.

Daily production reports create a "knee-jerk" reaction to common variation in the system. If you are constantly making decisions based on daily production reports, overall trends and special variation will never be spotted and quality will not improve. Actually, quality will decrease over the long run because inconsistency will result from a short-term view.

Striving to increase quarterly dividends to shareholders also contributes to American management's short-term view. Shareholders need to realize that this impedes functioning and improvement of quality as well as competitive position, and in the long run will cause the demise of the company.

Quarterly performance appraisals of management make no sense. Being reviewed every three months only reinforces a short-term view and discourages long-term commitment and perspective. Emphasis on short-term profits has led to shortsightedness and unifaceted thinking.

Frequent job-hopping by managers also demonstrates a conditioning to the short-term view. U.S. business schools and companies have reinforced this practice as a way of advancing one's career. In the short run, the individual probably does advance more rapidly. However, the costs to that individual, to his or her employees, to the companies, and to U.S. industry in general are staggering. These costs are not only monetary. People are affected by change, whether it is positive or negative. Change creates stress, which can lead to health problems, family problems, an inability to interact well with co-workers and supervisors, drug and alcohol problems, and performance problems. How can we cope with these long-term effects on the individual, family, company, U.S. industry, and American society?

New Long-Term Family View

The short-term view has not been successful; that is the bottom line. We have to do something else—we have to create and perpetuate constancy of purpose with a long-term view. Large organizations must begin to view themselves as families. Successful families endure and meet the physical and emotional needs of their members. They believe that they will exist for a long time to come and plan accordingly. Their members are united around common goals and are committed to each other.

Families that are struggling with meeting day-to-day needs, such as those on welfare or those with ongoing serious problems such as alcoholism or spouse abuse, are so absorbed in crises that they can't believe that there is another way to live. Their family style is one in which making it through the day is an achievement. These crisis-oriented families are no different than America's crisis-oriented organizations.

Successful families do much more than survive. They plan for the future and work toward a better life. They decide what they want and how to achieve it. For example, a family could decide that it wanted a larger home, or that the relationship between the parents and children needed to improve, or that it wanted to divide the family's chores differently. It could also plan more long-range objectives, such as saving money to send the children to college or for the parents' retirement. These successful families are no different from successful organizations. They meet today's needs and also plan for the future. They have a long-term perspective and believe that they will exist for a long time to come.

An important aspect of organizations viewing themselves as families is their commitment to their employees. If a company employs a policy of laying off workers during declines, the message is clear to all those workers who are laid off and also to those who are not: "We (the company) have no commitment to you as an employee; our commitment is to ourselves (management) and our shareholders." Imagine a similar scenario in a family. The finances are slim this particular Thanksgiving, so the family can only afford a small amount of food. If the family used a policy similar to the company policy above, the parents would tell two of their four children (probably the two younger ones) that they couldn't eat Thanksgiving dinner! It sounds absurd when you put it in that perspective, but that's exactly what is being done in American industry. For example,

> Greyhound Corp. forced 12,700 bus-line workers to take a 7.8% pay cut. But management's pay this year will jump between 7% and 10% from 1982's levels. The union was told pay cuts were necessary to compete. Management says Greyhound executive pay is below that of comparable companies.[1]

The results of management not giving employees a commitment to permanent employment and sending the message that management is not concerned with the well-being of the employee over the long-term are devastating. Trust and security are destroyed and are replaced by fear and anxiety. Employees who are fearful and anxious do not perform well, and these maladies are very contagious. They can completely demoralize a work force and can cripple the company's functioning.

In Japan, the "company" is viewed as the employees, not the physical assets, as in the United States. Therefore, more attention is paid to the well-being of employees as the most important aspect of achieving the organization's goals.

Stating Organizational Goals and a Philosophy

Another important aspect of organizations viewing themselves as families concerns organizational goals and a philosophy. Successful families not only meet everyday needs but they also plan for achievement of short-term and long-term goals, in line with their beliefs and values. All of the members of the family are aware of the beliefs, values, and goals, and the children are socialized into the family's philosophy as they grow. Having long-term goals makes decision making somewhat easier. If a family believes that education is important and that its long-term goal is for a child to pursue higher education, then the parents will forego buying a new car if their resources are needed to finance it. If a family has not thought about the education of its children and has no philosophy or unifying goals, the parents might decide to buy the new car and deplete their resources. Then if the child wants to go to college, the family could be thrown into a crisis.

Organizations also function better with a philosophy and unifying goals. Practical day-to-day decisions must be based on a consistent phi-

---

[1]*The Wall Street Journal* (Orlando, Florida), December 20, 1983.

losophy. There has to be a framework within which managers can operate; otherwise they can only respond to crises. Unifying goals help an organization through difficult times by providing a sense of purpose. A mission statement and operating philosophy are the written manifestations of an organization's unifying goals. The mission statement and operating philosophy must be lived and must be practiced by managers and employees. Stockholders, as well as customers and vendors, must also be aware of the company's unifying goals.

HOW POINT ONE RELATES TO THE OVERALL PHILOSOPHY

The Deming philosophy stresses a commitment to the never-ending improvement of quality. In order to make this commitment, a company must allocate resources for the innovation and redesign of products and services. If top management does not have a long-term perspective, these resources will not be allocated in a meaningful way. American companies must concern themselves with the problems of *today and tomorrow*. Management must have the view that the company will be in business in the future and must look toward innovation. Resources must also be made available for training, education, and research in order to improve quality.

A long-term perspective is an essential ingredient in never-ending improvement of the system, which replaces managerial overreaction to variation. This also leads to improved quality and management taking responsibility for the system. Part of this responsibility concerns the improvement of the company's competitive position and its ability to provide jobs for its employees.

Constancy of purpose provides a philosophy and a framework so that decisions can be made in a consistent manner. Managers under the Deming philosophy are concerned with the problems of today and tomorrow and inspire confidence with their long-term view of the company and its commitment to quality.

IDEAS FOR ACTION

Where We Are

Many companies have mission statements, goals, and operating philosophies. Unfortunately, these are all too often gathering dust on back shelves. They are lofty statements and vague generalities which have very little to do with the "real world" and do not guide the reader through the organizational maze. Sure, the first day on the job a new employee will be given the mission statement to read, along with several other papers, the most important of which will probably be the benefit forms. No one will discuss the mission statement then, or more importantly, when it should have been done—during the hiring procedure.

The process of (1) developing a mission statement, (2) making it a living document, and (3) socializing new employees to the mission statement is what is needed to begin the "journey to quality." If your company has a mission statement, the first thing that top management should do is to examine it. There probably is some good information there. However, you should bear in mind the following questions in assessing your statement and in rewriting it or in writing a mission statement from scratch.

Questions for Self-Examination

1. Does the statement reinforce the organization as something one should identify with and which deserves admiration from employees, customers, vendors, stockholders, and the community?
2. Does it provide a rallying point, uniting people so they feel satisfaction in working toward a common goal?
3. Does the mission statement focus on quality, continuous improvement, and customer satisfaction?
4. Does it stress the needs of employees with respect to their long-term value to the company as a critical resource?
5. Does the statement take a long-term view, committing the company to developing new products and services for the future, and putting resources into training, research, and education?
6. Does it take into account all those concerned with the company's ultimate survival, such as vendors, customers, stockholders, and employees?
7. Will company purposes, as established in the mission statement, remain constant despite changes in top management?

The above questions should help you organize your thinking about your firm's mission statement. The following sections should assist you in its development.

Developing a Mission Statement

The development of a mission statement is a long and arduous task. It should be spearheaded by top management, who has the responsibility for preparing it. However, there should be room for substantial input by employees, stockholders, lower-level management, vendors, customers, and the community. Once a statement is written, it should be analyzed, critiqued, and changed by those responsible for its preparation. The questions presented previously should serve as a guide in this process. When the mission statement is complete, it should be disseminated to management, employees, vendors, customers, and stockholders. These groups can then provide input for change. Remember, it may take years to develop a mission statement, and it is something that if used properly will be constantly under revision. In adopting the Deming philosophy, it is necessary to be patient and view all actions in the context of long-term change rather than a "quick fix."

Possible items for discussion in a mission statement include:

- Investors
- Customers
- Vendors
- Employees (hourly and salaried)
- Citizenship (community)
- Quality philosophy
- Distribution of profits
- Plans for growth
- Fields of interest (innovation, research, and development)
- Strategic mission and direction (long-term)
- Corporate relations
- Corporate objectives (long-term)

The following is an example of a mission statement that is congruent with the Deming philosophy:

XYZ ORGANIZATION
MISSION STATEMENT

The mission of the XYZ Organization is to continually improve the quality of our products and/or services to meet our customers' needs. This will be accomplished by creating an environment that encourages everyone in our extended process to cooperate in achieving that goal. It will allow us to increase productivity, better our competitive position in the marketplace, provide a reasonable return for our stockholders, insure our existence in the future, and provide stable employment.

Top management will lead this long-term effort by subscribing to and implementing the following 14 points:

1. Create constancy of purpose toward improvement of product and service, with a plan to improve competitive position and stay in business.
2. Adopt the new philosophy. We are in a new economic age. We can no longer live with commonly accepted levels of delays, mistakes, defective materials and defective workmanship.
3. Cease dependence on mass inspection. Require, instead, statistical evidence that quality is built in to eliminate the need for inspection on a mass basis.
4. End the practice of awarding business on the basis of price tag. Instead, depend on meaningful measures of quality, along with price.
5. Find problems. It is management's job to work continually on improving the system.
6. Institute modern methods of training on the job.
7. Institute modern methods of supervision.
8. Drive out fear so that everyone may work effectively for the company.
9. Break down barriers between departments.
10. Eliminate numerical goals, posters, and slogans that seek new levels of productivity without providing methods.
11. Eliminate work standards that prescribe numerical quotas.
12. Remove barriers that rob employees of their pride of workmanship.
13. Institute a vigorous program of education and retraining.
14. Create a structure which will push on the prior 13 points every day.

Critical factors involved in the XYZ Organization's operating philosophy are:

People.   We believe that the employees of XYZ are a valued and long-term resource. We will support and encourage employees' contributions and their personal growth. We believe that all employees are entitled to dignity, respect, recognition, proper training and supervision, and fair compensation. We will work cooperatively to establish a positive working environment in which:

- Teamwork is emphasized.
- Defect prevention replaces defect detection so we may move toward never-ending process improvement.
- Training is a continual process for all employees.

- Employees are encouraged to participate in the never-ending improvement of the process.
- Responsibility, authority and accountability are delegated as closely as possible to those performing the work. We believe that this will aid in creating an environment that will foster initiative, innovation, and risk-taking necessary to the employees' development.
- Vacancies are filled from within XYZ when appropriate talent is available, and it is consistent with the employee's long-range goals.
- An environment conducive to continuous job security for all employees will be provided. Employees should identify with and participate in the company through and beyond retirement.
- All necessary steps will be taken to provide a healthy and safe working environment for employees.
- Organizational goals and policies will be communicated regularly to employees to encourage their responsibility to communicate their ideas, opinions, questions, and concerns freely. Management will make every effort to respond.

Customers. We believe that customers' satisfaction with our products and services will determine our future existence, therefore:

- Our goal is to be recognized by our customers as an innovative, cost-effective, high-quality supplier. This requires thorough understanding of our customers' present and future needs.
- We will develop long-term relationships with customers. Employees will be encouraged to get involved with customers' needs. This involvement can improve the existing product, as well as stimulate the development of new products and technology.

Suppliers. We believe that suppliers are part of the XYZ commitment to never-ending improvement. We will establish long-term, trusting, and if appropriate, single-source relationships with our suppliers, and we will require statistical evidence of quality from them.

Community. XYZ Organization will make every effort to be a good corporate citizen of the community. We will:

- Conduct our business at all times in a fair, ethical and professional manner with customers, governments, suppliers, community neighbors, and the general public.

- Act as a positive influence in our community by encouraging employees to participate in local government and community affairs and by supporting community causes.
- Abide by all laws and regulations affecting our business and conduct active programs to insure compliance with anti-trust, health and safety, Equal Employment Opportunity and environmental laws and regulations.
- Improve community awareness of our operations.

Investors. We are committed to never-ending improvement of quality, and competitive position. We will strive to surpass our customers' needs, thereby succeeding as a company, insuring our existence in the long run, and providing shareholders with a reasonable return.

Planning. We advocate long-range planning. All short-term decisions will be consistent with long-term objectives. All people affected by the planning should be involved in it. It should take into account the long-range needs of employees, customers, suppliers, communities, and investors. Our commitment to the future must balance the needs of these five groups over the long term.

Making the Mission Statement a "Living" Document—Top Management's Tasks

Once a mission statement is formulated, it is management's task to make sure that it becomes a "living" document. Everyone in the organization must understand it and must integrate it into their day-to-day behavior. There must be consistency between what the mission statement says and what the company actually does. Management must provide the leadership and must act as a role model in this endeavor. It must be open to feedback which points out any discrepancies between its behavior and the mission statement. Management should be held accountable by employees, vendors, stockholders, customers, and the community for upholding the company's goals and philosophy as described in the mission statement. It must set an example of commitment to the principles, which will motivate others to join in that commitment.

As in a family where the parents must be the leaders in upholding the family philosophy and in guiding the family to its goals, top management must play the same role for the "corporate family." Lack of commitment or inconsistency will be noted very quickly, as any parent knows. If the lack of consistency can be communicated to the authority figure, and it is received by the authority as positive, then real communication can exist.

Making the Mission Statement a "Living" Document—
The Process of Positive Communication

For this positive interchange to take place, four elements must exist: (1) The manager has to communicate the desire to know when his or her behavior is at odds with the mission statement. An attitude that will encourage open expression of concerns on the part of workers, lower-level managers, vendors, customers, stockholders, and the community must be conveyed. (2) The manager has to act on the information received. Otherwise, people will begin to feel that they are wasting their time because of the lack of interest in their feedback. (3) The manager should reward and encourage feedback behavior. The feedback should never be held against an employee or a lower-level manager if it is given in an appropriate manner. (4) Employees have to be willing to take the risk of giving management feedback. They have to care enough about the organization and also have some basic trust in a new system that they don't know much about. This relates back to the first three elements necessary to open communication. If the attitude and actions of top management create the proper atmosphere, the employees will be much more willing to take the risk of giving feedback. This feedback and communication process is critical in the transformation of the organization. Management must realize this and must do everything it can to convey the importance of positive communication.

Making the Mission Statement a "Living" Document—
Tasks of Middle-Level and Lower-Level
Managers and Employees

An effective way of communicating to middle-level and lower-level managers and employees that top management intends that the mission statement be a "living" document is to have everyone write an interpretation of the statement. Departmental discussions can grow out of this, and input for revising the mission statement will emerge. Everyone, line workers included, needs to understand what the organization does and how it goes about doing it. Workers and lower-level and middle management will perceive this active role in company goals as a statement that the management is committed to constancy of purpose and is truly interested in their involvement in the process. It is this type of action on the part of management that begins to create an atmosphere of positive communication.

The hiring process is another area in which middle-level and lower-level managers can help make the mission statement a "living" document. A potential employee should be screened on his or her ability to perform the job. However, the candidate should also be assessed on his or her agreement with the company's mission statement. If a Personnel Department exists in the organization, these people are trained in the assessment of job applicants and should be thoroughly versed in the mission statement. They should be able to discuss it with potential employees and should be able to judge from their reactions, verbal and nonverbal, whether or not the applicants are in agreement with the company's philosophy. If there is no Personnel Department, this task will be carried out by lower-level and middle-level managers. If the applicant does not agree with the company's philosophy, there is no point in hiring him or her. Being qualified to perform a job is one important aspect of hiring someone; but if that person cannot become part of the company team, then efforts are worthless. It makes no sense to hire someone who will cause the company problems. It isn't fair to the company and its current employees, and it isn't fair to that person, who is being set up to be uncomfortable and fail.

Making the Mission Statement a "Living" Document— The Role of Stockholders and The Board of Directors

Stockholders should be aware of the company's mission so they can understand what the company is doing now and what it is planning for the future. It is the responsibility of top management to communicate the company's mission statement to shareholders.

The Board of Directors must be conversant in the organization's mission statement. In order to perform their tasks properly, they must have the long-term perspective afforded by a mission statement. Those Board members who are not aware of, or not in agreement with, the company's mission statement should be removed from the Board, if at all possible.

Socializing New Employees to the Mission Statement

New employees in our framework should be aware of the importance of the company's mission statement from the beginning. They already were exposed to it during the hiring process and have an initial commitment to it. It is now the organization's duty to formalize and strengthen this commitment through training and education. There must be an ongoing training program in the company's mission and operating philosophy.

Long-time employees can play a role in developing and carrying out this training. The Personnel Department can spearhead this effort by being given increased responsibility for training in this area and also for identifying those long-time employees who would be best suited to the job.

Retired employees could also play a part in the training effort, instead of being pensioned off and forgotten. Making use of long-time and retired employees is similar to a family in which older siblings and grandparents aid in socializing younger children into the family philosophy. This socializing effort can be an extremely rewarding and beneficial method for the organization and for all employees concerned.

POSSIBLE PITFALLS

Embarking on the "journey to quality" signals the beginning of a new era and a new spirit for an organization. Top management is infused with a spirit of change and growth, and this will filter down through the organization. However, the journey is also filled with possible pitfalls that must be overcome to succeed. We have encountered some that we will report here, but you will probably discover others in your journey.

Possible pitfalls include the following:

1. *Failure to plan for the problems of tomorrow.*

    It is not enough for management to plan and effectively deal with today's business problems. They must also be critically concerned about tomorrow's business problems. Management must continually plan for future developments in: customer needs and performance requirements, products and services, materials, methods, training and skills requirements, supervisory methods, costs of production and marketing, etc. Failure to plan for the problems of tomorrow can be deadly to an organization.

2. *Managerial zeal to complete the mission statement.*

    This will inevitably lead to the exclusion of input by certain groups or to the rushing of people. Remember, it is an extremely slow process, and that the process by which you come to the statement is extremely important also. The process of completing the mission statement says a great deal about how you are going to operate and communicates your intentions to others in the extended process.

3. *Behaving as if the mission statement is a fait accompli.*

    Being asked for your input into something that looks finished can certainly make anyone angry. If people are asked to contribute to the mission statement, they should be given a "working paper" and a clear message that it is not finished without their input and is open to change.

4. *Getting stuck in writing the mission statement.*

    Some managers or steering committees formed to write mission statements can become obsessed with the mission statement as an end in itself. They can become so bogged down in the actual writing of the company goals that they never use the statement. They never get past the sentence construction and actual wording of the document. Make sure there is at least one person involved in the writing of the mission statement who will keep it moving!

5. *Management's inability to prepare a mission statement.*

Even though the management in an organization may be creative and innovative, it may be unable to formulate a mission statement. This could be due to interpersonal problems between managers, resistance on the part of those who fear change, or the denial of problems on top management's part. If this is the case and somebody realizes it, help can be sought in the form of a consultant. A consultant can focus the group and can deal with the issues that have been paralyzing it. There is no shame in seeking help; at least you will get started.

6. *Thinking that the mission statement is cast in stone.*

Rigid adherence to a document only creates an inflexible system. Flexibility and adaptation are essential ingredients in our framework because we must deal creatively with the problems of today and tomorrow. Therefore, there must be room to change and grow. The company's goal statement should reflect this, or the organization will not be responsive to its vendors, customers, and others in the extended process.

7. *Forgetting the mission statement after it is written.*

This is a pitfall into which most organizations have fallen. Under the new framework, however, we cannot allow this to happen. As we discussed previously, everyone in the system has a role to play in making the mission statement a "living" document. Management must lead the way in remembering and living the company's mission.

8. *Believing that the mission statement will tell you how to behave in specific situations.*

A mission statement provides guidance and an overall picture of corporate philosophy. Although it may be of great help in making certain decisions, it is not constructed to be a guide for daily corporate living. A manager cannot become dependent on a mission statement in the absence of leadership skills. The administrator must know how to perform the tasks of a manager, incorporating the company's philosophy into these actions.

2

Understanding the Philosophy of Never-Ending Improvement

ADOPT THE NEW PHILOSOPHY. WE ARE IN A NEW ECONOMIC AGE. WE CAN NO LONGER LIVE WITH COMMONLY ACCEPTED LEVELS OF DELAYS, MISTAKES, DEFECTIVE MATERIALS, AND DEFECTIVE WORKMANSHIP.

DISCUSSION OF POINT TWO

Change is Needed

How many Americans still buy *only* American-made products? We would guess that there are very few, and that the number is dwindling as we write. What used to be an important element of our national pride—the quality of our goods and services—has become our national embarrassment. Foreign competitors have surpassed us by constantly improving their quality, while American quality has decreased. Dr. Deming states:

> We are in a new economic age. We can no longer live with commonly accepted levels of mistakes, defects, material not suited to the job, people on the job that do not know what the job is and are afraid to ask, handling damage, failure of management to understand their job, antiquated methods of training on the job, inadequate and ineffective supervision.
>
> Acceptance of defective materials, poor workmanship, and inattentive and sullen service as a way of life in America is a roadblock to better quality and productivity. We have learned to live in a world of mistakes and defective products as if they were necessary to life. It is time to adopt a new religion in America.[1]

Amen! We must adopt a new philosophy if we are going to regain our position in world markets. What we have been doing obviously has not been successful. We have to change or we will be left behind, watching others surpass us and wondering why they are succeeding. Perhaps we have already reached a low point, an abyss, and we are ready to embark on the long, agonizing process of change. The Japanese were at that point when Dr. Deming introduced his ideas to them. Japan was viewed as a

---

[1]W. Edwards Deming, *Quality, Productivity, and Competitive Position* (Cambridge, Mass.: M.I.T., Center for Advanced Engineering Study), p. 19.

purveyor of junk and "Made in Japan" was synonymous with low quality. The Japanese industrialists were ready to listen; they were open to change. Maybe top management in America is ready now. There are indications of this. Nashua, Ford, and Pontiac have recognized the need for a new philosophy and are involved in changing their corporations' goals to stress customer satisfaction and quality.

Customer Satisfaction

Customer satisfaction must become the focus of corporate thinking. Providing customers with goods and services that meet their expectations and needs at a price they are willing to pay is paramount. This can only be done by continually improving quality in a never-ending cycle. Corporations can no longer strive to increase profits by producing larger quantities of low-quality goods and services. This is a backward and illogical way to attack the problem. Under this philosophy, you lose customers because they are not satisfied with your low-quality products. You also have to charge higher prices for your low-quality goods because your costs to make low-quality or defective items are higher than those of a company producing very few defects and striving for never-ending improvement. Why would anyone buy a good or service that is of low quality and high price? This is the question we must ask in trying to understand the need for change.

Customers are not stupid or naive. They know what they want and what they expect to pay for a particular item or service. In fact, consumers are becoming much more aware of these issues through increased education and media attention. Consumers' motivation to get the most value for their dollars in the current economic climate has also contributed to this increased awareness. So, there is no way to fool the customer. Marketing quality products at a fair price is the only way to satisfy customers. If you satisfy customers, profits will increase in the long run; but don't forget, satisfying customers, *not* increasing profits, must be your primary goal. Remember, a price tag cannot be put upon the advantages of a satisfied customer extolling the virtues of your company's products or services.

Management's Misconception about Quality and Productivity

It is a common misconception among management that if you want to increase productivity, the only way to do so is to stress quantity and/or lower costs. We will demonstrate the fallacy in this thinking and show that if you want to increase productivity, the way to do it is by improving quality. Actually, through Dr. Deming's methods you can have it all. You will increase quality and productivity, lower unit costs, and cut prices. Your position in the marketplace will be strengthened, and you can feel secure that your company will exist for a long time to come. You will be able to provide stable employment and have the funds to innovate, train, educate, and please investors. Customers will be satisfied with your product, and employees will have pride in their work.

Since you're probably very doubtful of the above outcomes, let's demonstrate through example. Let's say the Universal Company produces 100 widgets per hour. However, out of these 100 units, 20 percent are defective. This has been the rate of production and the rate of defects, more or less, for the past ten years. All of a sudden, the Board of Directors demands that top management increase productivity by 20 percent. The directive goes out to the employees, who are told that instead of producing 100 widgets per hour, the company must produce 120. The employees, some of whom have been there for the past ten years, become fearful. They must meet the new demands, but they can't imagine how they will do it since they're already doing their best.

The employees react to the stress by cutting corners to meet the new quota. Since there has been nothing changed in the system—i.e., machines, incoming materials, and training—the total responsibility for producing more widgets falls on the employees. The employees try hard to please. They want to keep their jobs. They know that if they fail, they will be replaced. They become frustrated because they can't increase their rate of production, so they speed up and become careless. They don't tighten screws completely. They don't file parts smoothly. The pressure to raise productivity has created stress, frustration, and fear. It has also created a defect rate of 25 percent and has only increased production to 104 units, yielding 78 good widgets produced in an hour, less than the original 80. Management, out of its own frustration at not knowing what to do, continues to blame the workers, and even lays off a few. The workers' morale hits an all-time low, sick days reach a high, employees come to work high on alcohol and drugs, and conditions deteriorate.

This example demonstrates the old way of thinking about productivity and quality—that is, for productivity to increase, quality must suffer. Under the new philosophy, this isn't the case.

The New Way of Looking at Productivity and Quality

If quality improves, productivity increases. To increase productivity, management must stress quality not quantity. Let's look at another example to demonstrate the new way of looking at productivity and quality.

The Dynamic Factory produces 100 widgets per hour with 20 percent defective. Top management has been ordered by the Board of Directors to increase productivity by 20 percent. Top management of Dynamic, luckily, has just attended a seminar on Dr. Deming's philosophy. They do not panic; they do not transfer the responsibility for this productivity increase to the workers. They know that they are responsible, and they can accept that responsibility because they know how to handle the problem. They realize that Dynamic is making 20 percent defective products and thus 20 percent of the total cost is spent making bad units. If Dynamic's managers can improve the process, they can transfer resources from the production of defectives to the manufacture of additional good products. Management is able to improve the process by making some changes at no additional cost, so that only 10 percent of the output is defective.

The benefits that result are the following: (1) Productivity has risen. Dynamic now produces 10 percent more good units at the same cost. This creates an additional increase in productivity. (2) Quality has improved. Now, only 10 percent of the output is defective instead of 20 percent. (3) The cost per unit is also lower because the factory produces more units at the same cost. (4) The price can be cut accordingly. (5) Workers' morale goes up because they are not seen as the problem. They feel pride in the quality of their work and are motivated to communicate any problems in the system to management.

To sum this up, if you stress productivity, you will sacrifice quality and may even lower your output. Employee morale will plunge, costs will rise, customers will be unhappy, and stockholders will be concerned. On the other hand, stressing quality can give you all the desired results: less rework, greater productivity, low unit cost, price flexibility, competitive position, increased demand, larger profits, more jobs and more secure jobs. Customers get high quality at a low price, vendors get predictable long-term sources of business, and investors get profits. Everyone benefits and everyone shares in your success.

Some Thoughts on Defects

The new philosophy rejects commonly accepted levels of defects, rework, shoddy workmanship, and poor service. Consider the costs to your company for rework, waste, and redundancy, including costs for material, manpower, capital equipment, facility space, warranty, retesting, reinspection, shipping, customer dissatisfaction, schedule disruptions, and so on. These costs are staggering, and we can no longer tolerate this as "business as usual." Defects are not free. Somebody makes them and gets paid for doing so. If a substantial proportion of the work force corrects defects, then the company is paying to correct defects as well as to make them. If your process is in control and you are constantly striving to improve it, you won't be doing rework. (This will be discussed further in Chapter 5.)

A statement by management that defect rates should be 6 percent is an acceptance of the fact that 6 of every 100 items will be bad. This attitude has become pervasive in the American way of business. In Japan, they think about defects per million, so American acceptance sampling tables can't even be used!

> They're still laughing about this at IBM.
>
> Apparently the computer giant decided to have some parts manufactured in Japan as a trial project.
>
> In the specifications they set out that the limit of defective parts would be acceptable at three units per 10,000.
>
> When the delivery came in there was an accompanying letter.
>
> "We Japanese have hard time understanding North American business practices. But the three defective parts per 10,000 have been included and are wrapped separately. Hope this pleases."[2]

Managing for Success Instead of Failure

The above example certainly points out the ludicrous position to which American management has brought us. We manage for failure instead of success. Our attitude toward defects is one of *detection*—we expect them to be there. Therefore we assume that we will find them later on and hopefully can do something about them. In contrast, we should be involved in *defect prevention*, or making it right the first time. As we have shown, this is far more cost-effective and sound. Once we are in the position of defect prevention then we can work on never-ending improvement of the process, but it has to start with a positive, "Do it right the first time" attitude.

Another example of managing for failure is the writing of contracts. We create an arm's-length relationship between the buyer and the vendor so that it is easier to lay blame on each other. We concentrate on breach of contract clauses, which are, in essence, provisions for failure. To manage for success, the buyer and vendor should relate to each other as though they are part of the same company.[3] There should be minimal discussion of breach, and the focus should be on what needs to be done to succeed.

It is human nature for people to want to be a part of something that is successful and positive. If an organization adopts the new philosophy of

---

[2]*Toronto Sun*, April 25, 1983, p. 6.

[3]Organizations must comply with laws which govern their behavior.

constantly striving for the never-ending improvement of quality, filtered through with an attitude of managing for success, everyone will jump on the bandwagon. Employees, union officials, vendors, customers, and stockholders will want to become involved and will know that they are important to the process. This will help perpetuate the new attitude and will give impetus to the never-ending pursuit of quality.

HOW POINT TWO RELATES
TO THE OVERALL PHILOSOPHY

The foundation of the Deming philosophy is quality, its importance, how to improve it, and its benefits. Adopting the new philosophy is synonymous with adopting a "quality consciousness." This new "quality consciousness" is the backbone of an organization's mission statement, embodying it with spirit and direction. As stated earlier, a long-term perspective is required to implement this philosophy, but it should be a positive long-term perspective, in the context of managing for success, not failure.

The new attitude must be adopted if American business expects to regain its position in world markets. The new attitude is the key to creating a ripple effect in American business that will demand excellence and high quality in all products and services. The ripple effect can be seen in the example of the Ford Motor Company, which has already adopted the new philosophy and is implementing Dr. Deming's methods. Ford now requires its vendors to be trained in Dr. Deming's methods and to present statistical evidence of quality. Think of the profound impact! Hopefully, these vendors will not only improve their quality for Ford but also for all of their other customers. Eventually, everyone will be caught up in the journey for quality and never-ending improvement.

Adopting the new philosophy requires changing attitudes. This is difficult for many people because it involves moving from something that is known to something that is unknown. This creates mistrust, fear, and anxiety, particularly for people who are satisfied with the status quo. Top and middle managers probably have the most to fear. They have succeeded in the current systems and know how to negotiate them. They don't know what life in an organization that uses Dr. Deming's methods will be like and how they will fare. So, naturally they resist the change. During the transitional phase, when an organization moves from its current state to one that uses Dr. Deming's methods, knowing that the fourteen points comprise a navigational chart provides some security. This gives people who fear change a concrete sense of direction and may facilitate the altering of their views.

IDEAS FOR ACTION

Questions for Self-Examination

To help you assess where you stand on the quality issue, the following questions should be asked:

1. How do you define quality of your products and/or services?
2. Do your employees know what constitutes a quality job?
3. Do you push quantity to achieve productivity, instead of stressing quality?
4. How do you know whether you are pursuing quality?
5. What do you know about the problems of your customers in the use of your products/services?
6. Do your customers think that your products live up to their expectations?
7. How do your customers compare your products with those of competitors?
8. In relation to questions 5, 6, and 7, what information have you gathered and how?
9. Do you demand statistical evidence of quality from your vendors?
10. Do you work with vendors on improving their quality?

Raising quality consciousness involves changing attitudes, defining quality, removing barriers, and getting everyone involved. The following sections should assist you in the journey to never-ending improvement.

Changing Attitudes

If we are really serious about improving the quality of our goods and services in this country, we must make that attitude a prevailing force in everything we do. We have to stop being complacent and stop accepting shoddy goods and poor service. As consumers we can certainly do this, and probably do to some extent. You've probably written at least one letter or made at least one complaint regarding poor quality. It's frustrating to be on the receiving end of poor quality, that's for sure. Therefore we all have to work together toward changing the attitude that allows poor quality to exist. We all have to express our intolerance of poor quality and change our currently held attitudes.

Within organizations, top management must lead the way. Managers have to demonstrate a long-term commitment to improving quality in everything, from what is produced on the factory floor to relationships with customers and vendors. Management has to realize that continuous improvement in quality and productivity will result in a better competitive position. It also must believe that quality improvement will give rise to higher productivity and that quality and productivity are not opposing goals. Although top management has the job of defining quality and guiding the organization in its achievement of it, everyone in the organization, including middle management, supervisors, workers, secretaries, and other office staff, along with vendors and investors, must change his or her attitude regarding quality.

Defining Quality

Changing attitudes is a difficult task, but it can be made easier by giving people something more concrete to grasp. Defining what is meant by quality can create a common ground for discussion and can make clear what is expected of everyone.

Quality must be thought of as a customer-oriented philosophy. Quality should be defined as "surpassing customer needs and expectations throughout the life of the product." Definition of quality and commitment to it are top management's responsibility. Top management must infuse everyone else with the spirit of never-ending improvement.

Identify and Remove Barriers to Achieving Quality

As mentioned earlier, once a commitment to the new quality consciousness is stressed and quality is defined by top management, the next step is to transform the company from one that is involved in defect detection to one that is involved with defect prevention. Your organization must build quality in, not inspect defects out. Your goal should be continually reducing the number of defectives. As your organization achieves the above, it can begin surpassing specifications. At that point, customers' needs will have been met and exceeded, and customers will brag about your product or service and advertise for you.

It is easy to say that a company should "do it right the first time" but actually doing it is a different story because of the barriers that may exist. Even in an organization where top management is committed to quality and has defined it, barriers to achieving it still exist. Therefore an effort must be made to designate all employees as "barrier detectives." Their responsibility is to find out why work is less than perfect, and what can be done to correct the problems.

Many times the removal of barriers is easy to accomplish. One of the authors worked in a social service agency that provided family counselling services. The results of a client satisfaction questionnaire revealed that the families felt that they could not talk about their "real" problems with the social workers, so their problems were not being resolved. When the Director of the agency saw these results, he was ready to fire the entire social work staff. He called them into a meeting where he angrily read the results of the survey and demanded answers. No one dared to respond. Finally, a social work intern said,

> You know, my clients said that to me in the beginning, and I kept wondering why. Then I realized that I don't talk to my supervisor about real issues either because we have no privacy—the walls on all of the offices are only about 6 feet high, so everyone can hear what you say. No wonder the clients can't really talk.

The agency was committed to providing quality services to its clients; however, a real barrier existed. The way the offices were structured allowed no privacy for clients to discuss their most personal problems. It took someone outside of the system to recognize the barrier because those in the system had become so accustomed to it that they didn't notice it anymore. Although the Director realized that the condition of the offices was a barrier, he was reluctant to ask the Board of Directors for the money to renovate the office because the budget was going to be cut for the following year. He struggled with this issue, and eventually he decided that quality services were paramount, so he went to the Board with the request. Board members were amazed and outraged that the offices were in such a condition. They hadn't been aware of it, and they vowed to get the needed renovation as quickly as possible, even though the budget was tight.

This example points out the need for "barrier detectives" in all aspects of an organization. Committees can be organized in departments or across departmental lines. A consultant can be used as a barrier detective. Each organization has to determine which way would be the most effective. Whatever structure is set up to handle barrier detection, it is clear that it is extremely important and can be the impetus to substantial changes.

Get Everyone Involved in the Quality Journey

Top management is responsible for raising "quality consciousness." Part of this responsibility is to get everyone involved in the never-ending improvement of quality. This should begin during the initial employment interview and should continue throughout the hiring, training, and retraining processes. Hiring interviews should reflect the commitment to quality and should assess the candidate's attitudes in relation to quality, team work, pursuit of never-ending improvement, continuing education, and adaptation to new circumstances. Quality as an integral part of the mission statement should be emphasized, as well as emphasizing a positive approach to the new way of managing. Potential employees' responses to these areas will aid in the selection process. The discussions of these issues can constitute their initial socialization to the company's goals and philosophy.

Unions should also be included in the quality effort. They can be powerful allies in the quality journey and should not be overlooked. They can help in hiring, training, retraining, and education. Unionism's place in the Deming philosophy will be discussed in depth in Chapter 15.

Vendors also must be an integral part of the quality journey. Vendor relationships should be long-term, trusting, single-source (by item) partnerships in which both parties are actively involved in the never-ending pursuit of quality. Vendors should be able to offer statistical evidence of quality, and buyers should be able to offer a long-term commitment to helping improve the vendors' processes. Contracts should be written to stress quality and never-ending improvement, instead of breach and noncompliance. This will create a ripple effect as quality is demanded of more and more companies, they will begin to demand it from their suppliers, and so on.

POSSIBLE PITFALLS

Top management has to change its attitude and develop its quality consciousness. Then it has to get everyone else involved in the quality journey by defining quality and by identifying and removing barriers that interfere with the improvement of quality. This is a difficult process, and there are many pitfalls that can ensnare you as you attempt this process.

Possible pitfalls include:

1. *Top management continuing to push quantity while espousing a quality philosophy.*

    This contradiction will be noticed immediately by middle managers, employees, and union officials, who may then become "turned off" to anything having to do with the new philosophy. Your actions must match your words in order for others to believe that you are serious about quality and that you know how to achieve it. Workers know that improving quality increases productivity. In meetings with workers, Dr. Deming frequently asks: "Why does improving quality raise productivity?" The inevitable tip of the tongue response is "Less rework." You can't fool them with hollow statements.

2. *Top management's inability to define quality properly.*

It is very easy to get caught up in traditional definitions of quality such as "conformance to specifications." This is meaningless in the absence of information about customer needs and expectations. Your product could easily conform to arbitrary specifications and still not meet customer needs and/or expectations.

3. *The company's inattentiveness to customer feedback.*

Following from the prior pitfall, you must constantly obtain information from your customers to continually improve your quality. Companies have to have a system whereby they can properly receive, assess, and use consumer feedback in redesign; otherwise there can be no real improvement.

4. *Becoming overwhelmed by the amount of barriers uncovered.*

Any organization embarking on an honest appraisal of its barriers to quality will find numerous problem areas. It would be easy to become overwhelmed by the task of removing those barriers. You have to guard against this by prioritizing the barriers and systematically planning how to remove each one in its time. You've got to have patience and tenacity to follow through on your plans. If you do not handle the barriers in this way, you will either deny that the problems exist or you will scurry around trying to solve all the problems at once. Obviously, denial and/or scurrying will not lead to the desired goals.

5. *Getting "hung-up" with complainers.*

When people are asked, "What's getting in the way of our doing a quality job?" they'll tell you. The problem with this is that some people won't know how to handle this discussion appropriately. They'll be so glad that someone finally asked that they will barrage you with a litany of complaints, personal issues, old issues that have been rectified, and skepticism about conditions ever changing. Whoever does the barrier detection has to be aware that it is very easy to get caught up in listening to these people, but it generally is unproductive. Of course they should be heard, but you need to structure your time and interviews with them to get pertinent information. You also should make a point of reaching out to those employees who might not be as verbal or used to talking about these kinds of issues because their input is very important also.

6. *Ignoring the union.*

Union officials should be made aware of the company's interest in moving toward the Deming philosophy, from the very beginning.

They should be an integral part of the effort and should be included in the initial training of top management. In this way, they will feel a part of the process and not an afterthought. They will support the change and not sabotage your attempts. If they are left out of the process, they will most likely be adversaries and will tell their membership that this is another program designed to make more money for the company while exploiting the workers.

7. *Middle management's fear of change.*

   Middle managers' perception may be that they have a lot to lose if their organization changes the way it has been operating. Generally, they have succeeded under the current systems and know what they have to do to keep climbing to the top. So, they are reluctant to change their attitudes. They are particularly scared of the idea of reporting barriers because their job in the past was to handle problems and not report them to the higher-ups. They were only supposed to tell the boss positive things to demonstrate what good managers they were. Under the Deming philosophy, this has to change. Top management must help middle management see that it (top management) wants to be, and must be, involved in removing barriers to quality improvement.

8. *Continuing to blame vendors for poor quality*

   A company embarking on never-ending improvement of quality must become involved with its vendors' processes and must help them improve quality also. Making a product out of defective parts is pretty difficult. Vendors should have to offer statistical evidence of their quality. However, it is up to you to lead the way and "role model" through your own efforts what can be done to improve quality and how to do it. There should be a sharing of information, successes, failures, resources, etc., along with actual hands-on involvement in each other's operations. Continuing to blame vendors for your failure to achieve quality is a waste of energy that should be devoted instead to the never-ending pursuit of quality.

3

Replacing Mass Inspection with Never-Ending Improvement

CEASE DEPENDENCE ON MASS INSPECTION. REQUIRE, INSTEAD, STATISTICAL EVIDENCE THAT QUALITY IS BUILT IN TO ELIMINATE THE NEED FOR INSPECTION ON A MASS BASIS.

DISCUSSION OF POINT THREE

Imagine the following scenario: You are the manager of a supermarket, and from your office window on the second floor, you are able to survey the supermarket aisles. One day, while you are observing the goings-on, you notice two of your regular customers, Ms. Samson and Mr. Adams, shopping. Ms. Samson is proceeding up and down the aisles at a normal pace, occasionally comparing unit prices, and then continuing on in her usual manner. Mr. Adams is a completely different story. Who would have thought that he would open every package possible to inspect its contents for damage and count the pieces? But that's exactly what you see him doing. It takes him hours to complete his shopping, and he looks worn out by the time he reaches the checkout counter.

Since he has shopped in your market for several years, you're amazed that he feels the need to inspect all the products and doesn't trust you to offer quality goods. You go down to the checkout counter to talk to him, and Mr. Adams greets you by saying, "Lucky for me I checked everything today. I almost bought a box of toothpicks with two broken ones. You ought to be more careful with your stock." You thank Mr. Adams for the information and return to your office to ponder the meaning of all this.

Why would Mr. Adams, a prominent attorney who earns $150 an hour, spend 3 hours ($450) to do a 100 percent inspection of items purchased in a store that he has patronized for several years? This is the first time he ever reported to you that he found defective goods, and the cost of the defectives is probably less than one cent. How many hours (at $150 per hour) has Mr. Adams spent inspecting products he purchased from you? You begin to question Mr. Adams' intelligence and sanity until you remember that the supermarket chain you work for requires 100 percent inspection guarantees from its vendors.

You start to think about the time and money that must be spent to perform 100 percent inspections and you question the cost/benefit factors. You mention this issue to your supervisor, who tells you that it is company policy and an industry standard to require 100 percent inspection guarantees. He says that because so many defective products are made, it's the only way to ensure that you are providing quality goods for the customer. "Besides," he says, "if a customer has a complaint, we can always show him our 100 percent inspection guarantee. That gets *us* off the hook and makes our suppliers have to handle any problems." You wonder if there isn't a better way to provide quality goods for customers, but you get caught up in day-to-day business and forget about the issue.

The Mass Inspection Attitude

Mass inspection is a way of life in most businesses. It is an attitude born out of mistrust, misunderstanding, and failure to monitor and improve the process. If a company has little or no understanding of how to control or improve its process, there is no predictability. If this is the case, how can the company conduct business? How can it offer a product at a certain price and make sure it can deliver it? In the absence of a better solution, many companies choose to inspect everything they produce and to throw out or rework defectives—at a tremendous cost increase to the buyer.

The cost of the disposition of defective material is staggering. Aside from the cost of producing it (employees are being paid to make defectives), there are the costs to the purchaser. If an incoming part is defective, a purchaser can (1) return it to the vendor, (2) throw it away, (3) rework or repair it, (4) sell it to someone else, (5) use it anyway, (6) put it into inventory, or (7) downgrade it for another use. All of these options involve time and money, which will invariably result in a cost increase and/or quality reduction in the final product. There is a better way. We have to learn how to stop producing defectives in the first place, by employing Dr. Deming's methods.

Mass inspection implies that defects and mistakes are expected. Dr. Deming states, "Routine 100% inspection is the same thing as planning for defects, acknowledgment that the process cannot make the product correctly, or that specifications made no sense in the first place."[1] If we adopt the new philosophy described in Point Two, we will no longer rely on mass inspection because we need to move from defect detection to defect prevention to never-ending improvement. We can no longer tolerate the mentality that allows the expectation of defects. Mass inspection is also counter to the new philosophy because it takes a short-time view. Each

[1]W. Edwards Deming, *Quality, Productivity, and Competitive Position*, p. 22.

day, output is inspected for that day's sake. There is no integration of the results into the improvement of the process.

Problems with Mass Inspection

There are other problems with mass inspection. One is that it is too late. James Harbour, a consultant hired by Warner-Lambert, saved the company $300 million a year by helping plant managers tighten control of their manufacturing processes so that they could make products right the first time, thereby reducing inspection delays and customers' complaints. Harbour says, "If you don't make things right the first time, then no amount of testing will make you productive." He told top management that quality is not achieved by after-the-fact inspection, but by tight control of the process.[2]

Another problem with mass inspection is that it is not necessarily accurate. Play the role of inspector for a few moments and count the number of *f*'s in the following passage:

FINISHED FILES ARE THE RESULT OF YEARS
OF SCIENTIFIC STUDY COMBINED WITH THE
EXPERIENCE OF MANY YEARS.

Did you find six *f*'s? When this exercise is done in a group, more than half of the participants typically come up with the wrong answer. This demonstrates the fallibility of 100 percent inspection. A corollary to this is that 200 percent inspection is worse than 100 percent inspection because when two people perform the same task, neither one takes the responsibility for its outcome, and accuracy is further decreased.

Another problem with inspection is that it is often performed under pressure, which further decreases its accuracy. Think about what percentage of products are shipped during the last week of the month; it should be about 20 or 25 percent. But, in some companies, it is as high as 60 percent! Inspection performed under those circumstances is a total farce.

There have always been some people who believe if product inspections were carried out properly, quality would improve. However, inspection neither improves nor guarantees quality. Mass inspection at any stage in the extended process does not make a clean separation of good from bad. Only through an understanding of the extended process and a joint effort between buyer and vendor can quality be achieved.

[2] Steven Flax, "An Auto Man Tunes Up Warner-Lambert," *Fortune*, 3, No. 5 (March 4, 1985), pp. 71–78.

HOW POINT THREE RELATES
TO THE OVERALL PHILOSOPHY

Mass inspection is essentially checking goods with no consideration of how to make them better, improve the process, or achieve higher quality within the framework of the Deming philosophy. This is a waste of time. What we are striving for is never-ending process improvement and a commitment to examining the process over time. Moving from defect detection (inspection) to defect prevention to never-ending improvement is critical to the new philosophy. As inspection decreases due to improvement in the system, the massive inspection effort can be turned to further improvement, creating a spiral of quality.

Mass inspection impedes an ongoing, mutually beneficial relationship between a vendor and a buyer. This positive relationship is crucial to the implementation of Dr. Deming's methods. Knowledge of each others' processes and quality levels and working as a team are what is important. If the companies understand their own and each others' process capabilities, they have a much more meaningful base from which to work.

Mass inspection is managing for failure. Under the new system, our goal is managing for success. Mass inspection focuses on the negative, without offering any means of improvement. It is a dismal way of viewing life. Mass inspection also keeps us thinking short-term. We inspect each day, without considering the system and the long-term view. Improving the process over time is paramount, rather than counting how many defectives there are in a particular day.

IDEAS FOR ACTION

Questions for Self-Examination

To help you assess where you stand on the inspection issue, the following questions should be asked:

1. What inspection are you carrying out:
   (a) On incoming materials?
   (b) In process?
   (c) On final product?
2. How reliable is your inspection at each of these points, and how do you know?
3. What data do you have to show whether your inspectors are in line with each other?

4. Are your testing instruments or system of measurement valid?
5. How much material that goes into the production line is used in desperation?
6. How much material turns out to be totally unusable in the judgment of the production manager?
7. Are you paying for defective incoming products from your suppliers?

Let's see what we can do to eliminate the need for inspection on a mass basis.

Dr. Deming's Alternative to Mass Inspection

Dr. Deming advocates a plan that minimizes the total cost of incoming materials and final product. Simply stated, the rule is an inspect all-or-none rule. Its logical foundation has statistical evidence of quality as its base. Dr. Deming's rule for minimizing the total cost of incoming materials and final product is derived mathematically, and if you are interested in this, you are referred to Dr. Deming's book for the derivation of his rule.[3]

The rule for minimizing the total cost of incoming materials and final product is referred to as the "kp rule" and is not commonly known even to most statisticians. Therefore, working with a statistician trained in Dr. Deming's methods is critical if a company is going to successfully journey to quality. You are advised that a very general description of the kp rule is presented here to facilitate understanding:[4]

Let p = the average fraction defective in incoming lots of parts (which could be a day's receipt of material),
Let k_1 = the cost to inspect one part, and
Let k_2 = the cost to dismantle, repair, reassemble, and test an assembly that fails because a defective part was put into the production line.

(Determination of p, k_1 and k_2 must be guided by a statistician trained in Dr. Deming's methods.)

If k_1/k_2 is greater than p, then 0 percent inspection[5]. This means that if the percentage of incoming defective parts is very low, the cost of inspecting an incoming part is high, and the cost of the defective part

---

[3] Deming, *Quality, Productivity, and Competitive Position*, pp. 267–311.

[4] Ibid., p. 268, paraphrased

[5] Ibid., p. 269, paraphrased.

getting into production is low; therefore no inspection is needed. The rationale is that there is not much risk or penalty attached to incoming defective parts.

If k_1/k_2 is less than p, then 100 percent inspection.[6]   This means that if the percentage of incoming defective parts is high, the cost of inspecting an incoming part is low, and the cost of the defective part getting into production is high; therefore do 100 percent inspection. The logic here is that there is great risk and a penalty attached to incoming defective parts.

If k_1/k_2 equals p, then either 0 percent or 100 percent inspection[7].   Decision making as to whether 0 percent or 100 percent inspection should be done has to occur in this case. In general, if p is not based on a substantial past history, perform 100 percent inspection, for safety's sake.

The above rule is appropriate between any two points in the extended process, e.g., internally, in the vendor's processes, and between the firm and the vendor.

Example of the *kp* Rule

An automobile manufacturer is deciding whether to purchase $25 million worth of equipment that would perform tests of engines purchased from vendors. The following figures were determined:

1. The inspection cost to screen out incoming defective engines is $50 per engine ($k_1 = \$50$).
2. The costs for corrective action if a defective engine gets into production is $500 per defective engine ($k_2 = \$500$).
3. On average, 1 in 150 incoming engines is defective ($p = 1/150 = .0067$).

Consequently,

$$\frac{k_1}{k_2} = \frac{50}{500} = .1$$

Note that 0.1 is greater than 0.0067. Therefore, k_1/k_2 is greater than p, and the correct course of action would be to do no initial inspection on incoming engines, to achieve the minimum total cost.

[6] Ibid.

[7] Ibid.

If no engines are inspected, the automobile company would incur the $500 cost in 1 out of 150 engines. This translates into an average corrective action cost of $3.33 per engine ($500 × 1/150). By cutting out initial inspection, the company saved $46.67 per engine ($50 − $3.33), on average. Since the company purchases 4000 engines per day, this translates into a daily savings of approximately $187,000 (4000 × $46.67). (Not to mention the savings of $25 million not spent on testing equipment, interest on that money, and time freed up to work on improving quality!)

The next step in the pursuit of quality is for the automobile company to work with its engine vendor to reduce the proportion of defective engines.[8]

Rule for Chaos

The above kp rule applies to a process that is stable; that is, p is reliable because the process capability is known and can be predicted. This is the state to which Dr. Deming's methods will bring us, eventually.

However, we know that what currently exists in the real world is, for the most part, chaos. Systems and processes are not known, not predictable, and by nature variable. Until a process is in control, there is an alternative to continuing 100 percent inspection; it is Joyce Orsini's rule:[9]

If k_1/k_2 is less than 1/1000, then inspect 100 percent of the incoming lots.

If k_1/k_2 is between 1/1000 and 1/10, then test a sample of 200. If there are no defectives, then accept the remainder. Inspect the remainder if you find at least one defective item in the sample.

If k_1/k_2 is greater than 1/10, then do no inspection.

Use of this rule will also be helpful in working with a vendor to bring his process into control. A running record of the samples of 200 can be kept, and the number of defectives can be charted, sample by sample. Feedback to the vendor will be extremely helpful in identifying problems.

POSSIBLE PITFALLS

Eliminating the need for inspection on a mass basis involves fundamental changes in how an organization views its processes. Striving for never-

[8] Ibid., pp. 276–77, paraphrased.

[9] Joyce Orsini, "Simple Rule to Reduce Total Cost of Inspection and Correction of Production in State of Chaos," dissertation for the doctorate, Graduate School of Business Administration, New York University, 1982.

ending improvement is dependent on these changes to succeed. Possible pitfalls include:

1. *Ignoring the need for a statistician.*

   Point Three is the first place in Dr. Deming's philosophy that we obviously encounter the need for a statistician to have major responsibilities in the achievement of quality. As was demonstrated in the previous section, substantial benefits can be reaped when the kp rule is used. However, this rule can only be implemented by a statistician trained in Dr. Deming's methods. If your organization already has a statistician, and you decide to adopt Dr. Deming's methods, your statistician will be trained along with the entire organization. He or she will become integral to the process of changing your company to a "Deming company." If you don't currently have a statistician on your staff, it will be necessary to hire one or to retain the services of a statistical consultant. (See Chapter 16 for a discussion of statisticians.)

   If you ignore the need for a statistician, the consequences will be dire: You will not succeed in your efforts. Implementing Dr. Deming's philosophy relies on both humanistic and statistical aspects, and both are necessary for success.

2. *Lack of communication with vendors.*

   To go from defect detection to defect prevention to never-ending improvement, you have to work with your vendors to help them improve their processes. You have vital information regarding their output. If you truly want to improve quality, you must communicate with your vendors so that they know what the problems are. Failing to do so is tantamount to saying that you are unwilling to put forth the effort needed to succeed as a "Deming company." Vendor relations will be discussed more fully in the next chapter.

3. *Continuing to use acceptance sampling.*

   One of the biggest areas of resistance to Dr. Deming's methods comes into play in relation to Point Three. People who have traditionally used acceptance sampling tables in inspection procedures have a difficult time "buying into" the kp rule. Acceptance sampling procedures have become standard practice, and people balk at the suggestion of not using them. However, continuing to rely on the acceptance sampling tables, in lieu of Dr. Deming's kp rule, will seriously impede the quality effort.

4

Changing the Philosophy of Purchasing

END THE PRACTICE OF AWARDING BUSINESS ON THE BASIS OF PRICE TAG. INSTEAD, DEPEND ON MEANINGFUL MEASURES OF QUALITY, ALONG WITH PRICE. MOVE TOWARD A SINGLE SUPPLIER FOR ANY ONE ITEM, ON A LONG-TERM RELATIONSHIP OF LOYALTY AND TRUST.

DISCUSSION OF POINT FOUR

Purchasing on the Basis of Price Tag Alone

Dr. Deming states,

> Price has no meaning without a measure of the quality being purchased. Without an adequate measure of quality, business drifts to the lowest bidder, low quality and high cost being the inevitable result. . . . He that has a rule to give his business to the lowest bidder deserves to get rooked.[1]

However, in many organizations this is standard operating procedure. Our daily newspapers often point out the absurd results of government agencies purchasing from the lowest bidder. How many projects have gone substantially over budget, created unsafe situations, and lagged on way past the estimated completion date because of problems created by purchasing solely on the basis of price? Unfortunately, there are all too many such cases. Therefore consumers are becoming increasingly aware, through consumer education, that research on quality and price is the best way to purchase.

So, what happens to these same people when they purchase in the context of business? They are caught up in a system, a system that perpetuates buying solely on the basis of price. In a meeting that Dr. Deming attended, a buyer stated, "Any time I fail to give the business to the lowest bidder, I should prepare to leave. I'd be out of a job. This policy is set by

Much of the discussion in Chapter 4 comes from H. Gitlow and D. Wiesner, "Vendor Relations: An Important Piece of the Quality Puzzle," University of Miami Working Paper Series, 1985.

[1]W. Edwards Deming, *Quality, Productivity, and Competitive Position* (Cambridge, Mass.: M.I.T., Center for Advanced Engineering Study, 1982), p. 23.

management."[2] Management is guilty of shortsighted, uninformed thinking, which results in gargantuan problems down the line.

An Example of Decision Making in Purchasing

Three vendors submit bids to a firm for a large quantity of a certain part. Vendor A charges $11.00 per unit, Vendor B charges $10.00 per unit, and Vendor C charges $9.50 per unit. If the purchasing agent considers only the price tag, then Vendor C will get the contract. However, if the purchasing agent considers quality and price, another vendor might get the contract.

Let's say that Vendor A has been pursuing the never-ending improvement of quality, using Deming's methods, for some time. He has so improved his production process that only one unit per million is defective. Consequently, the effective price the firm would pay for A's good product is:

$$\frac{\$11.00}{(1 - .000001)} = \$11.00 \text{ per unit}$$

Vendor B has also been pursuing process improvement via statistical process control, but not as long as Vendor A. He has reduced his defect rate from 15 percent to 10 percent. The 10 percent figure has been stable over some period of time. The effective price the firm would pay for B's good product is:

$$\frac{\$10.00}{(1 - .10)} = \$11.11 \text{ per unit}$$

Vendor A is the better buy. However, both vendors have the organizational capacity to improve because they are in control of their processes, even if Vendor B is temporarily at a disadvantage.

Vendor C has no records showing the capability of his process to produce a good product. Consequently, the effective price the firm would pay for C's good product is unknown:

$$\frac{\$9.50}{(1 - ?)} = \text{unknown per unit}$$

It is a sure bet that Vendor C's defect rate is higher than A's or B's because he does not have his process in control. Hence, it is fair to ask Vendor C how he can have the lowest price. He might have had the material on hand in inventory, or from a cancelled, rejected, or returned order, and he wants to dump it at a low price.

To make matters worse, if the buyer has deadlines, he may be forced

---

[2]Quotation from Dr. Deming's personal notes.

to use the nonconforming material in desperation, at increased cost due to rework. This further exacerbates the effective price of material to the buyer. Vendor C's material may get prohibitively expensive; this is an unknown. Vendor B's effective price will increase, but within the boundaries of his predictable 10 percent defective rate. Vendor A's price remains constant and becomes continually more attractive.

When buying material or services, you must consider the total cost. The total cost includes the purchase cost plus the cost to put the material into production, and the total cost is strongly affected by quality. The policy of awarding business on the basis of price tag alone can actually drive good competition out of the marketplace.

The New Job of the Purchasing Agent

Modern purchasing must be performed by people able to judge quality. This requires education in statistics, supplemented by the experience of trial, error, and relearning. Further, purchasing agents must understand the problems encountered in using materials purchased. It is necessary that purchasing agents follow a sample of materials through the whole production process into complex assemblies, and then onward to the customer. They must learn how their purchases are "fitting into" the system, that is, meshing with the process to meet the needs of the customer. The following is a real example of what frequently exists in systems where there is absolutely no coordination between the purchasing agent and the user of the purchased item.

A hospital serves medium (versus rare or well done) steak to patients who select it for dinner. The performance desired is patient satisfaction, within nutritional guidelines. However, performance specifications are not used. Instead, a technical specification of 5 ounces of steak is substituted. It is assumed that patient satisfaction (performance specification) and 5 ounces of steak (technical specification) are equivalent.

Meanwhile, the hospital purchasing agent switched from meat Vendor A to meat Vendor B to secure a lower price, while still meeting the technical specification of 5 ounces. He did not discuss or inform the hospital nutritionist of his action.

The hospital nutritionist began receiving complaints from patients that the steak was tough and well done. She investigated and found that Vendor A's steaks were thick, while Vendor B's steaks were thin (and longer and wider). She realized, via statistical monitoring methods, that the thinner steaks cooked faster, given her usual preparation. She said, "If I had known that the steaks had been changed, I could have accommodated the change without creating patient dissatisfaction." The purchasing agent said, "I met the technical specification of 5 ounces."

This example demonstrates what can result when the purchasing agent remains isolated from the other members in the systems. The job of purchasing can be performed, based on technical specifications; but as we saw, unless this is coordinated and followed up in the system, customer satisfaction may not result.

Thus, the position of purchasing agent will become a complex and demanding one in a "Deming company." The buyer will have to learn statistical methods to assess quality and to make decisions. He or she will have to develop the skills necessary to interact with other employees and with customers to determine satisfaction or dissatisfaction with the item purchased. In the extended process, communicating the information back to the vendor for future reference will also be a responsibility of the purchasing agent.

Moving from Multiple to Single Source Relationships

Multiple sourcing is the commonly accepted way of doing business in America. Many buyer-vendor relationships are based on the belief that to prevent disastrous interruption of supplies from vendors, firms must maintain multiple vendors for each item. Several reasons exist for this type of behavior. Three of the major ones are: (1) protection against disaster, for example, acts of God, strikes, fires, explosions, fear of price increases, perceived increase in the vendor's bargaining position, vendor bankruptcy, vendor inventory shortages, vendor failure to meet promised delivery schedule, and vendor downtime; (2) vendor's inability to supply the required volume; and (3) vendor not possessing the technology or patents required to provide products. Only categories 2 and 3 provide potential excuses for multiple-sourcing items.

Costs of Multiple Sourcing

Firms pay a large price for multiple sourcing. Some of the costs are: (1) increased travel costs to visit vendor facilities, (2) increased paper work, (3) increased telephone expense, (4) loss of volume discounts, (5) spreading confidential information, (6) increased set-up charges, (7) increased investment in capital equipment and or test equipment which must be provided to the vendor, (8) increased inventory costs due to carrying multiple vendors' items and their spare parts, (9) increased training costs of maintenance personnel to work with multiple vendors' materials, (10) increased "jury-rigging" when repairs are effected due to an inadequate supply of items in the stockroom, (11) prolonged time for vendors at the low end of the production learning curve, (12) competitive and repetitive manpower to deal with multiple vendors, (13)increased tooling requirements (multiple dies, etc.), and (14) increased variation in incoming quality characteristics because of vendor-to-vendor variation. This last point is critical. Multiple vendors, each meeting required specifications, can generate products different enough to cause reset-up time and problems in production.

Problems with Multiple Sourcing

Multiple sourcing promotes arm's-length relationships between vendors and buyers, exactly contrary to what is required for quality. Multiple sourcing sends to vendors the message: "I don't trust you, so I will keep your competitors around to keep you honest." Multiple sourcing creates an antagonistic, short-term, price-dependent, inflexible relationship between buyers and sellers. In multiple sourcing, vendors may not be willing to alter their processes to meet a firm's revised specification requirements in accordance with the extended process concept. Why should they? They may have other customers for their product, or if another vendor is cheaper, the buyer will purchase from that vendor.

Rationale for Single Sourcing

Instead of spending a great deal of effort disaster-proofing a firm by creating a large supply base for each purchased item, management should search for a single supplier for each item who exhibits financial stability, labor stability, quality-conscious management, political stability, statistical process control, low or no downtime, dependable vendor relations, etc.

The supply base (per item) will naturally diminish when a firm requires statistical evidence of quality. This decrease will be the result of the inability of most vendors to meet the new requirement for quality. A firm will be lucky to find one vendor that can provide statistical evidence of quality.

Quality is promoted by encouraging long-term relationships between buyers and vendors that are based on statistical evidence of quality. These types of relationships must be single source in nature, for a given item. Only in a single-source relationship will a vendor be willing to modify his process to meet revised quality of design specifications at a reasonable price. Single sourcing sends to the vendor the message: "I trust you and want to do business with you in the long run."

Single-source relationships allow for the possibility that either the buyer or vendor made an error at the time of contracting. The error could have been due to one of many reasons, such as the vendor failing to anticipate changes in the cost of raw materials, or the buyer's failure to completely understand consumer needs. Regardless of the source of the error, the single-source relationship allows for open negotiation of the contract to meet the needs of the buyer and vendor, and ultimately, the customer.

Managers will not have the time to deal with more than one vendor (per item) in the context of a single-sourcing philosophy, due to the massive effort required to single source. Purchasing agents will not have time for more than one vendor per item because they will be statistically evaluating quality to make better informed and sensible decisions.

Managers must move toward single sourcing (for each item) to construct an environment in which all members of the extended process jointly pursue and benefit from quality. Reducing the number of vendors and requiring statistical evidence of quality will require time, learning, cooperation, and patience.

Example of the Benefits of Single Sourcing

A company had been buying cans from three different suppliers, playing one vendor against another to try to get a lower bid. In 1975, the vice-presidents of manufacturing, research and development, and purchasing took it into their heads that it might be better to have one supplier of cans instead of three; that by having one supplier, they might share the benefits of mass production and they might work with the vendor to improve quality. Moreover, although all three suppliers were delivering excellent cans, there were differences between the cans of the three different suppliers, and time was lost to change over from one supplier to another.

It is now six years since this company adopted the plan of having a single source supplier of cans. They are pleased with the results. Savings amount to $5,000,000 to date, and the supplier of cans now sends control charts every week, along with the cans that he supplies.[3]

Ford and General Motors are attempting to close the "quality gap" with their foreign counterparts, particularly the Japanese, by pressuring American steel manufacturers to improve their performance.

"To spur the improvement—and lessen the pain—the auto companies are rewarding the steel companies with bigger and longer contracts as well as other concessions.

One of the biggest concessions has been the move from so-called multiple sourcing to sole or dual sourcing in purchasing steel products. Now, 60 percent of Ford's steel requirements are met by single suppliers and another

[3]Deming, *Quality, Productivity, and Competitive Position*, p. 30.

10 percent by no more than two suppliers, according to Paul R. O'Hara, director of metals, petroleum, and materials purchasing for the company.

That is a clear break, he noted, from the pattern not too long ago when Ford would look to as many as six companies for a particular steel product, to encourage competition. Sole or dual sourcing affords suppliers "larger tonnages and better continuity," Mr. O'Hara said.[4]

Dr. Deming's work with Ford and General Motors is becoming apparent and is impacting on other industries with very positive results. If managers would begin to construct long-term single-source relationships based on statistical evidence of quality with vendors, all participants in the extended process would enjoy the benefits of improved quality.

HOW POINT FOUR RELATES TO THE OVERALL PHILOSOPHY

Dr. Deming's philosophy stresses the never-ending improvement of quality in the extended process. This must be achieved through attitudinal changes that reflect a long-term perspective and quality consciousness, as well as the use of statistical methods as a common ground for communication. Point Four discusses the need to award business on the basis of quality (along with price) and the implicit establishment of a long-term relationship between vendor and buyer. A "Deming company" will be buying both a vendor's process and the vendor's products. It will have to become involved in helping the vendor improve his process over the long run. This requires a long-term perspective and a willingness to get involved in real change as opposed to purchasing for one time only, with no concern for future needs.

Awarding business on the basis of price tag alone is managing for failure. If no thought is given to the quality of what is being purchased, and incoming materials are of poor quality, then the final product will also be of poor quality. Awarding business on the basis of quality, in addition to price, is managing for success. It leads to single sourcing, which results in higher-quality incoming materials.

A long-term perspective and quality consciousness are vital to the Deming philosophy. But, these attitudes must be backed up by actions and by the use of statistical methods. Statistical methods provide the means to measure, monitor, and improve quality in the extended process. Working with vendors to improve their processes necessitates the use of statistics as a common language within a long-term single-source relationship.

[4]*New York Times*, August 8, 1985, Sec. D, p. 1.

IDEAS FOR ACTION

Questions for Self-Examination

The following questions will help you analyze where your firm stands, in respect to purchasing quality products from vendors:

1. How do you choose a vendor?
2. Do you make your decision solely on the basis of price?
3. What are the effects of this practice?
4. Do your vendors supply you with statistical evidence of quality?
5. If not, how do you know what you are purchasing?
6. Do you single or multiple source vendors for each item?
7. What are your costs for multiple sourcing?
8. What kind of relationships do you have with your vendors?
9. What happens if you or the vendor make a mistake at the time of contracting?

Now that you are more aware of your current practices, let's look at what we can do to change them. Ending the practice of awarding business based on price tag alone involves (1) selecting the right vendors, (2) changing the job of the purchasing agent to maximize the amount of material purchased that is used with no problem, and (3) changing the way contracts are written between buyers and vendors.

Selecting the Right Vendors.   Modern qualification procedures are important when selecting a new vendor or reevaluating a current vendor. They must stress quality and enable the selection of vendors who are willing to improve their quality.

A vendor relations manual should be available to all vendors (potential and current). This manual should stress the importance of quality-related issues. The checklist below provides questions to assist in evaluating a vendor's quality effort, commitment, and ability to satisfy customers.

AREAS	*QUESTIONS*
Management	Does the vendor have an operating philosophy and mission statement which stresses quality consciousness?
	How does the vendor define quality?

(*continued*)

AREAS (cont.)	*QUESTIONS (cont.)*
Management (*cont.*)	Does the vendor's organizational structure aid his quality quest?
	Does the vendor socialize employees, vendors, customers, etc. into his quality efforts (e.g., training in philosophy)?
	Does the vendor follow Dr. Deming's 14 points?
Financial	Is the vendor financially stable, or does he have financial problems, which could interrupt supply?
Geographic	Is the vendor located in an area plagued by earthquakes, tornadoes, or other Acts of God which could interrupt supply?
Political	Is the vendor located in an area subject to political upheaval which could interrupt supply?
Personnel	Are the vendor's labor relations stable, or are they subject to strikes or work stoppages which could interrupt supply?
	Do the vendor's supervision, training, and educational programs stress quality?
	Do all of the vendor's employees receive training in statistical methods?
Design	Is the vendor willing to participate in joint quality (product development and design) planning?
	Is the vendor willing to share cost data that affects design issues?
	Is the vendor willing to discuss and modify product/service or process designs to meet the customer's needs?
	Does the vendor understand all relevant quality characteristics and specifications?

AREAS (cont.)	*QUESTIONS (cont.)*
Design *(cont.)*	Is the vendor committed to the problems of tomorrow and R & D?
Manufacturing	Are the vendor's physical facilities and maintenance adequate?
	Are the vendor's processes stable and capable? What evidence does the vendor have of the above?
	Does the vendor use Statistical Process Control? (More about this in Chapter 5.)
	Is the vendor geared toward never-ending improvement, defect prevention, or defect detection?
	What is the vendor's current and potential production capacity?
Purchasing	Is the vendor willing to work with the buyer to develop operational definitions for the critical quality characteristics of processes, product services, or specifications?
	Do the vendor's contractual arrangements stress or hinder quality?
	Does the vendor single source suppliers?
	Is the vendor a single source supplier for any customers?
	What is the structure of the vendor's single source relationships?
Inspection and Testing	Does the vendor use statistical methods to monitor, control and maintain laboratories, equipment, measurements, etc.? (More about this in Chapter 5.)
	Will the vendor cooperate with the buyer on tests and use of instruments and graphs?
	Are the vendor's laboratories, equipment, and measurements appropriate

(continued)

AREAS (cont.)	*QUESTIONS (cont.)*
Inspection and Testing (*cont.*)	for the customer's quality characteristics and specifications?
	Does the vendor use acceptance sampling procedures or the Kp rule?
	Does the vendor utilize statistical process control of product/service, process, etc.? (More about this in Chapter 5).
	Is inspection and test data used for defect detection, defect prevention, or never-ending improvement?
Quality Coordination	Do all areas in the vendor's firm use statistical methods for never-ending improvement of quality?
	Does the vendor "live" the extended process concept?
	Does the vendor have corrective action loops to resolve problems of process or product/service?
	What are the vendor's plans for the disposition of non-conforming material, non-conforming processes, and non-conforming procedures?
	Will the vendor use the customer's quality data and report forms?
	Will the vendor adhere to the buyer's request for submission of samples?
	Will the vendor adhere to the buyer's request for preparation of quality plans?
	Will the vendor adhere to the buyer's request for inspection, test and reliability information?
	Will the vendor adhere to the buyer's request for statistical evidence of quality?
	Will the vendor adhere to the buyer's request for procedures for making engineering changes?

AREAS *(cont.)*	QUESTIONS *(cont.)*
Quality Coordination *(cont.)*	Does the vendor provide aftersales service?
	Does the vendor provide logistical support and delivery?
Price	Is the vendor's price/quality package attractive?
Litigation Mindness	Do vendor attorneys participate in the formulation of the contract? Is it constructive or protectivist?
	Does the vendor have pending suits with other customers?

Only after the buyer has been satisfied on all the issues (and more) listed in the above checklist should the vendor be given consideration as a possible business partner.

Changing the Job of the Purchasing Agent.   Dr. Deming states,

> The purchasing managers of a company are not at fault for giving business to the lowest bidder, nor for seeking more bids in the hope of getting a still better price. This is their mandate. Only the top management can change their direction.
> Purchasing agents have a new job. It will take five years for them to learn it.[5]

Top management in the United States has to be willing to expend the time, money, and effort needed to retrain purchasing agents. In the long run, this is the only route that will lead us to improved quality. The purchasing agent must be trained to statistically evaluate a vendor's process, in order to select the vendor who has the most attractive quality/price package. After selection, the purchasing agent must work cooperatively with the vendor, giving feedback on the material purchased. Vendors need to know what happens to the material shipped in production, so that they may work toward never-ending improvement of quality. If the material sent is unsuited to the manufacturing requirements and has to be reworked, or it is totally unusable, or is put in inventory, the vendor needs to know this.

[5]W. Edwards Deming, "Improvement of Quality and Productivity Through Action by Management," *National Productivity Review*, 1, no. 1 (Winter 1981–1982), 18.

Changing the Way Contracts are Written
Between Buyers and Sellers

In a perfect world, both buyer and vendor would attempt to maximize their common good by cooperating to create quality products at the least cost. Unfortunately, the modern history of contracting does not tell a story of cooperation. Rather, it is concerned with the creation of arm's-length transactions and the assignment of risk.

We contend that the risks of producing quality products should be borne by both buyers and vendors, regardless of their skill in negotiating contracts. The inability of U.S. firms to compete with companies dedicated to "quality" (e.g., many Japanese companies) forces responsible management to reconsider its policies concerning contracting and quality.

Traditionally, assignments of risk are established when contracting parties reach agreement. The vendor has made a judgment that he or she can perform profitably, and the buyer assumes that the firm's needs have been articulated. However, both parties are exposed to the possibility that either one is wrong. The vendor could perform properly but still not satisfy the buyer's need. For example, if the review features of a contract reveal that the vendor is conforming to contractual requirements, but the normal variations inherent in the vendor's process are no longer acceptable to the buyer's need, the specifications must be redrawn. The new specifications may require greater effort and expense for the seller, who understandably demands an adjustment in price. It is at this point that the relationship of the parties is severely tested. When the original contract price was bargained for, the vendor was required to make an evaluation of the cost of performance. New specifications, possibly costing more money, will not be demanded by the buyer, who is in a very precarious negotiating position. Unless the parties have planned for this possibility, they will have to exercise considerable skill in amending the contract.

The Problem of the "Open" Price Term

An agreement whose terms are incomplete or vague cannot serve as the basis of a contract. The terms must be clear enough to enable the court to determine the parties' intention and to fix legal rights and duties. This requirement, if rigidly obeyed, is the natural enemy of the joint undertaking required to search for quality. The assignment of risk principle operates badly in today's marketplace. The vendor and buyer, at the time of the contract, do not have all the answers as to what type of performance by the vendor would satisfy the buyer's needs for the duration of the contract. In effect, there is a need for a true "open" price term if a quality search is to take place. Simply stated, the "open" price term recognizes that the parties have agreed in principle and operation to search for quality together.

Contracting and the Legal Code

The law operates efficiently if the vendor and buyer know how to express the required terms of performance. However, judgments of monetary cost (the vendor's evaluation) and worthiness (the buyer's judgment) are frequently premature at the time of contracting.

Fortunately, the law has relaxed its requirement of certainty in some of the material terms in a contract. The Uniform Commercial Code has validated the development of common law principles, in substantial ways. For example, agreements do not necessarily fail as binding contracts when the parties have omitted the price or time and place of delivery of the goods. The Code sets forth certain so-called "gap fillers" which apply, unless otherwise agreed. Accordingly, where no price is mentioned, a "reasonable price" governs.[6] Likewise, delivery at a "reasonable time" and at the seller's place of business governs when the parties neglect these terms.[7]

Code provisions are most helpful for quality purposes when they allow parties a margin for uncertainty (e.g., a reasonable price, a reasonable time, etc.). Even more pertinent is how the Code handles the term *price* in Section 2–305. This section grants the parties wide latitude in how price is determined since it allows the parties to agree to "a price fixed by the seller or the buyer." This unilateral grant of power is monitored for possible abuse by the Code requirement that it "means a price for him to fix in good faith" [Sec. 2–305 (2)]. The Code also allows the contract to expressly state that the price is left to be agreed upon by the parties.

The Quality Clause

The contracting parties must commit themselves to pursuing quality by acknowledging the merit of the extended process. Both agree that the process itself is being purchased and that the vendor is perfectly willing to have his behavior monitored and inspection procedures (for control and improvement purposes) instituted. Both acknowledge that either, or both, could be technically wrong in their specifications of the product. They agree to work toward quality at a fair price and place safeguards for both parties in the contract.

There are a number of ways in which this agreement could be ex-

[6]Section 2-305, Uniform Commercial Code, 1978 Official Text, American Law Institute and National Conference of Commissioners on Uniform State Laws (1978).

[7]Section 2-309(1), Uniform Commercial Code.

pressed. The following sample contract provides a formula for performance which recognizes the possibility of error by both contracting parties, yet binds each to make a good faith effort to produce a quality
product.

> THE PARTIES HEREUNTO AGREE to a plan for the production, delivery,
> and acceptance of a quality product and adherence to those practices which
> achieve such, including commitment to the "extended process," the presence
> of precise operating definitions (definitions you can do business with, to be
> discussed in Chapter 5), and the establishment and delivery of statistical
> control charts (also to be discussed in Chapter 5), all for the express purpose
> of monitoring, understanding, improving, and purchasing the vendor's
> process as well as the product. In specific furtherance of the above it is agreed
> as follows:
>
> FIRST. Recognizing the critical importance of operating definitions,
> the products herein named shall be operationally described as:
>
> SECOND. Vendor shall establish and maintain records of its process
> in manufacturing the described goods sufficient in timing, content, and
> number to provide the buyer with information allowing determination of
> whether the process is in control. The specifics of such statistical control
> charts shall be as follows:
>
> THIRD. The vendor shall establish and maintain records reflecting
> such information as shall be necessary for the buyer to effectuate Dr. Dem-
> ing's kp rule, i.e., a "p" chart. (See Chapter 5 for a discussion of "p" charts.)
> Communication of such information shall be at the times and in content as
> is described as follows:
>
> FOURTH. It is understood that the performance of the above three
> operations can singly, or in combination, result in the following conse-
> quences:
>
> A. Manufacture of the product may reveal that the operational def-
> initions mutually agreed upon do not fulfill the buyer's needs, i.e., quality.
> In such event, it is agreed that the buyer shall have the option to cancel the
> contract as regarding that product, provided however, the buyer shall be
> obliged to reimburse the seller for all expenses incurred in a good faith at-
> tempt to perform the contract under the operational definition agreed upon,
> plus a sum here fixed as a percentage of the expenses incurred. It is further
> agreed that the buyer is granted the option to redefine the description and
> contract with the seller at a price to be mutually agreed upon by the parties
> under Section 2–305 (1) of the Uniform Commercial Code, providing always
> that the Vendor may in good faith refuse to so contract where the facility
> does not have the capability to perform under the new contract description.
> "Capability" includes both technical and economic capability within this
> paragraph.
>
> B. The control chart provided by the vendor to the buyer may reveal
> that the process is in control, i.e., no abnormal sources of variation, yet it
> is determined by the buyer that such does not meet the buyer's needs (e.g.,

as a result of market research, service/sales analysis, etc.). In such event the same remedies and option set forth in Subparagraph A shall govern the behavior of the parties.

C. The control charts contemplated herein may reflect that the process is not in control (i.e., state of chaos). In such an event the vendor must bring the process under statistical control. The failure of the vendor to make meaningful initiatives to correct the process shall, as hereby agreed, be a breach and constitutes a substantial impairment of the bargain upon the passage of __ days from buyer's demand for assurance and correction, or after a reasonable period of time from such demand, whichever period is the shorter.

D. The control charts contemplated herein may reflect other deviations of process, e.g., runs or nonrandom patterns for points in control. Such manifestation reflects a system not in conformance with the contractual duty the vendor owes to the buyer. In such event the legal characterization and remedies set forth in Subparagraph C shall govern the behavior and rights of the parties.

If buyer and vendors would stop contracting to lay blame, via the creation of arm's-length relationships, and would begin contracting to create long-term single-source relationships, the pursuit of quality in the extended process would be greatly facilitated.

POSSIBLE PITFALLS

Changing purchasing practices involves upsetting many "givens" in the marketplace. It will be a difficult process and you will encounter many problems. Possible pitfalls include:

1. *Top management resisting single sourcing.*

   Most managers have had very little experience with the concept of single sourcing. It scares them because they immediately think of all the disasters that could potentially interrupt production. Unless management is committed to the new attitude and willing to gradually work toward single sourcing by item, success will not be achieved. Top management has to be trained to understand the benefits of single sourcing, as outlined in this chapter, and must be supported by the Board of Directors in its efforts.

2. *Not providing adequate training and supervision for purchasing agents.*

   The new role of the purchasing agents will substantially change the duties of people who may have been buyers for several years. These purchasing agents will need training in statistical methods, as well as ongoing support in adjusting to their new, more complex duties. Issues will arise, such as having to choose a new vendor when the old one has become a friend over the years. Supervisors must play a key role in working with purchasing agents to make this transition as smooth as possible. Without training and supervision, purchasing agents will follow the old rules, and this can have a devastating effect on the chances of improving quality.

3. *Purchasing agents resisting their new role.*

Since the new role of the purchasing agents is so different from the old, the new purchasing agents may be unable or unwilling to carry out their revised responsibilities. For these people, it is incumbent upon management to find other positions in the organization so that they can work in a capacity that suits their mutual needs. Those who are motivated to learn and accept the new responsibilities must be moved into the new purchasing positions.

4. *Management sending double messages about purchasing rules.*

Management must make very clear to purchasing agents what is expected of them under the new system. Purchasing agents can no longer be evaluated on choosing the lowest bidder. If management truly wants to achieve quality, then the message to the purchasing agents has to be crystal clear: "We want to change how we choose our vendors, and we are willing to work with you in training, supervision, and anything else that is needed to achieve that goal."

5. *Continuing to use "assignment of risk" type contracts.*

A major impediment to achieving the benefits of a trusting, single-source relationship with a vendor is the continued use of contracts that create an adversarial atmosphere between buyers and vendors. Lawyers need to be trained in the Deming philosophy so that they can work with firms to create contracts that encourage the pursuit of quality, rather than perpetuating a "sue for breach of contract" attitude. An organization's legal staff should be trained, along with the rest of the organization, in Dr. Deming's methods. In this way, the attorneys can develop a respect for the philosophy and an understanding of why contracting needs to change.

5

Improving
the System

*IMPROVE CONSTANTLY AND FOREVER
THE SYSTEM OF PRODUCTION AND
SERVICE, TO IMPROVE QUALITY AND
PRODUCTIVITY, AND THUS
CONSTANTLY DECREASE COSTS.*

DISCUSSION OF POINT FIVE

Responsibility for the System

Some American managers view their responsibilities as a narrowly defined piece of territory. Often this territory is limited to the legal liability that can be established in court. This concept of limited liability and the rise of complex bureaucratic structures have diffused responsibility for corporate misdeeds to the point where chief executives of corporations rarely are disgraced for even gross misconduct by their companies. Contrast this with the resignation of Japan Air Lines' President, two days after a JAL 747 crashed, killing over 500 people. In Japan, this resignation was anticipated because it is traditional for chief executives to take responsibility for corporate calamities. This example is dramatic, but it does point out the philosophical underpinnings of the difference between many American and some Japanese companies. Taking responsibility for the system is the only way top management can function if we hope to turn America's corporate deterioration around.

A major roadblock to quality in America is that management believes that the workers are responsible for all the trouble. Managers think that there would be no problems in production or service if only the workers would do their jobs the way they were taught. This just isn't so; the workers are handicapped by the system, for which management is responsible. Management is responsible for the entire system and for all of its various processes: (1) the design of product or service, (2) the measurement of the amount of trouble with the product or service, (3) The assignment of responsibility for action to remove the cause of the trouble, etc.

Improving the Process

According to Deming, improving the process means

> continual reduction of waste and continual improvement of quality in every activity: procurement, transportation, engineering, methods, maintenance, locations of activities, instruments and measures, sales, methods of distribution, accounting, payroll, and service to customers.[1]

Continual improvement of the process results in less rework, downgrade, etc., and higher quality. This leads to a continual rise in productivity, bringing higher profits and improved competitive position. Therefore, management should be critically interested in improving the process.

"Interest" is all very well, but more is needed if any real transformation is to take place. Statistical methods can have a profound impact on process improvement, quality, productivity, costs, and competitive position. Unfortunately, statisticians in the United States have failed to communicate this potential impact to management. Furthermore, business schools, for the most part, don't teach the material needed to help potential managers do their jobs successfully. People in management need to know about statistical methods for quality control, not just establish a Quality Control Department. Quality control must be a learning process in which everyone in the company participates, under the direction of a competent statistician.

Improving the process is the key to increasing quality and productivity, and to reducing unit costs. Process improvement is aided by using appropriate operational definitions of product/service and/or process quality characteristics, and by reducing the variation in a process and moving it toward the desired level, while following the Fourteen Points.

Operational Definitions

Management's attempts to improve the process have to begin with precise definitions of specifications, products/services, jobs, etc. Such definitions are meaningless unless they bring about increased communication between the involved parties. Operational definitions are definitions with which people can do business. They are a prerequisite for an understanding between buyer and vendor, management and labor, inspectors and workers, etc. They must have the same meaning for all parties concerned,

---

[1]W. Edwards Deming, *Quality, Productivity, and Competitive Position* (Cambridge, Mass.: M.I.T., Center for Advanced Engineering Study, 1982), p. 30.

over time. An operational definition consists of: (1) a criterion to be applied to an object or to a group, (2) a test of the object or of the group,
and (3) a decision as to whether the object or group did or did not meet
the criterion.[2]

Here's an example of the confusion that can be caused by the absence
of a precise definition of what's being produced. The label on a shirt reads
"75 percent cotton." What does this mean? Three-quarters cotton, on the
average, over this shirt, or three-quarters cotton over a month's production? What is "three-quarters cotton"? Three-quarters by weight? If so,
at what humidity? By what method of chemical analysis? How many anal-
yses? Does "75 percent cotton" mean that there must be some cotton in
any random cross section the size of a silver dollar? If so, how many cuts
should be tested? How do you select them? What criterion must the average satisfy? And how much variation between cuts is permissible? Obviously, the meaning of "75 percent cotton" can only be stated in statistical
terms.[3]

Importance of Operational Definitions.   Major quality and productivity problems can arise when inspectors who are responsible for finding defects are inconsistent in their judgments over time, or when inspectors are inconsistent with each other. Workers will be confused over what
is acceptable or what is defective. They need an operational definition of
a defective product.

Operational definitions establish a language for process improvement. An operational definition puts communicable meaning into a specification. Specifications like *defective, safe, round, 5 inches long, reliable,*
etc., have no communicable meaning until they are operationally defined
in terms of a criterion, test, and decision rule. Everyone concerned must
agree on an operational definition before process improvement can proceed.

Example of an Operational Definition.   A firm produces washers.
One of the critical quality characteristics is "roundness." The following
definition is an operational definition of roundness, as long as the buyer
and seller agree on it.

Step 1: Criterion for roundness.

(a) "Use calipers that are in reasonably good order." (You
perceive at once the need to question every word.)

[2]Ibid., p. 323.
[3]Ibid., pp. 334–45.

"What is 'reasonably good order'?" (We settle the question by letting you use your calipers.)

"But how should I use them?"

"We'll be satisfied if you just use them in the regular way."

"At what temperature?"

"The temperature of this room."

(b) "Take six measures of the diameter about 30° apart. Record the results."

"But what is 'about 30° apart'? Don't you mean exactly 30°?"

"No, there is no such thing as exactly 30° in the physical world. So try for 30°; we'll be satisfied."

(c) If the range between the six diameters does not exceed .007 cm, we will declare the washer to be round. We have determined the criterion.

Step 2: Test for roundness.

(a) Select a particular washer. (We could at this point specify some sampling scheme.)

(b) Take the six measurements and record the results in cm— 3.365, 3.363, 3.368, 3.366, 3.366, and 3.369.

(c) The range is 3.369 to 3.363 cm, or a 0.006 cm difference. We test for conformance by comparing the range of 0.006 cm with the criterion range of less than or equal to 0.007 cm (step 1).

Step 3: Decision rule for roundness.

Because the washer passed the prescribed test for roundness, we declare it to be round.

If a company has workers who understand what "roundness" means and a customer who agrees, the problems the company may have had satisfying the customer will disappear.[4]

Sources of Variation

Consider a manufacturing process that produces tubes with an average diameter of 1.50 inches. It is not realistic to expect every tube's diameter to be exactly 1.50 inches. We should expect some variation, depending on how the measurement was rounded off.

[4]H. Gitlow and P. Hertz, "Product Defects and Productivity," *Harvard Business Review*, September–October 1983, pp. 138–39.

Variation in a process (or product/service) is natural; it should be expected. But, it is a wild beast that must be controlled. As discussed earlier, there are two sources of variation in all processes: *special* and *common*. Special variation is due to an assignable or specific cause. For example, if a rod-cutting machine is knocked out of calibration by a new operator, it will result in special variation. Common variations are present in all parts of a process, an entire department, or a whole company, and can create high costs and low productivity and quality. Let's say that we produce a tube with a 1.56-inch diameter. Is the .06-inch discrepancy a special variation in the process? Or is it a common variation that we ought to expect (variation inherent in the system)? If it is a special variation, we would want to intervene and, say, adjust the machine. If it is not, we shouldn't intervene. In fact, by adjusting the machine without cause, we'd run the risk of creating more system variation and problems down the line.[5]

Some researchers estimate that special variations cause 15 percent of the problems in a process, while common variations cause the remaining 85 percent. Dr. Deming believes that as much as 94 percent of all system variations are caused by common sources. Some examples of common variation are listed below:[6]

1. Hasty design of component parts and assemblies. Inadequate tests of prototypes. Hasty production.

2. Inadequate testing of incoming materials. Specifications that are too stringent, or too loose, or meaningless. Waiving specifications.

3. Failure to know the capabilities of processes that are in a state of statistical control, and to use this information as a basis for contracts, both for quantity and quality.

4. Failure to provide production-workers with statistical signals that will tell them how they are doing and when to make some change.

5. Failure to use [statistical] charts as a measure of the faults of the system, and of the effect of action taken by management to reduce them.

6. Failure to write job-descriptions that take account of the capability of the process.

7. Inadequate training of workers, with the help of statistical controls.

8. Settings of machines chronically inaccurate (fault of the crew responsible for settings).

[5]Ibid., p. 132.

[6]W. Edwards Deming, "On Some Statistical Aids toward Economic Production," *Interfaces*, 5, no. 4 (August 1975), 2.

9. Instruments and tests not reliable. Consequent demoralization and loss from false reports and false signals. Loss from needless retesting.
10. Smoke, noise, unnecessary dirt, poor light, humidity, confusion.

Confusion between common and special causes of variation leads to frustration at all levels, more variation, higher costs, and lower productivity. Management may react to variation by blaming the workers if it does not understand and is not able to distinguish between the two sources of variation.

Workers are usually powerless to act in the presence of common causes of variation. Common causes of variation are system problems, and management owns the system. Workers just labor in the system that management created and rules. They cannot do much about machines or test equipment that is out of order. They can report such events, but management must do the follow-up and make the necessary changes. Workers cannot change the specifications and policy for procuring incoming materials either, and they are not responsible for the product's design. These are all part of the system, and only managers can change the system.[7]

Control Charts.   Since workers should not be held accountable for system problems, managers must know how to identify special and common causes of variation so that they'll know when and how to take action on the process. The only way to identify common and special sources of variation in a process is through the statistical signals that control charts generate.

A control chart is a chart with a base line, frequently in time order, on which measurements or counts are represented by points that are connected by straight lines. An example of a control chart of daily percent of defective products is pictured in Figure 5–1.

A control chart has a center line and an upper and lower control limit. The center line reflects the process's average. The control limits provide statistical signals for action by management by indicating the separation of common and special variation. These charts are extremely useful for studying product properties, process variables, costs, errors, and other management data.

The use of control charts must be supervised by a competent statistician who can train an entire organization in their construction. Interpretation must be guided by the statistician because he or she has the experience necessary to assess the meaning of the data, special versus common variation, and degree of variation. Then, management can make informed

[7]Gitlow and Hertz, "Product Defects and Productivity," pp. 132–33.

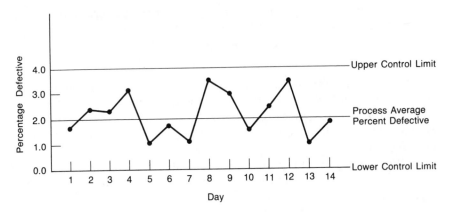

Figure 5-1   Percentage of defective products produced daily.

decisions and take action to improve the process. Later in this chapter, we will present a detailed description of control chart construction and interpretation.

Managerial Action on Special Variation.   If a control chart is analyzed, and a sample value falls within the upper and lower control limits, and if a trend or some other systematic pattern is absent, the variation is probably common. However, if a sample value falls outside the control limits, and/or if trends and other systematic patterns are present, the variation is probably special. Once management has established that a cause of variation in a process is special, it should be eliminated. After management has eliminated all assignable causes of variation in a process, it has a stable process that is in statistical control.

A process is called *stable* if it exhibits only common variation—variation due to the limitations inherent in the process. The advantages of achieving a stable process are:[8]

1. Management knows the process's capability and can predict its performance, costs, and quality levels.
2. Under the stable process, productivity is at a maximum and costs are at a minimum.
3. Management can measure the effects of changes in the process with greater speed and reliability.
4. If management wants to alter specification limits, it has data to back up its argument.

[8]Ibid., p. 136.

A stable process that produces too many defects will do so as long as the system remains the same. Only management can change the system.

Managerial Action on Common Variation. A process cannot be improved until it is in statistical control. Until a process is stable it is an unknown entity. Once statistical control has been achieved, managers can improve the system by shifting the process average closer to nominal, or the desired level, or by reducing the amount of common variation. Consider the example below.

An industrial laundry had a problem. The washroom operators were spending a great deal of time rewashing clothes, at a high cost. Via control charts, it was established that the trouble was common to all washing machines and all operators; hence it was common and environmental. Management's brainstorming deduced that low-quality detergent was the cause of the problem. The owner of the shop had been purchasing low-quality detergent at bargain prices. The loss of machine and man time had cost many times the savings on the cheap detergent. Buying higher-grade detergent stopped the problem dead in its tracks.

The above action could only have been implemented by management. The operators, who were being blamed for the problem, could not have solved the problem themselves.

HOW POINT FIVE RELATES TO THE OVERALL PHILOSOPHY

Making a commitment to constantly improve the system necessitates a long-term perspective. Analyzing, understanding, and improving the process are ongoing tasks that stretch out into the infinite future. Management must be able to deal with the day-to-day issues of the organization and also move toward never-ending improvement. The scope of never-ending improvement is vast and overwhelming, but Point Five of the philosophy offers some very tangible ways of improving the system.

Constantly working to improve the system is managing for success. Quality achievement becomes management's primary objective. Moving from defect detection to defect prevention to never-ending improvement gives management a guide in its quality journey. When management understands the sources of process variation, acts to achieve a stable process, and reduces common process variation, quality results. The organization succeeds through management's taking responsibility for improving the system.

Constantly improving the process is strongly tied to stopping mass inspection. Achieving a stable process is necessary so that you can use the *kp* rule and minimize inspection costs (See chapter 3 for a discussion of the kp rule). This works cyclically because the time and money saved from minimizing inspection can then be put back into further improvement of the process.

Vendor relations depend heavily on operational definitions to facilitate communication and to avoid potential conflicts. Working with vendors to improve their systems, as well as constantly improving your own system, is an integral part of the Deming philosophy. Vendors will have to get involved in process improvement if they are to remain in the marketplace.

IDEAS FOR ACTION

Questions for Self-Examination

Constantly improving the system necessitates analyzing where the problems are and who is responsible for them. Looking at the following questions can help you determine your organization's position and needs:

1. What proportion of the troubles that you have with quality and productivity are the fault of (a) the production workers, and (b) the system?
2. What are you doing to make quality and productivity everyone's job?
3. What methods are being used in your business to improve the system?
4. What changes have you made recently in the system?
5. How did you decide to make the changes?
6. Once you find problems in your organization, how do you begin to work on them?
7. Do you continually evaluate all of the elements of your system?
8. Do you make use of statisticians in your quality effort?

Your answers probably do not yet reflect the quality consciousness that will be evident in a "Deming company." Some basic procedures must be implemented to achieve this level of awareness.

An Overview of Never-Ending Improvement

Statistical methods are vital in working toward never-ending improvement. Everyone in the organization will need to learn basic techniques under the guidance of a master statistician to participate in its transformation. However, the environment in the company must demonstrate the new commitment to quality, a long-term perspective, and a growing trust between management and workers before statistical methods can be used. This may be an extremely difficult and painstaking process. It will also take time, probably a year or more, for everyone to be made aware of the new philosophy and to begin to trust the new attitude.

Management must provide basic statistical training to all employees. Hourly employees will need less theoretical content and more "how to" information. If a union is present, it must be fully informed about the objectives of the statistical effort to avoid conflict. Union officials must be included in the training sessions and should be enlisted as change agents if they accept the new philosophy.

Implementation of statistical methods should be gradual. Start with a pilot project rather than a massive effort that involves the whole organization. The pilot project must be chosen carefully. It should be something that has a high probability of demonstrating improvement and providing a model for how to solve a problem.

The Shewhart Cycle

An overview of the steps required to manage never-ending improvement is shown in Figure 5-2, known as the Shewhart cycle. The steps are listed below.

Step 1—PLAN (P): Collect data upon which a plan can be constructed for what needs to be accomplished, in a given time frame. Next, determine what actions must be taken to realize the plan. For example, in a sales department, prepare a daily or monthly sales and a visitation plan after fully examining customer needs.

Step 2—DO (D): Take the necessary actions that further the plan developed in Step 1. In this example, this translates into executing the sales and visitation plan.

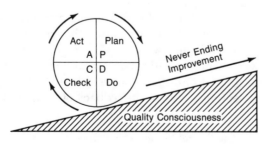

Figure 5-2   The Shewhart Cycle.

Step 3—CHECK (C): Check the results of our actions by collecting data to make sure that we have achieved what we planned. This means checking the sales and visitation records to see that they met the plan and satisfied the customer.

Step 4—ACT (A): Act by making the changes to the plan that are needed to better achieve customer satisfaction and to continue what we did that was successful. In the example discussed in Step 1, this translates into finding out if the customer is happy with the sales and visitation schedule. If the customer is not satisfied, changes are needed, and the information should be fed back to the preceding steps. If the customer is satisfied, feedback is necessary to ensure continued satisfaction. The PDCA circle creates never-ending improvement in the extended process and can be used in managing any subprocess.

Correct judgment is necessary to determine the proper actions to solve existing problems and to improve jobs correctly and efficiently. Judgment and action must be based on facts or data. Deciding on the nature of the data to be collected for a particular problem is the first step in quality improvement. Views not backed up by data are more likely to be opinions, exaggerations, and mistaken impressions, although data collection can result in invalid information if it is not done correctly.

The right data for the right problem, collected accurately and analyzed properly, can yield important information for action. But data without context or inaccurate data can be invalid and sometimes harmful to the problem-solving process.

Tools for Managing

Problem solving in an organized, directed fashion is sometimes difficult because people aren't familiar with step-by-step methods to attack a problem. Brief descriptions of several problem-solving tools follow to provide the reader with an overview of the various techniques.

Flow Chart or Diagram. A flow diagram is a tool used to describe a process. It shows the sequence of events which comprise the process. A flow chart usually begins with inputs, shows the transformations which occur to those inputs, and ends with outputs. Flow diagrams are particularly useful in visualizing operations and in aiding in planning and coordinating responsibilities of different areas. Figure 5–3 is an example of a flow chart representing a system for feedback of quality of design studies.[9]

[9]J. M. Juran, *Quality Control Handbook* (New York: McGraw-Hill Book Company, 1951), pp. 42.11.

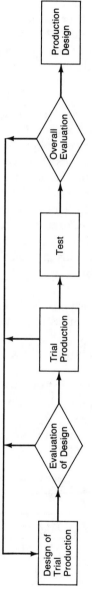

Figure 5-3   Flowchart of quality of design study.

Check Sheets.   Check sheets are forms used to collect data about problems, completed tasks, job assignments, etc. The best way to understand check sheets is through an example.

Table 5-1 shows a check sheet set up by a steel mill to collect information on injuries between January 1 and May 31. The check sheet allows management to generate a list of injuries, determine the number of injuries per month (by type), and know the frequency of different types of injuries, over time.

Pareto Analysis.   "Pareto analysis" is a method of separating the most important characteristics of an event from the least important characteristics of an event. It is a way of isolating the *vital few* from the *trivial many*. The vital few are the factors that account for the largest part of the total. Data are gathered and recorded on check sheets, which will eventually go into the construction of a Pareto chart. Once the chart is constructed, the major causes of a problem can be isolated and investigation can begin. Table 5-2 is an example of a check sheet, and Table 5-3 is a Pareto diagram of injuries in a steel mill. As you can see, 76 percent of the injuries are back strains. This information could lead to a directed program of accident prevention.

Brainstorming.   Brainstorming is a form of creative thinking. Brainstorming is designed to get unrestricted ideas about a particular topic from all members of a group.

Brainstorming sessions follow the three-step procedure listed below:

1. Each team member makes a list of ideas.
2. The team members sit in a circle and take turns reading one idea at a time. As the ideas are read, they are displayed so that all group members can see them. This procedure continues until all the items

TABLE 5-1   Injury Check Sheet

Type of Injury	January	February	March	April	May
		Month			
Back strain	̶H̶H̶ /	̶H̶H̶ ̶H̶H̶	̶H̶H̶ ̶H̶H̶	̶H̶H̶ //	̶H̶H̶
Acid burn					/
Hand cut	/	////	/		
Ankle sprain	/			/	
Foreign object in eye				/	/
Leg cut		/			

TABLE 5-2   Summary of Injury Check Sheet

Source Document:	Injury Report Form
Dates:	January 1–May 31
Location:	Anywhere, U.S.A.
Department:	Steel Mill

Type of Injury	Check	Subtotal
Ankle sprain	//	2
Back strain	//// //// //// //// //// //// //// ///	38
Hand cut	//// /	6
Foreign object in eye	//	2
Acid burn	/	1
Leg cut	/	1
Total		50

on everyone's list have been read. If an item on someone's list has been mentioned by another group member, that person should read the next item on the list. Cross-conversation is allowed only for clarification concerning a group member's item.

3. Once all items have been read, the group leader asks each person in turn if he or she has any new items. This process continues until no group members can think of any new items.

Fishbone (Cause and Effect) Diagram.   The fishbone diagram is a graphic way of analyzing problems (effects) and the causes that contribute to them. Brainstorming is used in a group setting to creatively bring forth

TABLE 5-3   Injury Pareto Diagram.

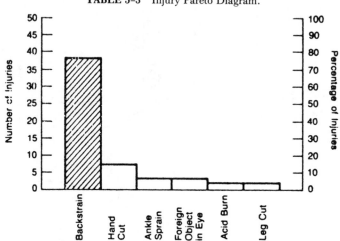

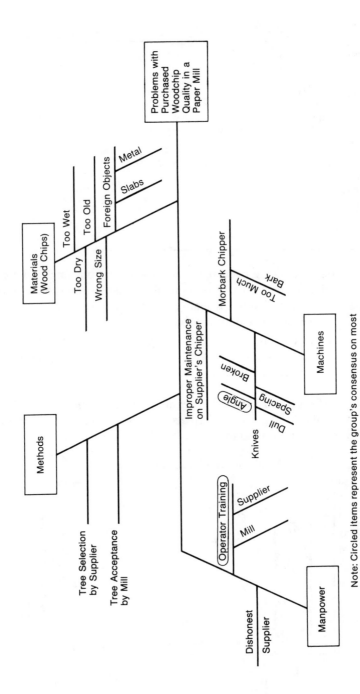

Figure 5-4 Cause and effect diagram of purchased chip quality.

Note: Circled items represent the group's consensus on most probable causes.

ideas which are used in the construction of the fishbone chart. Figure 5-4 is an example of a cause and effect diagram analyzing the problem of purchased wood chip quality in a paper mill. Once the causes are isolated and prioritized, corrective measures can be implemented or data collection can begin to determine if the isolated cause is a significant problem requiring corrective action.

Histogram. A histogram plots the frequency of each particular measurement in a group of measurements. It is a bar graph that depicts a frequency distribution. Figure 5-5 is an example of a histogram that shows the case hardness depth of cam shafts from two vendors. Histograms provide valuable information concerning the variability present in a process. This figure shows the increase in unit-to-unit variation which occurs when two vendors are used for a particular item, as opposed to one vendor.

Scatter Diagrams. Scatter diagrams show the relationship or correlation (but not cause and effect) between any two characteristics. If pairs of measurements about two characteristics are obtained and plotted, they form a scatter diagram. Further, if the points cluster around a straight line, there is a relationship or correlation between the two characteristics.

For example, a manufacturer of steel sheets wanted to determine if

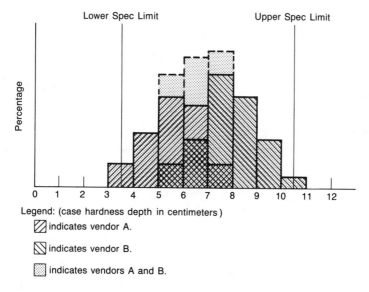

Figure 5-5 Histogram of case hardness depth of cam shafts from two vendors.

an inexpensive and nondestructive test of hardness (Brinnell hardness) could be substituted for an expensive and destructive test (tensile strength). The manufacturer collected data on the Brinnell hardness and tensile strength of twenty randomly selected steel sheets. He plotted the data to create a scatter diagram (see Figure 5–6). This figure shows that a strong relationship exists between the two methods; hence the Brinell test could be used, at a great savings.

Control Charts.   You will recall that control charts are used to study variation in a process to differentiate between common and special sources of variation. Walter Shewhart, a physicist with Bell Labs, did much of the early work of describing variation in statistical terms. By the early 1920s, Shewhart had developed control charts to monitor and analyze variation over time. Table 5–4 and the next five figures (Figures 5–7, 5–8, 5–9, 5–10, and 5–11) illustrate the construction of a control chart and demonstrate the impact that control chart usage can have on management's course of action.

Suppose you want to examine the keypunching operation in a data processing department. First, consumer research must be performed to determine what the critical characteristics of the keypunching operation are to the customer. Some possible characteristics are no typing errors, no transposition errors, no warped cards, no off-punched cards, no folded cards, and no bent cards. This information is further refined in service call

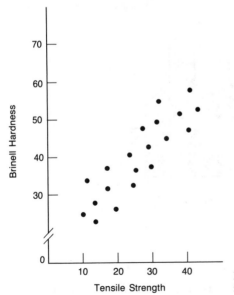

Figure 5–6   Scatter diagram of two tests for hardness.

TABLE 5–4   Raw Data for Construction of Control Chart

Day	Number of Cards Inspected	Number of Defective Cards	Proportion of Defective Cards
1	200	6	.03
2	200	6	.03
3	200	6	.03
4	200	5	.025
5	200	0	.0
6	200	0	.0
7	200	6	.03
8	200	14	.07
9	200	4	.02
10	200	0	.0
11	200	1	.005
12	200	8	.04
13	200	2	.01
14	200	4	.02
15	200	7	.035
16	200	1	.005
17	200	3	.015
18	200	1	.005
19	200	4	.02
20	200	0	.0
21	200	4	.02
22	200	15	.075
23	200	4	.02
24	200	1	.005
TOTAL	4,800	102	

analysis by speaking with customers concerning problems they are having with keypunched cards.

You must construct a flow diagram to clearly define the keypunch process. Operational definitions are then established for all process/product characteristics important to customers. This includes determining the best sampling plan to collect data on the customer-specified characteristics. Then you determine a sample size, let's say 200 cards per day. Take random samples of 200 cards from each day's output and check them in respect to the customer defined characteristics determined above. Table 5–4 shows the proportion of keypunch cards that fail to meet one or more of the critical customer characteristics; i.e., they are defective.

Figure 5–7 is a plot of "proportion defective" (column 4 in Table 5–4) against "day" (column 1 in Table 5–4). Figure 5–8 then shows the computations you'll need to construct the center line (in this example, the average proportion defective (p) for the process) and the upper and lower control limits (UCL and LCL). Remember: you will have a statistical expert to

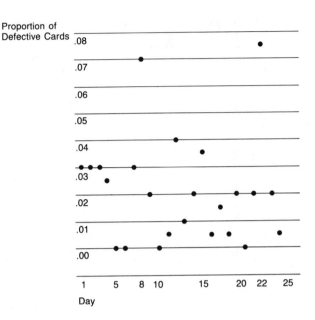

Figure 5-7 Plot percentage of defective cards against day. (Reprinted with permission of *Harvard Business Review*, September/October 1983, p. 134.)

guide you in the use of control charts. Next, you construct the control chart (Figure 5-9) by connecting the points plotted in Figure 5-7 and drawing the center line and upper and lower control limits across the points.

Finally, you analyze the control chart. If a sample value falls within the upper and lower control limits, and if a trend or some other systematic pattern is absent, the variation is probably common. If, however, a sample value falls outside the control limits, the variation is probably special. The control chart shown in Figure 5-9 is just one of many kinds of control charts, each of which has a special purpose.

Acting on Special Variation.   By comparing Figure 5-7 and Figure 5-9, the reader will see how difficult it is to differentiate between the two causes of variation with the naked eye. Figure 5-7 does not allow managers to distinguish between the two sources of variation, while Figure 5-9 clearly shows that on days 8 and 22, something special happened, not attributable to the system, to cause defective cards to be keypunched.

When a manager determines that the cause of variation is special, he or she should search for and eliminate the causes that are attributable to a specific worker or group of workers, a machine, or a new batch of raw materials, and so on.

Brainstorming, used in conjunction with cause and effect diagrams,

Figure 5-8 Computation of center line and control limits. (Reprinted with permission of *Harvard Business Review*, September/October, 1983, p. 135).

---

p = $\dfrac{\text{Total number of defectives over time frame under investigation}}{\text{Total number of units examined over time frame under investigation}}$

$$= \frac{102}{4,800} = .02125 \rightarrow .021 = \text{Center line}$$

UCL $= p + 3 \sqrt{\dfrac{p(1 - p)}{n}}$

$$= .02125 + 3 \sqrt{\frac{(.02125)(1 - .02125)}{200}}$$

$$= .02125 + 3 \,(.010198)$$

$$= .05184 \rightarrow .052^*$$

LCL $= p - 3 \sqrt{\dfrac{p(1 - p)}{n}}$

$$= .02125 - 3 \sqrt{\frac{(.02125)(1 - .02125)}{200}}$$

$$= -.00934 = 0.0 = 0.0\% \,^{**}$$

---

*If the upper control limit is .052 and a sample of 200 cards is randomly drawn from the process, then the UCL can be restated in number of defective cards $[10.4 = (200)(.052)]$. Hence, if 11 or more defective cards are found in a sample of 200 cards the process is declared out of statistical control.

**A negative percentage is not possible.

p = average proportion defective for the process,
UCL = upper control limit,
LCL = lower control limit, and
n = sample size.

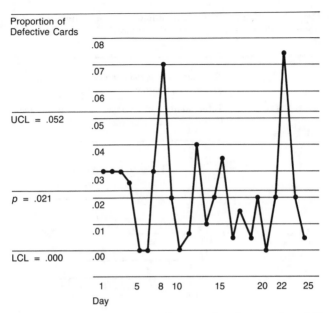

Figure 5–9 Control chart, or P-chart. (Reprinted with permission of *Harvard Business Review*, September/October 1983, p. 137.)

is useful to help determine the special sources of variation causing the key-punch operation to be out of control. This enables management to set policies which will eliminate sources of special variation, leaving it with a stable and predictable process.

For this example, let's say that management found that on day 8, a new keypunch operator had been added to the work force, and that the one day it took the worker to acclimate to the new environment probably caused the unusually high number of keypunch errors. To ensure that this assignable cause would not be repeated, the company instituted a one-day training program.

Investigation of day 22 showed that the night before, the department had run out of cards from the regular vendor and did not expect a new shipment until the morning of day 23. Consequently, the department purchased one day's supply of cards from a new vendor. Management found that these cards were of inferior quality, which caused the large number of keypunch errors. To correct this assignable variation, management instituted a revised inventory policy and operationally defined acceptable quality for keypunch cards.

After eliminating the days for which assignable causes of variation were found, managers recomputed the control chart statistics:

$$p = \frac{73}{4400} = 0.01659 \rightarrow 0.017$$

where

upper control limit = 0.044
lower control limit = 0.000
p = average proportion of cards with errors

Figure 5-10 shows the revised control chart next to the original chart. The process is now stable, in statistical control. The capability of the process has become known and predictable.

In summary a stable process that produces an unacceptable number of defects will continue to do so as long as the system remains the same, and only management is responsible for changing the system.

Acting on Common Variation. Once a process reaches stability, which is not a natural state but an achievement, management is ready to act on the system to improve productivity and quality. Checksheets used in tandem with Pareto analysis are extremely useful to determine causes of common variation and to prioritize them for action. Managers can improve the system by:

1. Shifting the process average. For example, management may want to decrease the proportion of defects or increase the average output.
2. Reducing the amount of variation. Management should continually work to decrease the amount of variation to obtain a more consistently uniform product.

Certain inputs and procedures, such as labor, training, supervision, raw materials, machines, and operational definitions, define the system. To improve the system, management must alter these factors. Again we stress that only management has the responsibility and authority to make these changes. Workers on their own cannot affect the system.

How can management set about changing the keypunch process to improve quality and productivity? Management can help employees produce more error-free cards consistently by instituting actions that improve the process, reducing the average proportion of defective cards and the amount of common variation.

In this example, checksheet and Pareto analysis resulted in management changing the lighting in the keypunch area. Management deter-

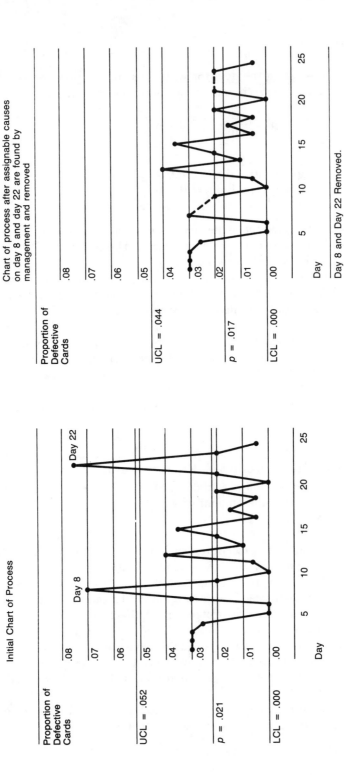

Figure 5-10 Control charts for keypunchers. (Reprinted with permission of *Harvard Business Review*, September/October 1983, p. 137.)

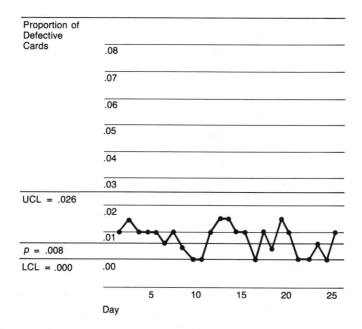

Figure 5-11 Chart of process after training and procedure changes have been implemented by management. (Reprinted with permission of *Harvard Business Review*, September/October 1983, p. 137.)

mined that poor lighting contributed to poor quality among all the keypunch operators. Figure 5-11 shows the new control chart after management installed new lighting. The average proportion of keypunch cards with errors has decreased from 0.17 to .008, and the process variation has decreased as well.

It is important to stress that the concepts we've been discussing encompass more than just control charts. Companies may use control charts without any understanding of the approach we're concerned with, namely, management's responsibility for improving the system, no habitual dependence on final inspection, quality consciousness, and long-term perspective, etc.[10]

POSSIBLE PITFALLS

Introducing the use of statistical methods is a difficult and critical process. There are many pitfalls that must be avoided in working toward neverending improvement. Some pitfalls are:

[10]Gitlow and Hertz, "Product Defects and Productivity," pp. 133–36.

1. *Management attempting to reach never-ending improvement only through automation and, capital investments.*

   This may be necessary, but overall system improvement using statistical methods may minimize the need for capital investment and can enable the organization to achieve its goals.

2. *Management's inability to create an atmosphere that is conducive to the workers' acceptance of their new tasks.*

   Employees are going to experience many changes in the implementation of Point Five. They will be required to go through training to learn statistical methods, which will substantially alter their jobs. If management has not created an environment that recognizes the difficulty of this and has not offered substantial support and freedom to express doubts and concerns, workers will reject the use of statistical methods.

3. *Management attempting to improve the process without the guidance of a competent statistician.*

   Managers must know enough to know that they don't know. A statistician trained in Dr. Deming's methods or one who can be trained is essential to the journey to quality. A statistician will help the organization through training and overseeing the use of statistical methods. He or she will initially train top management in the organization, set up a pilot project once the corporate environment is ready, guide the data collection and analysis, and continue training. Without the assistance of a statistician, results are impossible to achieve. If a company works with a statistician, then its managers can gain an understanding and appreciation of variation in a system. This will prevent management from taking action when no action is necessary or from taking inappropriate action.

4. *Managers' reluctance to make improvements that reduce their level of responsibility.*

   Since the use of statistical methods usually leads to simplification of the process, managers may fear that their departments will be less complex, changing the need for management. Departments might be merged or eliminated, depending on what the new system demands. This is threatening to managers because they don't know what their responsibilities and position will be in the new system.

5. *Management's insensitivity to labor's resistance to using statistical tools.*

   Employees who have been working at a job for several years feel that they "own" their jobs. They know them inside and out and immediately mistrust an outsider (statistician) who purports to tell them what their jobs are. Management must be sensitive to this issue and must work with the consultant and employees to enable acceptance of the new methods. One way to do this is to involve union leadership in training from the very beginning. If union leaders understand that the statistical tools are not being used to punitively measure the amount of work done by employees, then they can ease problems in the transition phase. If the union is left out and doesn't grasp the goals of the new philosophy, then it will understandably undermine any efforts to use statistical methods.

6. *Using statistical methods as as policing tool.*

Statistics in a "Deming company" are used constructively for the purposes of never-ending improvement. However, some companies and managers view statistics as a way of keeping tabs on what the employees are doing. Using statistics as a policing tool only creates and fosters an atmosphere of mistrust and pettiness, rather than creating an atmosphere of never-ending improvement.

7. *Creating a separateness between "the real job" and "statistical methods."*

Everyone has to integrate statistical methods into their day-to-day job functions because never-ending improvement *is* the job. Jobs have to be redefined and prioritized to demand statistical thinking and application. Once Dr. Deming's methods are adopted, they must filter into the everyday workings of the organization. If they do not become part of everyone's job, then they will tend to be seen as an extra, an add-on, and quite possibly will be ignored or put off until the "real job" is done.

8. *Premature large-scale use of statistical methods by hourly workers.*

Anyone who supposes that quality, productivity, and competitive position can be achieved by massive immediate use of control charts and other statistical techniques by hourly workers will doom his own career and carry his company along with him.[11] Statistical methods require awareness concerning their use and interpretation. Premature use of control charts will leave workers wondering, "What do I do with this control chart? How do I read this control chart?" This will seriously negate efforts to change the corporate culture and will impede transformation.

9. *Politicalization of changes needed for never-ending improvement.*

Statistical work will result in organizational changes. Organizations must be careful not to allow these changes to become excuses

---

[11]W. Edwards Deming, *Quality, Productivity, and Competitive Position*, p. 48.

to redress old grievances. For example, one of the authors was in a plant that required installation of a sampling station. By the time the blueprint for the station was complete, it looked like a mini-palace. The parties involved were trying to use the sampling station as a way to get something they had been denied in the past. This politicking delayed the quality effort.

6

Instituting Modern Training Methods

DISCUSSION OF POINT SIX

There is a great deal of training going on in American organizations today. Some companies have their own training departments. In other firms, consultants are brought in, or employees are sent out to receive state-of-the-art training. Expensive equipment is often required to show films, videotapes, and slides. Programmed instruction and computers are also utilized. Training has become a very expensive, time-consuming process. The question is whether it is worth it. Certainly workers need to be trained to perform their jobs. However, training, as it is currently implemented, needs to be totally overhauled. It must be integrated into the new philosophy and be guided by the new attitude. Too often, training is used by management as a response to a problem, instead of as an ongoing integrated approach to employees' growth and development. In our new philosophy, employees are our most important assets. We must make a commitment to expend the time, effort, and money to train them so that they can adopt the organization's philosophy and do their jobs properly, and then assess whether they are achieving personal and organizational objectives.

Training in the Organization's Philosophy

When a new employee begins, orientation to the company's philosophy of commitment to never-ending improvement must occur. *All* employees should be taught about Dr. Deming's Fourteen Points initially, although this will be an ongoing process. The organization's goals should also be discussed. The idea of discussing these issues with all employees will seem very strange to some managers, trainers, and supervisors. But, how can you expect employees to work with you to achieve organizational goals if they don't know what the goals are? Training must demonstrate to the employees that they are an important part of the team. It can initially help the new employees feel more relaxed and comfortable in a difficult situation. If employees are screened well and hired because they agree with the company's philosophy and goals, this aspect of training should aid in reducing new employee anxiety. Knowing that they are working with people who have similar beliefs and values about work is important to the initiation process.

Job Training

Once an employee is trained in the company's philosophy, learning how to perform the job is necessary. In many organizations, this means on-the-job training and involves assigning a new employee to an experienced worker who does the actual training. There are several problems with this method, among which are: (1) the experienced worker may not be a good teacher; (2) the new worker may be forced because of time pressures to produce before being really ready; (3) the experienced worker may leave out some explanations because of being so accustomed to doing the job; and (4) the trainee learns only the particular job tasks. The last issue is particularly important to an organization that wants to become a "Deming company." Employees in the new system must be trained to perform their jobs, but their "job" is much more broadly defined to include an understanding of the organization's product or service and the quality characteristics associated with that product or service. This means that the employees must understand operational definitions and specifications in order to perform their jobs. The employees need to get an overall picture of what is being done, not just learn the specific parts of their job.

Employees also must understand the extended process and where they fit in the process. They should know about the process within their own organization as well as the vendor's and customer's jobs. Frequently the vendor and customer will be production workers within their own company. Dr. Deming raises an important question: "How many production workers ever saw the next operation, their customer?"[1] This lack of coordination within the system reinforces the employee's view that just performing the job tasks is enough. At a seminar given by one of the authors, a woman whose job title was "100 Percent Inspector" related that she once asked management what product the component she was inspecting went into. She was told that "she didn't need to know." Of course she didn't *need* to know if all that is expected of her is to mechanically perform her task. But management should see her as an integral part of the system and

---

[1] W. Edwards Deming, *Quality, Productivity, and Competitive Position* (Cambridge, Mass.; M.I.T., Center for Advanced Engineering Study, 1982), p. 194.

should train her to understand the entire process, instead of viewing her as a dehumanized robot. The problems in morale and employee relations that this attitude creates are staggering. Management must begin to view workers as human beings who deserve the opportunity to learn and develop within the context of their job situation.

Requirements for Training

Management must view training as part of everyone's job, not an add-on or an extra. Time and money must be budgeted for training, and a great deal of thought should go into its planning. Input from all levels of the organization is important in needs assessment for training. Once the needs are assessed, a training procedure should be established. This should include formal class work, experiential work, and instructional materials. (Training techniques will be presented later on in this chapter.)

The most important part of any training is evaluating when someone's training is completed. Unfortunately, the methods generally used to do this are woefully inadequate. Evaluations by the trainer and/or trainee are subjective and have no factual base. Pre- and posttests attempt to gather statistical information but are frequently one-shot deals that offer no long-term perspective or plan for improvement. Dr. Deming's approach is much more integrated and provides a fair, objective way of assessing when someone is adequately trained.

Using Statistical Methods

Statistical methods must be used to learn when training is completed and also can determine the worker's capability. By using control charts, workers can see whether they are in control. If not, then they can use more training. Once in statistical control, employees can work on never-ending improvement. However, if workers are in statistical control, then more training will not improve performance or change the capability of the process. They must be trained using new methods, or screened and given a new job with proper training. Further, it is possible that someone who is in statistical control can lose it. So, more training can be beneficial. Workers will also need training if product specifications are changed because that essentially changes their jobs.

Results of Poor Training

Poor training (which sometimes translates into no training) can cause several major problems in an organization:

1. Poor quality is caused by differences between workers, between inspectors, and between workers and inspectors. This happens because people don't know what their job is. They haven't been properly trained, and the result is a variable standard of quality.
2. Employees fear causing physical harm to themselves or others because they don't know correct procedures. Employees may also fear being caught doing something wrong by the supervisor or by their co-workers.
3. Barriers are created by poorly defined job boundaries. Conflicts often result because people are unsure of what their jobs are and how they interact with the other jobs in the process.
4. Workers lose their pride of workmanship. They don't know what to do, how to do it, or how it fits into the overall picture. They are embarrassed at not knowing and are reluctant to ask questions because they have supposedly been trained.
5. Stress levels for everyone in the organization are high because personal and organizational goals are not being met.

Results of Proper Training

Training that offers employees a share in the overall philosophy and goals of the organization, an understanding of their job as more than just a mechanical task, specific procedures to do their job properly, and a way of evaluating when training is complete results in many positives for an organization:

1. Quality is improved because everyone knows the job and is in statistical control pursuing never-ending improvement.
2. The process's capability is known, and the company can offer statistical evidence of process control to customers. This obviously makes the firm an attractive vendor.
3. Workers are secure in their jobs. They no longer fear causing harm or being caught by their supervisor. They have become involved in a process that encourages asking questions and solving problems.
4. Barriers between workers are broken down. Since everyone knows what his or her job is, boundaries are clear, and conflicts will significantly decrease.
5. Workers regain a sense of pride in their work. They feel they are valuable, and they become more open to improvement and learning.
6. Stress levels decrease. Organizational and personal goals are being

met, and the whole atmosphere is more positive, encouraging better working relationships and higher morale.

HOW POINT SIX RELATES TO THE OVERALL PHILOSOPHY

In the Deming philosophy, people are viewed as an organization's most valuable long-term resource. No other company asset improves with age like an employee. Management must help people, through training. Then they will flourish and constantly improve. People want to do a good job, but they need to understand what their job is and to feel a part of the extended process. Modern training methods involve a long-term perspective because use of control charts implies commitment over time, with consideration of variation in the system. Training becomes a process, not an entity that is completed for the sake of completing it, without a means to measure its effectiveness.

Modern methods of training help to create the new corporate environment and provide a positive attitude that is necessary to compete and succeed in the new economic age. Training is set up to help the worker succeed and improve his or her performance, instead of setting the person up to fail and suffer loss of morale. By operationally defining what is expected of the worker and gearing training to improve what the worker already knows, management creates a positive experience. This feeling is generalized to feeling good about the organization, about the work being done, and about himself or herself.

Training workers to achieve statistical control results in improvement of quality. The system's capability is known, and the company knows what it is able to produce consistently and at what price. This is vital information to customers and can make the firm a much wanted supplier. The company can continue the journey for never-ending improvement once it has a stable process. It is extremely important that the workers understand that the never-ending process of improvement is a goal and that they are a part of that effort. If management clarifies its belief that the workers will not be blamed for problems of the system, then the workers will honestly and accurately perform their jobs. They have nothing to hide because they will understand common and special causes of variation and statistical control.

IDEAS FOR ACTION

Responding to the following questions should indicate where you stand in relation to training in your organization.

Questions for Self-Examination

1. Is training in your organization tied to your mission and goals?
2. Are new employees often thrown into a job situation with minimal or no training?
3. Do new employees know clearly what is expected of them?
4. Are new employees trained in the philosophy and values of the organization?
5. How do you know when training is completed? Is there a way of measuring its effectiveness, or is it over when it's over?
6. Is management responding to problems by throwing training at the workers in an attempt to "do something"?

Your answers to the above questions can provide you with some insight into your company's training philosophy. Your organization probably spends money on training, but is it helping you to achieve your goals? In the Deming philosophy, training is a vital link between management and employees that sets the stage for never-ending improvement.

Setting Up a Training Program

A general model for setting up any type of training program is provided below.

Identify Organizational Objectives and Goals.   Management must first have a plan for the organization and must work with the Training Department so that the trainers have an overall picture of the organization currently, and in the future. Trainers have to know if any major changes are anticipated that will impact on the training effort. Management should see training as a link between itself and the rest of the organization. Information about the mission and philosophy must be communicated, and to a large extent, this is accomplished through training.

Identify Organizational Goals That Will Be Met Through Training.   Management has to develop an "action plan" to meet its goals. Within this framework, certain goals can be achieved through training. Management should identify these objectives and should work with the trainers to formalize a plan for training in these areas. Examples of the types of training are listed below:

A. *Organizational philosophy and goals training* could aid in meeting a goal of socializing everyone to the mission statement, in an ongoing fashion.

B. *New employee orientation* will be beneficial in achieving a goal of making everyone aware that quality is the company's major thrust.

C. *Supervisory training* could help in gaining supervisory support for the Deming philosophy, statistical thinking, and never-ending improvement.

D. *Management training* could focus on teaching managers the Deming philosophy and how to think statistically.

E. *Team building* could be beneficial in changing the corporate culture.

F. *Problem-solving techniques* would relate to the organization's journey for never-ending improvement.

G. *Job training* should be geared to the pursuit of quality in the extended process.

Developing training programs that are connected to the overall goals of the organization is extremely important. Management has to use training as part of an "action plan," not as a reaction to a problem.

Analyze What Needs To Be Taught. Trainers should work with managers, supervisors, and employees to analyze the needs in a particular area. Let's say you want to set up training for new employees. A needs assessment should be performed to determine what the new employee should be taught. For example, input should be obtained from management as to the needed training in organizational goals and philosophy. Supervisors should be consulted as to the training needs in departmental and company rules and policies, orientation to the workplace, and the nature of supervision. And employees should be consulted and observed to obtain information about the "job," its tasks, and its place in the extended process. A trainer can only perform the job when a valid needs assessment has been performed and he or she sees how the particular training fits into the overall picture.

Develop the Training Program. There are as many approaches to training as there are trainers. Much of one's own personal style is transmitted in the training process, so the trainer has to be comfortable with the methods and media that are used. Autonomy must be given to develop the program around the strengths of the trainer, while meeting the needs of the trainees. In general, training should contain a variety of methods and media because different people learn differently. "Job" training should include: (1) formal class work, (2) experiential work, (3) clear instructional materials and (4) the use of statistical methods.

Formal Class Work. Formal class work to convey certain cognitive information and to orient new employees to the organization and its philosophy and goals is necessary. Trainers can provide many types of learning experiences through the use of books, workbooks, audio-visual techniques (audio tape, video tape, film, slides, overhead projectors, charts, etc.), programmed learning, computer-aided learning, role-playing, discussions, case studies, and lectures. Varying the use of the methods and media will help keep the attention of adult learners. Classroom work must be planned very carefully so that the presentation is relevant, informative, interesting, factual, and well-organized. Employees will turn off and tune out if they feel that the training doesn't meet their needs.

Experiential Training. Experiential training is a must. Most jobs use techniques that can only be learned through practice. The ideal situation is an apprenticeship, with an expert in the field. Since this is not generally feasible, alternatives are on-the-job training, or simulated environment training. On-the-job training has certain disadvantages, which we have discussed, but where there is no alternative, it must be used. If you can designate certain employees as trainers and teach them how to teach, on-the-job training can be beneficial. Pressure must not be put on the trainee to perform initially, and a trusting atmosphere should prevail. Simulated environments can be helpful because employees are not under pressure to produce in the actual job site. They can become familiar and comfortable with the job before they actually have to do it.

Instructional Materials. Workers must have clear, concise tangible instructions that describe (1) the product(s) and/or service(s) of the organization, (2) the quality characteristics, specifications, and operational definitions, (3) the company's philosophy and goals, and (4) the job of the worker, vendor, customer, and supervisor, etc., in the extended process. This will provide employees the opportunity to integrate all of these aspects of their "job" and the ability to refer to the materials when they have questions.

Use of Statistical Methods. Statistical methods must be used to monitor training and to determine when it is completed. This was discussed earlier in this chapter, so only a brief example will be provided here.

Before training, a machine operator's control chart of the proportion of defectives produced per day looked like that shown in Figure 6-1. Training was instituted and monitored through control charts. Eventually the worker was able to bring his process into control (see Figure 6-2).

Once the worker was in control, training was complete. If the worker loses control of the process or the specifications change, then training should take place again.

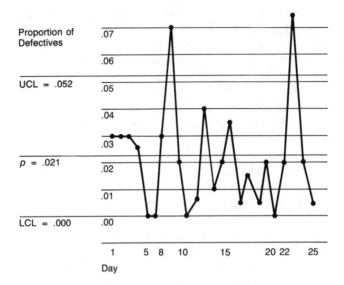

Figure 6-1 Cutting machine operator's control chart before training. (Reprinted with permission of *Harvard Business Review*, September/October 1983, p. 137.)

Implement the Training Program.   Once organizational goals and objectives and needs assessments are incorporated into the preparation of a training program, training should be implemented. This stage in the process seems obvious; however, implementation is not always that simple. Logistics, changes in priorities, and resistances are some of the issues that can impede the training effort.

Logistical issues such as deciding on a time that is good for everyone to participate in training, the location, who is to attend, and how long the training should last arise and often are interwoven with interpersonal

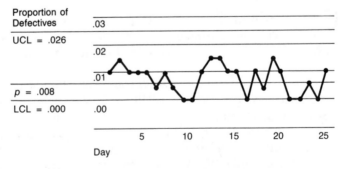

Figure 6-2 Cutting machine operator's control chart after training. (Reprinted with permission of *Harvard Business Review*, September/October 1983, p. 137.)

and political matters of the organization. Every effort must be made to support the training effort and overcome these logistical issues. Management should step in when necessary to reinforce the trainer's efforts.

Implementing a training program can often be impeded by management who requested the training in the first place. Managers often change their priorities, so that a training program that was of utmost importance one week can be scrapped the next if there are budgetary changes, staff cuts, or production deadlines. Trainers must do everything they can to help managers maintain a long-term perspective in respect to training. Training that has been planned as an outgrowth of organizational objectives and philosophy must proceed in spite of short-term obstacles.

Resistance to training is a common phenomenon. People are fearful of change and often don't like being placed in a learning situation because of past difficulties or not wanting to expose their perceived inadequacies. The trainer must be aware of these resistances and must deal with them directly. Whether it is a group of managers who are resisting the idea of carrying the responsibility for the system, or it is an employee who keeps doing a task the "old" way, the trainer should confront the individual(s) with the attitude that is getting in the way of training. When resistance is pointed out, people generally acknowledge it and, in time, with help, can work through it and proceed with learning. In those cases where resistance is so great as to preclude learning, training is inadvisable until the person is ready.

Evaluation of Training.   Evaluation of training is really customer feedback. Trainees are the customers, and trainers are the vendors in the process. Trainers need to find out from their customers if they have met their needs. That is, are they helping trainees do their jobs and meet customer needs? The trainer must accept feedback, model openness to learning, and create an environment that encourages free-flowing expression of feelings. In this way, the training process becomes a model of the extended process that everyone can experience.

Feedback can be given in questionnaire form or verbally, or a combination of both. Trainers should alter their training programs based on customer feedback to more closely meet customer needs the next time around. Never-ending improvement is as important in training as everywhere else in the organization.

POSSIBLE PITFALLS

Training is extremely important in changing an organization from its current state to a "Deming company." The entire organization, including top management and union officials, should participate in training in the new philosophy and methods. There are several pitfalls that can impede the training process. Among them are:

1. *Management using training as a reaction to problems.*

   In the absence of a comprehensive philosophy of management and long-term goals and objectives, management will seek short-term solutions to problems. It is very easy to throw training at a problem, instead of analyzing the problem, discovering what the real issues are, and formulating and implementing a plan for dealing with it. This reaction is only a "band-aid" solution that may improve the problem in the short run, but over time will not solve the problem and may create more problems.

2. *Management jumping on the bandwagon for every new training fad.*

   Types of training and trainers seem to increase daily. New methods based on emerging research abound, and it is becoming difficult for a manager to know what type of training to implement. Some managers become enthralled with every new fad or technique that emerges, with little thought to the long-term consequences for their staffs. In the 1970's sensitivity training was popular and seemed to fit into the people oriented type of organizations that were emerging. Managers later found out that the training brought a lot of personal and interpersonal issues to the surface, but it did not really resolve them. It actually created more problems by frustrating people. Training *must* relate to the organization's long-term goals and objectives in order to be effective. People should not be subjected to managerial interest in a passing fad, in lieu of meaningful training that helps them do a better job.

3. *Continuing to rely on on-the-job training.*

   Management has to give up the notion that employees can train each other. It is management's responsibility to provide employees with the tools to do their jobs. One of those tools is proper training. Dr. Deming considers reliance on on-the-job training a serious disease in American industry. Resources have to be committed to educate and develop personnel since they are so vital to the company's success.

4. *Using training as a punishment.*

   In some organizations, an employee is sent to training because of inability to do the job. Usually, the employee can't do the job because proper training wasn't provided initially. The employee is punished because the system has failed. Proper training has to be implemented for all employees and must be monitored through statistical methods to know when training is completed.

5. *Trainers' resistance to the use of statistical methods.*

Many trainers and organizational development specialists are "people" people. They probably have had no training or experience in statistical methods, job definitions, operational definitions, etc., so they may resist the new type of training. Trainers have to be educated in the new philosophy so that they can understand that its main thrust is helping employees do their jobs properly. Management and the statistical consultant should work very closely with the training department so that the trainers "buy into" the new philosophy and their role in it. Trainers' resistances should be addressed openly, and fears should be allayed. This will help the trainers when they have to deal with employees' resistances.

6. *Labor's resistance to the new type of training.*

Employees, as they begin to participate in the new training, will not initially trust the new philosophy and will view the use of control charts as threatening to their jobs and seniority. They may see monitoring their performance as a test, rather than as a helping mechanism. Management, trainers, and supervisors must help them accept the new training in the context of the philosophy of never-ending improvement. This will be a long process. Union officials should be trained in the Deming philosophy so that they can support the new methods of training. Otherwise, they will view the use of statistical methods as documentation of employee failures, rather than as a method for the elimination of problems within the system.

7. *Failure to realize that training is a process requiring never-ending improvement.*

Management has a tendency to believe that when people have completed training, they are "trained." Training is a process that should be constantly refined, over time, by the trainers and the trainees. Input from all levels of the organization will be needed to continually improve the training process. Otherwise, training will be a waste of time, omitting the components of learning, growth, and development that have to take place. Viable training is a long-term process that needs support from top management if it is to succeed.

8. *Delaying implementation of the training.*

Once people are trained, they should be given the opportunity to use what they have learned as soon as possible. This will substantially reinforce their learning. If people have to wait to use what they have gained in training, they may forget a significant amount of information and/or skills.

7

Supervising
Never-Ending
Improvement

DISCUSSION OF POINT SEVEN

Consider the following scenarios:

"**The Not Tall Enough Employee**". An hourly employee in man-ufacturing is called into his supervisor's office. He says to himself, "Uh-oh, what did I do this time?" and nervously approaches his meeting. When he arrives, the supervisor tells him that he has been watching him this morning and noticed that he wasted a lot of time. The worker, who felt like he was doing a particularly good job this morning, is surprised but says nothing. The supervisor says that every time the worker needed a particular stock item he had to go and get a ladder to reach it, wasting time that he could be using on the production line. The supervisor tells the worker to do something about it and dismisses him.

The worker is troubled. He wants to do better but wonders what to do. Should he ask someone else to get the stock for him? Should he ask the supervisor to put the stock in a more accessible place? Maybe he should quit his job because he's not tall enough? Or worse, maybe he'll be fired. What will happen to his family if he loses his job? By the time the worker returns to the line, he is fearful, demoralized, and uncertain. For the rest of the day his output slows down and its quality is diminished.

"**Who Inspects the Inspectors?**" Marsha and Mo, who work next to each other on the production line, are called into the supervisor's office. Marsha is praised for a low defect rate, while Mo is berated for producing too many defectives. Mo is confused. He doesn't understand why there should be such a difference between himself and Marsha. They started on the job at the same time; they were trained together; they work at the same pace; and they seem to do the same things. Mo says he'll try to do better, and Marsha and he return to the floor. On the way, Marsha says, "I don't understand it. You and I work the same. What's going on here?" Mo is glad to get some support from his co-worker but still feels badly because he's doing a poor job and doesn't know how to improve. Nobody realizes that the difference between Marsha and Mo is negligible. The real difference is between the inspectors, John and Joanne. John inspects Mo's output; he is extremely critical. Joanne inspects Marsha's output; she is lenient and accepts most anything. The problem is a variable standard of what is acceptable between inspectors.

"The Sales Manager Gets Sold Short".   A District Sales Manager for a company that makes shoelaces is meeting with the Vice President of Sales for her annual performance appraisal. The Vice President commends her on her hard work, her ability to work well with subordinates, and her loyalty to the company. "But," he says, "your district's sales haven't met this year's quota, so we can't possibly give you a raise." The Sales Manager is taken by surprise. She says, "Everyone knows that the reason sales are down is because the importers are getting such a high market share. They're able to provide better quality laces at lower prices. What can I do about that?" The Vice President says, "Well, maybe we can send you for some training on how to motivate employees so they'll sell more. That should help improve your sales for next quarter. You'll just have to work harder to get that raise."

Current Supervisory Practices

What do the previous situations have in common? They demonstrate the poor supervision that is inflicted upon workers and managers. People are penalized for problems in the system; they are blamed for things that are completely beyond their control. In the case of the "Not Tall Enough Employee," the worker is blamed for being resourceful enough to find a way to do his job. If management really wanted him to do his job, it should take responsibility for the system and move the stock someplace else or give the employee a job that he is capable of performing. If management accepts the system as it is and doesn't change anything, then it must accept the employee's way of coping with the problem and not penalize him.

In the second scenario, "Who Inspects the Inspectors?" a very important issue is raised. Inspector variability caused by different perceptions of what is "good," fuzzy operational definitions, or inspectors' being out of control can play havoc with quality. Supervision based on inspection without a standard of quality is a farce and leads to demoralization of the work force.

Managers themselves are subject to poor supervision by being blamed for things that are beyond their control. Management's dealing with poor supervision may not be a day-to-day confrontation, however; it is usually distilled in the performance appraisal. The scenario "The Sales Manager Gets Sold Short" tells a familiar story. The Sales Manager is being punished for the poor quality/high cost of the product, in relation to the importers' products. Instead of the firm taking a hard look at its goals and its barriers to achieving quality, and implementing a plan to deal with the problems, management is doing nothing. The Vice President is the embodiment of management without reason. What can the Sales Manager do to improve the quality of the product, bring down its price, and make it competitive in the marketplace? Plenty, if the system were operating properly, and she could provide customer feedback to the design and production people. As the system stands, though, she can do nothing but be another victim of management's ignorance. How frustrating to work at a job and know you are doomed to failure! The Vice President's feeble attempt at encouraging the Sales Manager with the promise of training demonstrates management's misunderstanding of where the problem lies. Until management takes responsibility for the system, change cannot occur.

Management's Responsibility

Management must understand and must do something about variation in the system before supervision of workers can be truly meaningful. Immediate action should be taken by management to bring the system into control. Special causes should be removed. Inherent defects, bad incoming parts, machines not maintained, fuzzy operational definitions, tools not designed for the job, and shifts passing the buck to each other to meet quotas—all are barriers to quality that must be found and eliminated. When management does this, employees will know that it cares about improvement and that it knows how to achieve it.

An example of the result of management not acting on special problems was cited in an interview with John F. Mee:

> The leader of a foundry wanted more productivity. He asked the foreman why he wasn't getting it. The foreman was disgruntled and said he didn't believe the leader really wanted more productivity. "Why do you think that?" the leader asked.
>
> He was told that if he really wanted improvement, he would have removed numerous obstacles, such as faults in the tool room, faults with the way orders were written, faults with specifying proper standards. Even some

of the machinery wasn't up to the job. The foreman pointed out, and he was right, that these faults could only be corrected by the boss, and the boss had not corrected them. So, he assumed the boss didn't really want better production.[1]

Once special causes are removed, common variation will remain in the system. At that point, it is management's responsibility to tighten and hone the system to reduce common variation. Blaming workers for mistakes that are caused by common variation is very unfair. Workers are unable to do anything about those defects that are caused by common variation. Telling a worker about a mistake that is due to common variation is charging the worker with the system's problems. Supervisors who do this are creating frustration and stress for their employees.

Supervisors' Responsibility

Instead of focusing on the negative, policing, and searching for individual wrongdoing, supervisors should strive to create a positive, supportive atmosphere in which their relationships with employees are free from fear and mistrust. Building this type of relationship is the key element in good supervision. In this context, an employee will be open to learning, development, criticism, assistance, and change. Dr. Deming states, "The aim of supervision should be to improve the performance of man and machine, to increase output, and simultaneously to lighten the load of the production worker, to make his job more interesting as well as more productive."[2] A supervisor should be a coach, helping people to do better all the time in the journey for never-ending improvement.

The purposes of supervision should be to:

(a) Advance training,
(b) Remove barriers,
(c) Create an environment in which the worker can take pride in his or her work,
(d) Show workers how they fit into the extended process,
(e) Stress quality and
(f) Help improve the worker.

Supervisors should be trained in statistical methods so that they can help employees achieve statistical control and pursue never-ending im-

[1] Understanding the Attitudes of Today's Employees," *Nation's Business*, August 1976.

[2] W. Edwards Deming, *Quality, Productivity, and Competitive Position* (Cambridge, Mass.: M.I.T., Center for Advanced Engineering Study, 1982), p. 193.

provement. They can then train employees properly and know when training is completed. Another important task of the supervisor is to remove barriers in the system that impede the workers' performance of the job. This will go a long way in winning the workers' trust and in helping them take pride in their work. The supervisor should help the employees see where they fit into the whole picture. Organizational goals and philosophy should be imparted, and the employees should learn their importance in the extended process. The quality consciousness of the company should be stressed by supervisors, in their role as intermediaries between top management and workers.

Workers' Responsibility

If the nature of supervision is going to change, workers need to give the new system a chance. They have to be willing to trust the new environment and policies, to learn new techniques, and to develop a different way of relating to their supervisors. This will be difficult because in many cases it will be necessary to change long-established, ingrained patterns and habits. Managers and supervisors must make the initial effort to demonstrate their commitment to the new philosophy. If employees perceive it as a real commitment, then they will eventually accept the new type of supervision.

HOW POINT SEVEN RELATES TO THE OVERALL PHILOSOPHY

Supervision is a critical link between top management and workers. Instituting modern methods of supervision is key in changing an organization to a "Deming company" because supervisors wield a lot of power in their interpretation of management's edicts and actions. Supervisors essentially represent management's follow-through since workers rarely have contact with top management. If top management espouses the Deming philosophy but supervision of employees remains essentially the same, workers will not believe that management is serious. Therefore, management has to work closely and carefully with supervisors to ensure their acceptance of the new philosophy and the carrying out of their new responsibilities. Management has to provide a role model for supervisors, helping people accept change and creating a supportive environment.

The new supervision concretely demonstrates a long-term perspective. Using control charts to monitor the worker's performance necessitates a long-term view because the worker is looked at over time, rather than on a day-to-day or hour-to-hour basis. By using control charts and by changing the nature of supervision from day-to-day policing to working on process control and considering variation, the supervisor is clearly communicating management's long-term commitment.

Another way that the new supervision demonstrates long-term commitment is through the amount of time and resources that are now devoted to employees and their learning and development. No longer are employees thrown on the job with little or no training and left to find their own way in the system. The supervisor's job in a "Deming company" is to promote the growth and development of the employee through a long-term trusting relationship. It is within the context of this relationship that the new philosophy is made real for the worker, and the employee can believe that top management cares about its workers.

Instituting modern methods of supervision is managing for success. It generates a positive atmosphere because supervisors are not policing workers and blaming them for the handicaps of the system. The worker is treated with dignity, trained and supervised properly, and knows what the job is so that performance can improve. Employee morale improves; workers become more interested in their jobs and perform even better. Then, supervisors and management develop confidence in the workers, which further raises employee morale. Employees want to be involved in problem solving rather than griping, and management is open to their participation. It is a cycle of positives that is set in motion by the new supervision and attitude.

As workers feel better about their jobs and rekindle their pride of workmanship, they do a better job and quality improves. Through modern methods of supervision, the worker understands the job better, performs it better, and is coached and supported to seek never-ending improvement. The new quality effort and emphasis filter down to employees through good supervision. Through competent supervision, the worker also understands the extended process and where he or she fits into it. Workers know how they relate to their co-workers, the customers, the vendors, the community, and the organization as a whole. Employees feel a part of an important process and can identify with the philosophy and goals of the company.

IDEAS FOR ACTION

How you view supervision will become more evident after you have pondered the following questions.

Questions for Self-Evaluation

1. Does supervision in your organization take place within the context of a supportive relationship?
2. Do supervisors feel that they must police the workers, or otherwise the workers will slack off and productivity will decrease?
3. Do workers fear their supervisors because interactions with them are generally blaming sessions?
4. Are workers aware of what their job is, and how they fit into the extended process?
5. Is a spirit of teamwork evident in your company?
6. Are performance appraisals used to determine raises and promotions?
7. Are employees penalized because of poor inspection procedures?
8. Are resources being provided for continued learning and development on the job?
9. Does your organization reward and punish based on common variation?

Thinking about the above questions should raise some issues about supervision to which anyone who works in an organization can relate. Many people have been a supervisor and a supervisee and have had good and bad experiences in both roles. Supervisor-supervisee relationships have some elements that mirror parent-child relationships, such as nurturing, discipline, dependence, ambivalence, and power. These are highly charged issues for most people, and they carry over to the supervisory relationship. When most people talk about work to their family, friends, and co-workers, their supervisors are usually the focus of the conversation because they are prominent figures who represent parental approval or disapproval. Since the supervisory relationship is so important and is so entangled with past experiences with authority figures, we need to lay out a plan for establishing and maintaining supportive, objective, and fair supervision.

Proper Training for Supervisors

The first step that should be taken in changing supervision to a Deming approach is training the supervisors. From top management to line supervisors, all should be trained in the Deming philosophy and worked with continually to overcome resistances and to incorporate the changes into their daily actions. In the new system, the responsibilities of supervisors change dramatically. Supervisors, who previously may have only been responsible for pushing people to meet quotas, will now have to establish constructive coaching relationships with employees, use statistical methods, understand variation and the extended process, and create a supportive, trusting atmosphere in their departments, among other things. Obviously, these people are going to need a great deal of training themselves before they can be expected to make such radical changes. Some of them may not be emotionally or intellectually capable of making these changes. If this happens, an assessment should be made by management as to where the person would function well in the organization, and that person should be reassigned.

Training for supervisors should include indoctrination into the Deming philosophy, statistical methods as described in Chapter 5, relationship building, coaching, leadership skills, creating a supportive environment, treating the employee as a total human being, emphasizing interpersonal communication, stress reduction, and training methods. Supervisors have to be given the tools to carry out their new responsibilities. Most of them will welcome the opportunity to learn and grow in areas that they know will help the organization, the workers, and themselves.

Supervisory Do's and Don't's

The following are some basic *do's* and *don't's* for supervisors who use Dr. Deming's methods. They are simple statements which can help supervisors clarify some of the more important aspects of their new jobs.

Do's

1. Create an atmosphere of trust and support.
2. Encourage two-way communication.
3. Promote teamwork and interrelationships.
4. Stress quality, not quantity. (Supervisors must have the autonomy to stop the line when defectives are being produced. Repairs should be made immediately, not passed on to the next shift.)
5. Help workers understand their place in the extended process.
6. Randomly assign inspectors to workers and check for problems using statistical methods.
7. Use control charts to monitor and improve the workers' ability to do his job.
8. Meet on a regularly scheduled basis with workers to provide feedback and listen to their concerns.

Don't's

1. Blame workers for problems beyond their control.
2. Manage on numbers and quotas.
3. Create a reign of terror.
4. Reward and punish based on common variation.
5. Use statistics to police employees.
6. Ignore employee problems, i.e., stress, alcohol and drugs, family.
7. Haphazardly meet with workers as their only supervision.

Performance Appraisal Systems

Performance appraisal systems have been both criticized and praised by experts in organizational behavior, by personnel specialists, by people that evaluate, and by those who are evaluated. Much has been written about the validity of evaluation and the various ways of approaching performance appraisal. The frequently voiced goals of performance appraisal are:[3]

(a) To help or prod supervisors to observe their subordinates more closely and to do a better coaching job.
(b) To motivate employees by providing feedback on how they are doing.
(c) To provide back-up data for management decisions concerning merit increases, transfers, dismissals, and so on.
(d) To improve organizational development by identifying people with promotional potential and by pinpointing development needs.
(e) To establish a research and reference base for personnel decisions.

Overall, a review of the literature and practice reveals that a performance appraisal does not help most people meet the above goals. It is believed to be a necessary evil. Most people don't like it, but they don't see any alternatives. It can be made more palatable if it is done within the setting of a positive supervisory relationship, and if supervisees are receiving ongoing feedback and assistance in reaching their goals. But, objectivity and fairness are almost impossible to attain.

Press a human resources executive even at a good company to tell you how well the formal performance appraisal system is working, and after sighing, he's likely to confess that it isn't working quite like everyone hoped it

[3]Winston Oberg, "Make Performance Appraisal Relevent," in *Harvard Business Review Performance Appraisal Series;* reprinted from *Harvard Business Review,* January-February 1972, p. 40.

would—doggone managers just don't seem to be willing to give anyone low marks. At super-system Exxon, for instance, the cornerstone of the appraisal system is a forced distribution of performance—only 10% of people in a given area can be evaluated as in the top category, only 25% in the next bracket, and so on.[4]

These are only a few of the problems with performance appraisals.

The new philosophy totally rejects performance appraisals because they:

(a) Destroy teamwork,
(b) Reduce initiative and risk taking,
(c) Create overly precise and useless measures of performance,
(d) Don't distinguish between people and the system,
(e) Increase variability of performance, and
(f) Focus on the short term.

Teamwork is destroyed because people are concerned with their own success and lose sight of their importance in the extended process. Everybody acts to impress the supervisor to gain a good rating, as opposed to being concerned with the common good. Let's say a bank teller devises a particularly efficient way of organizing the tasks of her job. Under the current system, she may keep it to herself to earn a higher rating, in comparison to the other tellers. She is actually shortchanging her co-workers, who might benefit from using her methods, and in the long run, the customer. Ultimately, the consumer is the one who suffers as a result of individual success over the common good, and this has to change.

Initiative and risk taking are seriously reduced under the current system. People focus on meeting their goals and objectives, so creativity is stifled. Employees want to fit into the mold of what the supervisor perceives as appropriate. Someone with a different idea or method may not express it for fear of "rocking the boat," looking foolish, or being a threat to the supervisor. Hiding accomplishments is encouraged under this system. An employee who can surpass a goal in one time period will hold back and spread out the success over two time periods to make sure that he or she can meet the next period's goal, too.

Performance appraisal systems usually rank employees from "outstanding" to "poor," utilizing several categories or gradations. This ranking system creates an overly precise and meaningless statement about the employee's performance. For example, employees who are extremely vocal about their dissatisfaction over their performance rating frequently benefit

[4]Walter Kiechel, III, "Picking Your Successor," *Fortune*, December 10, 1984, p. 240.

from upward bracket creep because raters don't want to deal with fundamental issues.

Performance appraisal systems also do not distinguish between the people and the system. Even though people are only one element in a process, they are held responsible for the outcomes of the process. There are many other factors in a process, such as materials, machines, methods, and other people, that influence the results. The employee does not have control over all of these elements, and therefore, should not be rewarded or punished based on randomness in the system.

Variability of performance is increased through performance appraisal systems. Employees react to the appraisal and change their behavior to earn a better rating for the next rating period. Understanding of variation tells us that the employee is reacting to common variation in the system, probably overadjusting his or her behavior in the opposite direction, and creating more variability in the system. An example of managers creating variability in the system is naming an "Employee of the Month." All those employees who are not chosen tend to change their behavior to imitate the one who was picked (or burn out in frustration), making their performances more variable. If our objective is to reduce variability in a system, then performance appraisals must be abolished.

Performance appraisal systems encourage short-term thinking. Managers and employees break down years into quarters, months, weeks, days, and hours, depending on their place in the organization. Evaluations, ratings, or counts done at these time intervals only perpetuate the current short-term view. A long-term perspective is necessary in fairly assessing people's abilities and guiding employees in their careers.

The New Approach to Performance Appraisal

Ford's Chairman, Donald E. Petersen, charged an employee group to study performance appraisals and recommend changes. He stated,

> We believe our personnel evaluation system is a possible barrier to continuous improvement and quality performance. . . . We do know that the emphasis of any such system must be on developing teamwork throughout the corporation to meet customers' needs. There is untold waste of human resources with traditional evaluation systems.[5]

William W. Scherkenbach, Director of Statistical Methods for Ford Motor Company, has created an appraisal and development system based on Dr. Deming's philosophy. Scherkenbach says,

[5]As quoted in an article by William W. Scherkenbach, "Performance Appraisal and Quality: Ford's New Philosophy," *Quality Progress*, April 1985, p. 40.

The principal purposes of an appraisal and development system should be to nurture and sustain individual employee contribution to the continuous improvement of the organization as a team and to provide an assessment or evaluation of performance for the employee and management.[6]

Ford's new appraisal and development system is based on the Deming philosophy and requires an understanding of variability in the distribution of skills in the firm (the system). The assumption is that in any organization almost all the people are "within the system," and it is impossible to distinguish them from one another. If management is unhappy with the firm's distribution of employee skills, it has no one to blame but itself. After all, management hires, trains, and supervises the people in the firm.

It is devastating to employees to be this year's above-average employee and next year's below-average employee, all due to common variation in the system. So, the new evaluation recognizes that there are virtually only three possible positions: (1) within the system, (2) outside the system on the high side (or superior performance), and (3) outside the system on the low side (or inferior performance). Figure 7–1 depicts what this looks like. This method assumes that most employees are "within the system" and should receive pay raises and bonuses based on seniority. Those people who are operating outside the system demonstrating superior performance should receive special attention, for example, merit pay.

Teamwork is important for promotion. A manager finds out if someone should be promoted by talking to his supervisor, customers, suppliers, co-workers, etc., because people are promoted on the basis of their ability to work as a team. Anyone who is outside the system on the high side is considered a special person and should be treated as such; they will be

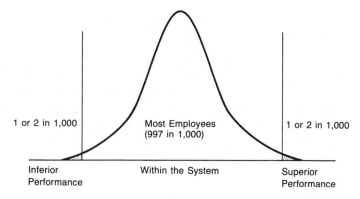

1 or 2 in 1,000   Most Employees   1 or 2 in 1,000
                         (997 in 1,000)

Inferior   Within the System   Superior
Performance   Performance

Figure 7–1 Distribution of employee skills.

[6]Ibid., p. 44.

rare. Those people operating outside the system on the low side need special development or replacement attention by management.

For illustrative purposes, let us examine a sales office with six salesmen. All have the same responsibilities and opportunities. The number of new accounts generated by each salesman in the past six month period is recorded in Table 7–1.

Table 7–1

Name of salesman	Number of new accounts
Allan	7
Fred	16
Mark	8
David	4
John	9
Phil	10
Total	54

The company's policy calls for semi-annual reviews of performance to determine who should be rewarded or punished. Based on traditional thinking, it appears that the company should reward Fred and punish David.

Examining the same issue from the perspective of a "Deming company" results in the following calculations:[7]

$$\text{Average number of new accounts per salesman} = \frac{54}{6} = 9$$

$$\text{Upper Control Limit (UCL)} = 9+3\sqrt{9} = 9+3(3) = 18$$

$$\text{Lower Control Limit (LCL)} = 9-3\sqrt{9}=9-3(3)=0$$

The laws of probability predict that the number of new accounts generated by a salesman during the six months under study are expected to fall between 0 and 18. This large amount of variation is attributable to the sales system. All salesmen are in the same sales system, and they all deserve the same percentage pay raise. No one should be rewarded, and no one should be punished. The sales system should be improved.[8]

If Fred had generated 26 new accounts (instead of 16) the sales system's statistics would be:

---

[7]These calculations are based on a C-Chart.

[8]Pay level is determined by seniority.

$$\text{Average number of new accounts per salesman} = \frac{64}{6} = 10.67$$

$$\text{UCL} = 10.67 + 3\sqrt{10.67} = 10.67 + 9.80 = 20.47 = 21$$

$$\text{LCL} = 10.67 - 3\sqrt{10.67} = 10.67 - 9.80 = 0.87 = 0$$

In this scenario, Fred *is* outside the sales system on the high side (he is above 21). Investigation by Fred's manager led to the realization that Fred had developed a better telephone procedure for screening potential customers. Fred should receive merit pay because he is outside the sales system and provides guidance for improvement for all within the system.

A note about "golden boys" and "super stars." Who are they? How do we know? The answer is simple. If someone is above the Upper Control Limit for their job for seven time periods in a row, this demonstrates that they are superior and deserve special attention.[9] They will be extremely rare.

Ford's pilot program has been launched, and the following are its critical features:[10]

1. Emphasis on management's responsibility to coach and counsel employees.
2. Reduction of the number of appraisal categories to three or four categories, instead of the original and arbitrary nine. Nine categories provided an overly precise and meaningless statement of employee performance.
3. Stressing teamwork and making it a part of the appraisal system.
4. Encouraging open two-way communication by retaining most evaluations (those of employees "in the system") at the supervisory level and only forwarding those of employees "outside the system" to higher management.

The results are far from in yet, but the direction is clear. Performance appraisals must reflect the new philosophy if consistency is to be maintained. Employees have to feel that they are valued by the organization and that they are supported in their efforts. The new system is the only way to promote teamwork in a meaningful way. Management will find this new system a particularly difficult aspect of the Deming philosophy.

[9] A run of seven is considered unlikely by most statisticians and would indicate a special circumstance. The criteria for being above the upper control limit must include teamwork.
[10] Ibid., p.46.

In the past, most managers have benefited from the standard type of performance appraisal. Their careers have been catapulted by excellent evaluations, and they believe that if you're good, the system will reward you. Overcoming this type of thinking will be hard, but if change is to take place, this obstacle must be removed.

POSSIBLE PITFALLS

Changing the way supervision is practiced is a very important element of the journey to quality. It involves major alterations in people's day-to-day existences at work. Problems that might impede your efforts include the following:

1. *Believing that a degree in management from a business school prepares someone for supervising employees.*

    Business schools do virtually nothing to teach students about human behavior, a philosophy of business, teamwork, and statistical methods, in a meaningful way. Courses are taken in some of these areas, but nothing is integrated to provide the framework for a supervisory approach. Students graduate believing that they can manage other people, and what's worse, they are hired to do so and given very little additional training. This perpetuates the horrendous supervision that abounds in many organizations today.

2. *Ignoring concerns about chain of command.*

    Supervisors may be uncomfortable with the new type of leadership and the new philosophy of the organization. They may be concerned about losing their authority because their new roles demand a more humanistic approach to their supervisees, along with increased teamwork. Lines of authority may get confused for some supervisors who are unable to assume their new roles and still maintain their status as authority figures. Also some supervisees may attempt to manipulate their supervisors or usurp power, based on the new philosophy. Management needs to send a very clear message to all: "There is still a chain of command, even though we are functioning more as a team." Supervisors should be backed up by management in any instances where an employee attempts to manipulate the system.

3. *Using statistics as a policing tool.*

    Statistical methods are an excellent supervisory aid if they are used in the context of a supportive, trusting relationship to problem-solve with the supervisee. If they are used as a policing tool, the relationship between supervisor and supervisee will invariably be one of fear and mistrust. For example, using statistics to generate comparisons between shifts only serves to create competition between shifts and to destroy teamwork.

4. *Failing to view the worker as a whole human being.*

Employees are people with lives outside of the organization. Supervisors have to see them as such and understand their needs and problems which can impact on their work lives. Taking a long-term view can help supervisors support an employee through illness, family problems, or substance-abuse problems. If the employee is seen as a valuable resource to the organization, these difficult times that everyone experiences occasionally should be looked on as temporary and surmountable, not as something for which the worker is penalized.

5. *Continuing to reward and punish employees.*

"Employee of the Month" programs seem so positive. If someone does an outstanding job, it follows that he or she should be rewarded. On the other hand, if someone is doing a poor job, he or she should be put on report or docked pay or whatever else is deemed an effective punishment. The reality is that the consequences, positive and negative, are a farce because they are usually based on common variation beyond the worker's control. Management has to gain an understanding of this and stop using these unfair methods.

6. *Ignoring the union in the implementation of the new supervision.*

Union people have to understand supervision with statistical methods. They must be involved in training in the Deming philosophy, from the beginning, so that they can understand the type of supervisory climate you are trying to create. Otherwise, they will think that this is just a more sophisticated, precise way to police employees, and they will sabotage your efforts.

7. *Maintaining the current performance appraisal system.*

Believing that current performance appraisals are dynamic, flexible, and useful is a delusion on the part of management. Unfortunately, management created the performance appraisal system, and it has an emotional attachment to it, which is difficult to sever. But it must be cut to make way for a more realistic, humanistic approach that encourages teamwork and quality.

8

Driving
Out
Fear

*DRIVE OUT FEAR, SO THAT
EVERYONE MAY WORK EFFECTIVELY
FOR THE COMPANY.*

DISCUSSION OF POINT EIGHT

Imagine waking up every morning, getting ready to go someplace that makes you feel insecure, anxious, afraid, and inadequate. You do this day after day, week after week, month after month, and finally, year after year. This kind of thing starts to take its toll. Your stress levels increase, your health deteriorates, your family relationships suffer, your job performance diminishes, and you burn out. You question why you continue to do this but realize you have no other options. It seems like a bad dream, one in which you are sentenced to a life of misery, with no way out. This sounds like an extreme situation, and it is. However, it is a situation in which millions of workers in the United States find themselves today. How many people that you know actually like their jobs? How many wake up in the morning, looking forward to a day at work? We would guess that they are very few and far between. Most people find work an unpleasant experience, not necessarily because they don't like what they *do* but because of the climate in which they do it. A critical element in this negative environment is fear. It is an enormous problem that has devastating results.

Fear can cause physical and physiological disorders such as breaking out in a rash, an increase in heart rate, a rise in blood pressure, a decrease in salivation and the secretion of digestive juices, and changes in the nervous system. This is only a partial list of disorders that can lead to behavior changes, emotional problems, physical problems, and in extreme cases, death. Stress-related illnesses are rampant; current research is demonstrating a causal relationship between stress and illness that can no longer be denied. Employees may turn to drugs and alcohol to dull their sense of fear and to help them make it through the day. This, of course, compounds their problems and that of the organization. Absenteeism rises because of stress-related illness, depression and other emotional problems, family difficulties, and burnout. All of these maladies impact heavily on an organization.

An employee participating in a climate of fear experiences poor morale, poor productivity, stifling of creativity, reluctance to take risks, ineffective communication, and reduced motivation to work for the best interests of the company. So, employee fear is important not only to that individual but also to supervisors and to the organization. The economic loss to the company is impossible to measure, and society in general is hurt in the long run. Management has a moral obligation to ensure the physical and emotional health of its employees for their well-being and that of the organization. Unhealthy employees cannot possibly participate in improving quality and productivity. They are too busy trying to deal with their own problems. Fear, which is a causal factor of many of these problems, must be reduced and eventually eliminated.

Unfortunately, many managers use their power to create fear, instead of working to drive it out of the organization. They have been trained and reinforced to believe that the way to get someone to do something is through coercive power. Workers believe that they will be punished if they do not perform. Of course, this generates fear, which impedes their performance and is counterproductive. Having power over someone does not necessarily mean that the person has to fear you and your actions. It is possible for managers to project an image of teamwork, concern, and support and still maintain their role as "the boss." Rewarding people for good work has been demonstrated to be much more effective than punishment or the threat of punishment.

Historically, management's behavior that promoted an atmosphere of fear was responsible for the formation of labor unions. Workers were receptive to labor union organizers because they feared for their jobs, their health, their sustenance, and their continued exploitation by management. Whether you believe that labor unions are positive or negative, they might never have emerged if it hadn't been for management's creation of fear in the workplace. Labor unions would never have endured if employees were able to overcome their feelings of insecurity and anxiety.

What Causes Fear

Fear emanates from a general feeling of being powerless because of someone (a manager) or something (the organization) that has control over important aspects of your life. It is the nature of a hierarchy to favor those on top over those on bottom, and everyone in the organization is aware of that. Specific elements of a system can increase the fear that exists by virtue of your position in the organization. These elements are: (1) lack of job security, (2) possibility of physical harm, (3) performance appraisals,

(4) ignorance of company goals, (5) failings in hiring and training, (6) poor supervision, (7) lack of operational definitions, (8) not knowing the job, product, and/or specifications, (9) failing to meet quotas, (10) being blamed for the problems of the system, and (11) faulty inspection procedures. These issues, except for number 9 (failing to meet quotas), have been discussed in previous chapters. Quotas and their harmful effects will be taken up in Chapter 11.

Fear in the system is not limited to line workers. Supervisors and managers have many of the same fears, along with others, like loss of status because of reorganization, hostile takeovers by conglomerates, and making a wrong decision. Vendors, in the extended process, are also affected by fear. They fear cancelled orders, being forced to accept lower prices, and loss of customers. Customers fear being taken advantage of by the vendor in price and/or quality, not having recourse to rectify problems, and loss of resources.

Fear is common in our society at large. We fear political change, nuclear war, flying in airplanes, medical examinations, crime, people of other races and religions, and what our children might be doing when they're not with us. We have become accustomed to the emotion of fear, as well as the pain that it often fosters. However, fear does not serve a purpose. There is no reason to perpetuate it in organizations; people are dealing with enough personal and societal fears and don't need additional insecurities from the workplace. Instead, what is needed is a consistent, supportive environment that stresses teamwork and concern for the individual as a whole human being.

HOW POINT EIGHT RELATES TO THE OVERALL PHILOSOPHY

If quality is to improve in all aspects of organizations, then the quality of work life must improve for everyone. We're not talking about more employee benefits or seminars on stress reduction or exercise breaks, although there is nothing wrong with any of these things. They just don't address the critical issue. People need a consistent, supportive, nonthreatening, secure environment in which to work. This can only be achieved through top management's commitment to treat people in a manner that allays fears and anxieties. Top management has to be given that same type of atmosphere; boards of directors and stockholders cannot motivate managers by fear. Otherwise, the mandate will be to use fear on subordinates to achieve goals.

Setting up long-term goals that are consistent with the new philosophy will aid in driving out fear. People will be impressed with the new goals of improved training and supervision, not blaming workers for problems in the system, and removing barriers that rob the hourly worker of pride of workmanship (Chapter 12)—all of which are indicators of management's commitment to reducing fears. Using control charts to monitor workers involves a long-term perspective that will eventually reduce fear. The workers will become more open and honest about discussing barriers to performing their jobs because they will sense that problems will be acted upon. When fear is in the system, everyone in it operates for short-term gain at the other's expense, instead of as a team with a long-term perspective. When fear is decreased, workers cooperate to ensure the long-term survivial of the company.

Driving out fear involves managing for success. Management provides the workers with adequate training, good supervision, and proper tools to do the job. Management measures performance fairly by using control charts to separate problems of the system from those of the worker. People are treated with dignity, and fear is removed from the environment. When all of these elements are in place, people want to work with management for the overall good of the organization and to share in its success.

IDEAS FOR ACTION

Thinking about the following questions that relate to fear in your organization will assist you in your journey to quality.

Questions for Self-Examination

1. Do your employees feel secure in the job?
2. Does your company practice staff layoffs in economically depressed times?
3. How do layoffs affect employee morale?
4. Has the company developed job descriptions that incorporate clear operational definitions and quality characteristics?
5. Do employees ask questions about their jobs?
6. Have employees been thoroughly trained about their jobs?
7. Does your company use traditional performance appraisal systems?
8. Does the performance appraisal system provide a road map for improvement?
9. Does your company use quotas or numerical goals?

10. What are the consequences for an employee who doesn't meet the production goal?

11. Does your firm rely heavily on inspection?

12. Is there pressure on inspectors because of job quotas and shipping deadlines?

13. Is there pressure on inspectors from production-line workers who may be affected by inspection results?

14. What has the organization done to ensure a safe working environment?

15. How are employees affected by unsafe conditions in their environment?

16. Does your company encourage cooperation and a free flow of information between departments?

The above questions should aid in uncovering things in your organization that cause fear. Once you are aware of these issues, you must deal with them to eliminate fear in the workplace. Just because most organizations function with a fearful atmosphere doesn't mean that it has to be that way. Management's commitment to change this situation in a consistent ongoing effort can eventually result in a real change in the environment.

Eliminating Fear Starts at the Top

One of the authors became the supervisor of a unit that had been run for years in an atmosphere of fear generated by a tyrannical supervisor. The prior supervisor treated line workers with disdain, did not allow them access to necessary information, created rifts between departments, did not provide adequate training, and showed favoritism toward certain employees. The author, as the new supervisor, had to work with the employees to overcome all of the fear and negative feelings that permeated the atmosphere. Treating all employees fairly and with respect, providing training, and maintaining a consistent atmosphere of support and teamwork paid off eventually. The workers began to trust and work as a team. The time period involved was about two years. The changes didn't happen all at once; it was a period of gradual change. At the end of this time, workers were much more positive about their jobs, the unit, their co-workers, and the supervisor. They related openly and were willing to raise problems and to work with the supervisor on their solutions. The quality of service to clients improved dramatically, and never-ending improvement was pursued. The workers were happier in their jobs. They experienced less stress because they had the support of each other and the supervisor, and they felt better about the quality of the service they were providing. Overall, a negative job situation was turned around to a positive one.

Driving out fear is difficult, but the following ideas should offer some assistance to those who desire change in the organization's environment. First of all, the Board of Directors and top management have to send a clear message throughout the organization: "Management by fear is no longer an acceptable leadership style." To do this, the Board and Top management must believe it themselves and must provide a model for the type of management that is desired. Managers have to direct the effort to eliminate fear, but mostly it will be accomplished through their actions. Any new managers or supervisors that are hired should be screened carefully as to their personalities and their ability to integrate into the new environment. The selection of candidates is critical. In choosing between two potential managers, the right personality type, an openness to learning, and the ability to work as a team member are much more important assets than a degree from an Ivy League college, given that the requisite skills are equal. Current managers and supervisors will need training and support to change their behavior. They will have to analyze their own personalities and determine if they are in fact doing things to promote fear. They can gauge this by employee responses. Supervisors can also help each other by providing feedback if they observe supervisor-employee interactions that are destructive.

The Board of Directors and top management should consider the concept of lifetime employment as a way to allay fear. However, the authors advocate this practice only if it is done in conjunction with the implementation of Dr. Deming's Fourteen Points. Lifetime employment, such as tenure for college professors and teachers and the Civil Service system, is generally a perpetuation of mediocrity. It does provide the workers with security, but it does not provide the necessary philosophy and methods to pursue never-ending improvement of quality.

Remove Physical Dangers

The first thing management must do is to ensure the employees' right to a safe working environment. Everyone has to feel secure that the workplace is not an incipient source of physical danger. Stringent safety standards should be delineated and reviewed periodically, with input from all levels of the organization. Machinery and equipment must be properly and routinely maintained. Workers should be trained to report problems, and management should respond quickly to employee reports of hazards on the job. No employee should be punished for refusing to operate a machine that is not working properly and could cause physical harm. Possible danger in the work environment must be clearly explained to employees so that they can decide for themselves whether they want to work in it. Fear of physical harm can demoralize employees and can totally destroy management's credibility. If management wants to create an atmosphere of trust and support, safe working conditions are a visible message that the welfare of the workers is paramount.

Training and Supervision's Focus

Training for everyone in the company's goals and mission will aid in reducing fear. This should be done on an ongoing basis to provide a constant link between top management and the rest of the organization. Top management needs input from everyone to make the company's goals achievable, and lower-level managers and workers need to know the direction that top management is taking. Since this is a fluid process, training and communication must take place in that context. Management's actions should be understood with hope and trust as opposed to fear and suspicion.

Training in operational definitions, quality characteristics, jobs, products, and specifications is very important. Not knowing what the job is can create a great deal of fear for workers. Dr. Deming says, "People on the job are afraid to enquire more than three or four times into the job: what is the job, what is acceptable, and what is not."[1]

Supervision should focus on never-ending improvement to increase productivity and should stop relying on quotas or numerical goals which are counterproductive. The use of statistical process control should eliminate the need for mass inspection. Mass inspection instills fear because it isn't uniform, and it only creates further confusion about what the job is.

Supervisors need to understand natural variation in the system so that workers are not blamed for problems beyond their control. The focus should be on the extended process and the fostering of teamwork. Supervisors should be ready and willing to help workers and to listen to their problems. This doesn't mean that management gives up the right to disagree with a worker or its right to make decisions. Rather, it encourages respect between management and workers, speaking openly about issues of concern, and working together to improve the organization. Opportunities for workers to be creative should be supported. Workers should be able to express themselves through their products or services and should be allowed to develop to their maximum potential. Performance evalua-

---

[1]W. Edwards Deming, *Quality, Productivity, and Competitive Position* (Cambridge, Mass.: M.I.T., Center for Advanced Engineering Studies, 1982), p. 33.

tions should be eliminated; rewards should be based on quality, team-work, seniority, and the advancement of the organization's goals.

Interaction within the Organization

Channels of communication should be opened. This could take the form of small discussion groups meeting on company time, a council of representatives from all ranks and departments, or occasional mass meetings of all employees and supervisors to discuss company policies and problems. All of these structures are helpful in driving out fear and making everyone feel a part of the larger organization. Employees must be willing to invest time and patience in communicating with management. Management has to be willing to share corporate knowledge and information. Organizations can no longer deprive workers of necessary information, particularly when health is at stake. Collective bargaining with unions should be in good faith and should strive for unification and mutual cooperation. This will be a difficult and lengthy process, but support from the union is a major factor in reducing fear.

POSSIBLE PITFALLS

Eliminating fear is one of the first things that should be acted on in the organization's journey to quality. It can bring about tremendous changes if management is sensitive and responsive to people's concerns. Potential pitfalls include:

1. *Avoiding the problems of people.*
   Dr. Deming feels that "the fundamental problem in American business is that people are scared to discuss the problems of people."[2] Managers want to deny that people have problems and fears. They walk around with blinders, trying to attend to their "managerial duties." They are able to keep their distance from workers because of the absorbing layers of middle management, whose job is keeping a lid on problems. What these managers are ignoring is that their job *is* dealing with employees' problems, eliminating their fears, and encouraging their development as people. Human beings have emotions that strongly influence their behavior. Their fears are a barrier to their emotional well-being and their job performance. Managers have to relate to employees on a person-to-person basis and should

[2]Private conversation with Dr. Deming.

accept their employees' anxieties as normal emotions that can be dealt with and ameliorated. After all, managers have experienced the same fears and should be able to communicate this to their subordinates.

2. *Believing that you have eliminated fear when it still exists.*

Employees, knowing that management's goal is to drive out fear, may become very compliant and begin telling management how wonderful everything is, how well the new program is working, and how understanding the supervisor has become. If this occurs at a very early stage in the transformation process, it is a signal of resistance to any *real* change. Employees are just placating management, while fear is still a major factor in the organization. Another signal that all is not really well is the strengthening of the organizational grapevine as a source of rumors that generate more fear. The grapevine can be turned into a positive force later on in the change process if key people in it "buy into" the new system. It is management's task to be aware of these situations and to rectify them through communication with employees over time.

3. *Not planning for the new fears that the philosophy will create.*

Management's concentration on driving out existing fears may involve a serious oversight. Implementation of the new system may introduce new fears into the environment, such as the fear of opening up and revealing oneself and a mistrust of management's new attitude. These new fears will have to be foreseen and be dealt with in training and supervision. Management may feel that it has traded in one set of fears for another, and it is frustrated. However, ignoring the new fears will not make them go away. They can be handled properly if management addresses them and works with employees and the union to alleviate them.

9

Breaking Down Organizational Barriers

*BREAK DOWN ORGANIZATIONAL
BARRIERS—EVERYONE MUST WORK
AS A TEAM TO FORESEE AND SOLVE
PROBLEMS.*

DISCUSSION OF POINT NINE

Barriers exist in organizations. This is a fundamental fact of corporate life. Statements like "Those guys in accounting have no idea what we go through here in production. They have it so easy, sitting back in their comfortable chairs all day, and going out to lunch," and "The Vice Presidents don't understand how hard it is for us department heads to hold onto employees with the terrible salary and benefits we offer. Those guys don't care; they're making enough," and "Why can't those union people stop making trouble for us? We're doing the best we can to keep this company going. They'll just have to accept layoffs this year" are all examples of barriers in the organization. The first is a statement of barriers between departments, the second depicts barriers between middle and upper management, and the third is an example of barriers between management and union.

Organizations are not created with barriers. A new organization starts out with team spirit, unity, and cooperation. However, these attitudes quickly disappear as people's roles become functional and as problems in communication, competition, and fears arise. Barriers impede the smooth flow of a process, and everyone in the process suffers, most notably the customer. When there are barriers in the system, rework and costs are increased, and quality and customer satisfaction are decreased. Dr. Deming states,

> People in research, design, purchase of materials, sales, receipt of incoming materials, must learn about the problems encountered with various materials and specifications in production and assembly. Otherwise, there will

be losses in production from necessity for rework caused by attempts to use materials unsuited to the purpose.[1]

Types of Barriers

Barriers exist in many places within the extended process. Internally they exist within the organizational structure and between levels of the hierarchy, and externally they exist between the firm and the other elements in the extended process.

The internal organizational structure gives rise to barriers between departments, and barriers between areas within departments. Competition, personal grudges, different ways of looking at a problem, and different priorities are common barriers to communication between departments and areas within departments. In some organizations, the barriers between departments become so great that a new person entering the system is told immediately with whom he or she can communicate and whom to avoid. Barriers between departments can become very intense struggles based on long-standing grudges or perceptions.

For example, if the head of finance was given a substantially higher pay raise one year, and all of the other department heads were angry, they might hold a grudge against that department head. Over the years, as the other department heads ignored or angrily communicated with the finance department head, he or she would turn to upper management for more positive communication. This would further serve to widen the gap between departments. If this continued for a few years, the finance department would be seen as management's "pet" and would be resented by people in the other departments because of its perceived special status. The finance department would be cut off from the rest of the organization, and everyone would suffer.

Barriers also exist between areas within departments. This can mean different divisions of a department or even various shifts. For example, one of the authors was visiting a factory where shift C was undercooking the last batch of material processed in order to increase its shift's output. The direct consequence of this was that shift D always began from square one. So, shift D also began to undercook its last batch of material in order to increase its production. Eventually, all shifts were undercooking material, and quality was forsaken for increased output.

Within the organization, barriers also exist between levels in the hi-

[1]W. Edwards Deming, *Quality, Productivity, and Competitive Position* (Cambridge, Mass.: M.I.T., Center for Advanced Engineering Studies, 1982), p. 35.

erarchy. Poor communication between employees and supervisors, supervisors and middle management, and middle and upper management is common. The lower-level people feel that the upper-level folks don't understand their day-to-day problems, and those on top think that their subordinates don't see the "big picture." Resentments, based on the nature of these relationships, are compounded by the build-up of actions that denigrate or demean the subordinate. For example, if supervisors are not involved in middle management's planning for its area's objectives, they will feel useless and will cease trying to provide input. Resentment and anger will increase and may result in sabotage of middle management's objectives. Once again, everyone will suffer.

The organization's interaction with the other elements in the extended process also gives rise to barriers. There are barriers between the firm and its vendors, the firm and its customers, union and management, and the firm and the community, including retirees from the firm. These barriers can have a great deal of impact on the organization. A company's relationships with its vendors, customers, union, and community can mean success or failure for it in the long run. Creating barriers between the firm and the customer, for example, leads to omitting the customer's input into product development and redevelopment. This could spell disaster because products will be designed without taking into account customer needs. Creating barriers between the organization and the community instead of fostering a good working relationship with it could result in the community's boycott of the product or of the service being provided. Again, barriers are the cause of problems that affect everyone in the system.

Reasons for Barriers

Barriers are caused by many different things or combinations of things. Following is a discussion of several reasons for barriers, which is not intended to be exhaustive. Each organization has its own particular causes of barriers, but those below are common to most firms or agencies.

1. *Poor communication or lack of communication.* Poor communication could occur between departments, within departments, between bosses and subordinates, or within the extended process. It creates barriers because people feel excluded, confused, scared, or demeaned. An example of lack of communication in the extended process is a social service agency locating a group home for emotionally disturbed adolescents in a residential neighborhood without first discussing issues and concerns with the community. This could

result in intense fear and anger and may create barriers between the agency and the community.

2. *Ignorance of the organization's overall mission and goals.* Ignorance leads to the pursuit of individual departmental or area goals as opposed to working for the overall good.

3. *Competition between departments, shifts, or areas.* Competition is often encouraged by management as a way to motivate employees. Actually, it results in underachievement overall.

4. *Decisions or policies lacking specificity that require interpretations.* If top management leaves questions that lower-level managers and supervisors have to answer, the result will surely be conflicts and barriers arising out of differences of opinion.

5. *Too many levels of management that filter information.* Too many levels can lead to a game of telephone, with the initial message being totally unrecognizable by the time it reaches the last person.

6. *Fear of performance appraisals.* Supervisees can never be totally honest with supervisors because they have to hide flaws to gain a good rating.

7. *Quotas and work standards.* Quotas and standards lead to hoarding of resources by individuals, areas, or departments to meet them.

8. *Differences between departments.* Accountants, engineers, production people, and marketers, for example, speak different languages and have different work cultures. There are different norms of behavior among these groups which make it difficult for them to communicate. Barriers can easily be built up when the accounting people work in beautiful, clean, air-conditioned offices, and the production people work in an ugly, dusty, hot environment.

9. *Decisions and resource allocation without regard to social memory.* In *The M-Form Society*, Ouchi discusses the concept of social memory. He says that a group can give up something for the common good as long as this is remembered and the group is eventually rewarded for it. A sense of community and civic-mindedness will exist in this type of environment.[2] In the corporate world, an example would be a department that voluntarily gives up an opportunity to have its offices redecorated because another department needs the money. If this department is not remembered for this act and eventually rewarded for it, resentment will occur and will create barriers.

[2]William Ouchi, *The M-Form Society* (Reading, Mass.: Addison-Wesley Publishing Company, 1984), Chapter 1.

10. *Jealousies over status and salary.* Jealousies create barriers because professionals and paraprofessionals often do some of the same tasks, yet they are paid vastly different salaries and accorded different degrees of status and respect by the organization.

11. *Personal grudges and interpersonal problems.* Some people just can't get along with each other. Whether their differences are based on a long-standing grudge about being passed over for a promotion, a co-worker's annoying habits, or the fact that a department head reminds another one of his brother whom he dislikes, conflicts between human beings exist. These often become intertwined with work issues and can create barriers to communication.

HOW POINT NINE RELATES TO THE OVERALL PHILOSOPHY

Breaking down barriers requires a long-term perspective. These barriers were created over a long period of time, and it will take time and patience to remove them. A long-term view must be maintained to continue the effort needed to work on these problems. Management must see that these efforts will pay off in the long run, that is, that they will eventually result in improvement of quality and customer satisfaction.

If an organization is to adopt the new philosophy of never-ending improvement of quality in the extended process, then staff areas have to work as an integrated whole. Vendors should be involved and be communicating freely. Customer surveys and employee surveys should be done to break down barriers between the organization and its consumers and employees. Labor unions and management have to remove blocks that impede their cooperation. Removing barriers to communication between all of these entities in the extended process is an important aspect of adopting the new philosophy.

Training has to be used as an aid in reducing barriers. The content of the programs, the way they are structured, and who participates are all critical elements in setting up training. The actual content of training can include overcoming communication barriers, dealing with problems between or within departments, or boss-subordinate relationships. However, the structure of the training and the selection of participants can be just as important in breaking down barriers. For example, training could take place across departmental lines, for all the first-line supervisors, in employee drug and alcohol problems. This would certainly get supervisors communicating with each other about common areas of concern. And providing training for a particular department in safety should include everyone, from the department head to the line workers. This will also help open dialogue between the department head and his or her subordinates.

Supervision in a "Deming company" should stress the extended process. Employees must understand the importance of communicating with their vendors and customers, who are frequently other employees in the system; e.g., Engineering's customer is Production, or the vendor to the employee on the line is the previous employee. Supervisors can help employees break down barriers in the system by modeling this activity themselves, in their relationships with employees, with other supervisors, and with department heads, etc. Performance appraisals should be eliminated under the new system, removing a major cause for barriers between supervisors and supervisees.

IDEAS FOR ACTION

Driving out fear and breaking down barriers between staff areas will go a long way in signaling the arrival of the new system and the eventual phasing out of the old one. The following questions will help you discover areas for improvement in this endeavor.

Questions for Self-Examination

1. Do you feel a sense of working together toward common goals with everyone in your organization?
2. Is it clear to you how your department relates to all of the others in the company, and how it fits into the general flow of the organization?
3. Has management clarified the organization's relationship to vendors, customers, and the community?
4. Is information shared and cooperation stressed between and within departments?
5. Are there barriers to teamwork?
6. What are those barriers?
7. Do the barriers affect the quality of the company's products and/or services?
8. Do obstacles in communication affect your morale and that of other employees?
9. Has management attempted to break down the barriers that exist, or does it perpetuate them?

The above questions should help you focus your attention on the issues of barriers in your organization. Clearly, something must be done to eliminate them and to promote teamwork and cooperation. Management should take the following action to effectively break down barriers.

Change Attitudes

Changing attitudes will be a constant, ongoing process in a "Deming company." The particular attitudes that need to be changed in breaking down barriers are: (1) identifying with specialized departmental goals instead of with the organization's unifying goals, (2) seeing the company as an isolated entity as opposed to part of an extended process, and (3) individualizing work as opposed to team cooperation.

As we have discussed, changing attitudes is a difficult task. If management is embarking on the journey to quality, action will already have begun in socializing everyone to the mission statement (Chapter 1). It will be an ongoing process that will offer clear direction and will unite everyone in a common purpose. This will aid in changing employees' identification from their specific department or area to the organization as a whole. They will be able to share the philosophy and overall goals with everyone else in the company and to understand their importance in the overall picture.

The second attitude that needs to be altered is seeing the organization as an isolated entity. Everyone in the firm must be educated about the extended process and must understand the role of cooperation in it. No longer can a manager manage or an employee do the job without regard to vendors, customers, the community, and other elements in the extended process. The new philosophy of never-ending improvement has to go beyond the boundaries of the particular job or department. Supervision and training must stress the extended process and the employee's role in it. Area visits to customers and vendors, both internally and externally, can provide valuable learning experiences for everyone. Information about the firm's process, how their materials are used, and how they can improve will be gathered during these visits and can provide a basis for attitudinal change.

Changing from individualizing work to team cooperation is the third attitude that needs attention. People have to be shown that teamwork will help them do a better job than working in isolation. Management has to demonstrate that individual efforts are simply not as effective as cooperative ones. Individual efforts can create barriers that diminish quality and customer satisfaction, while increasing rework, costs, and employee frustration. Actual examples of these instances should be discussed and be explored in training and supervisory sessions, with people from all of the areas involved. Cause and effect diagrams can be very useful in isolating barriers. Once the disadvantages of isolation and management's stress on teamwork are made clear, people in different departments and in different areas within the departments will be more willing to work on breaking down barriers and cooperating in a team effort. This change in attitude will also be facilitated by restructuring the organization based on teams, training in team building, and performance appraisals based on teamwork, all of which will be discussed in the following sections.

Open Lines of Communication

People in organizations have to start talking to each other, trusting each other, and working cooperatively. The ultimate goal of never-ending improvement of quality throughout the extended process has to supersede differences, jealousies, competition, and "protection of turf."

Management must emphasize direct verbal communication instead of memo writing, which should be limited to very rare occasions. This will force interaction and will reduce paranoia about information flow to higher-ups in the organization. One of the authors was consulting in an organization that was changing over to the new philosophy. He spent a great deal of time working with one particular middle manager who was very angry and resistant to the idea of teamwork. Upon further investigation, the consultant found out that the manager was angry at another manager because he only communicated by memos. He said, "The guy is driving me crazy. All he does is send me memos. How can I trust him, work on a team, and let him know what my problems are?" The consultant asked if he had ever told the other manager that this practice bothered him. He said that he hadn't, but thought it was a great idea and would try it. When the consultant returned the next time, he was greeted by a very pleased manager. The manager reported that he had spoken to the other manager, who said that he didn't realize his memo writing bothered anyone, and he would stop immediately. From then on, the originally angry, resistant manager became much more open to the new philosophy and methods.

What management should introduce and stress is open communication. Top management has to model this behavior by maintaining open offices, accessibility to employees, and getting involved in day-to-day interaction with employees. This will lay the foundation for similar interaction between staff areas and within the extended process.

Opening lines of communication also involves the confrontation of barriers and resistances. Supervision and training should be geared to helping people accept responsibility for behavior that creates barriers and should help change such behavior to a more positive stance. Again, management has to model the acceptance of its responsibility for behavior that feeds into the problem if it expects workers to be able to do so.

Resistance to change is to be expected, and supervisors and trainers must be keenly aware of how to help people deal with it and work through it. Forcing people to change is not the answer. Understanding the dynamics of change is necessary to support people through a difficult process, such as opening up lines of communication in a previously closed system. Publicizing efforts and results of the transformation of the organization can be very valuable to improving communication. Whether newsletters, videotapes, area visits, or scheduled meetings are used, people need to know what's happening throughout the company. Change is exciting, and employees want to share their growth, suggestions, and questions with each other. Management should encourage and participate in all these efforts.

Organizing and Structuring Teams

Since most organizations operate with a highly specialized structure that divides tasks into departmental areas, a great deal of thought and care should go into restructuring for teamwork. Employees must be allowed the opportunity to share their knowledge and feelings about how to organize teams for the achievement of organizational goals. In this way, they will have a stake in the success of the new structure.

Teams can be set up within departments or across departmental lines. Work teams, training teams, purchasing teams, hiring teams, and supervision teams are examples of teams that can function inter- or intradepartmentally. Interacting with people from other areas can be an important stimulator for professional development and for cross-pollination of ideas. Teams can be set up on a time-limited basis to examine a particular problem or institute a pilot project. Or, the teams can be ongoing, such as a team that guides the implementation of the Deming philosophy. No matter how organizations are restructured to create teams, management must attempt to reduce excess layers of middle management, and must take into account how to best implement the new philosophy.

Teams have to be given autonomy to function and to take action. Supervisors and managers can be available for consultation, as needed by the team, but should not make decisions for the team. Team members have to be open and direct with each other. There can be no holding back on information or cliques within the team. Team members will learn each other's strengths and weaknesses and should try to capitalize on everyone's strong points. For example, if one team member writes well but is less verbal in meetings, the group should designate that person the secretary and should continually work toward developing his or her verbal skills. Each person is different and has a unique contribution to make to a team.

Teams need a mechanism for communicating problems in the system back to management. They have to be assured that they will be heard and will be taken seriously; otherwise, they will feel their efforts are in vain and will become demoralized. Management can be regularly or periodically involved in team meetings, depending on the particular team. Whatever method is used, management has to follow through on issues that have been brought to its attention by the teams; otherwise it will lose credibility.

Training for Teamwork

Working on a team will be a new experience for many people. They will have had no training or model of teamwork to follow. Therefore, training will be very important if teamwork is to succeed. Just putting a bunch of people in a room together does not a team make! People will have to be instructed and supervised in how to work together. Training and supervision in team organization and development should be instituted at all levels. Education in team decision making and consensus, power struggles within teams, the nonverbal team member, the attention-seeking team member, how to develop team objectives, the benefits of teamwork, and conflict resolution are all key in helping people understand the nature of teamwork and how to move the team along in its stages of development.

Evaluations and Rewards Based on Teamwork

A natural consequence of changing attitudes, opening lines of communication, and organizing and training for teamwork will be the need to change the evaluation and reward system to incorporate the new team structure. Evaluations and rewards will have to reinforce the avowed emphasis on working, growing, and improving together. They should be based on contributions to teamwork and never-ending improvement (Chapter 6). Everyone should have input into the new system, and team members will be involved in rating each other. The new evaluation system, as an outgrowth of a comprehensive, ongoing plan that incorporates the elements discussed in this chapter, will be a welcome alternative to traditional practices.

POSSIBLE PITFALLS

Breaking down barriers in organizations is a difficult endeavor, but its rewards are great. Following the plan outlined in this chapter will help eliminate obstacles to communication and teamwork. Pitfalls that may impede your efforts include:

1. *Management's fear of losing the chain of command.*
   Managers, who are take-charge people, may have a difficult time giving up some control to the teams. They may see it as undermining their authority and may not be able to give the team the autonomy it needs to function. The role of the manager will change, and some managers will have a difficult time accepting this.

2. *Management's denial that barriers exist.*
   Managers like to believe that they are doing a good job at working with their people. The news that people in their department don't communicate with them or each other is generally greeted with denial and avoidance of the problem. Barriers can be so strong and so engrained in an organization that the thought of removing them is absolutely overwhelming. The way some managers deal with this is to deny that problems exist. Top management frequently won't acknowledge the barriers between departments and likes to think of the organization as "one big happy family."

3. *Management not eliminating special facilities and/or privileges.*
   Management's stated desire to remove barriers and its failure to act on the visible manifestations of them, i.e., privileges and differential facilities, will send a double message that can ignite hostility and resentment. Maintaining physical facilities that are substantially different between staff areas, while espousing an equality philosophy, will destroy efforts to break down barriers. Separate parking areas, special clothing, and different dining, recreational, and bathroom facilities perpetuate the notion that some people are better than others and destroy the sense of unity. Dealing with these "real" issues demonstrates a commitment to change and raises management's credibility.

4. *Assuming that the Training Department is free from barriers.*
   The Training Department is crucial to the transformation of the organization, and management has to frequently rely on it in the journey to quality. It is very important that management take a long, hard look at that department, its interactions with management, other departments, and within itself. Just because these people are trainers and have information about teamwork, improving com-

munication, and conflict resolution doesn't mean that they can effectively handle these issues themselves. Also if barriers exist between the Training Department and other departments, effective training will be very difficult.

5. *Continuing to view an area as different or special.*

Some departments in companies see themselves as "specialized," "more professional," or somehow different from the other departments. They will try to perpetuate barriers based on the idea that barriers are acceptable because their departments are so unique. This attitude may be supported by management who views an area as special and treats it as such. An example would be management bringing in an employee from the "superstar" Engineering Department to consult with the purchasing agent when the buyer did not request assistance.

6. *Perpetuating the belief that an area is second-string.*

People in departments like Engineering and Production tend to think that areas like Personnel, Administration, Training, etc., are less important, "softer" areas. The view that the company doesn't really need these "soft" departments to survive is common among those who actually make the products or provide the services. "What do we need administration for? All they do is cause us hassles. We don't need those jokers sitting in their offices making decisions about what we do in the field," is a frequently heard lament that demonstrates the disdain with which some departments view others. Management has to work on eliminating these beliefs.

7. *Failing to deal with people's fears.*

Efforts at breaking down barriers can be sabotaged by fearful employees who are scared of change. They have learned how to get along in the old system; they know it and are comfortable with it. But they are unsure what their role will be in the new system and are consequently scared. They will tend to cling to something familiar—the grapevine—which can become a very negative, destructive force. It can distort information, reinforce old barriers, create new ones, and generally wreak havoc on attempts to transform the organization.

8. *Ignoring "turf protection."*

Many organizations have a history of people fighting to gain and maintain control over certain areas. Once that control is gained, people don't want to give it up. In order to remove barriers, though, they will have to work as a team and communicate more. This will be especially difficult for those people who won their "turf" through extended in-fighting, sabotage, and inflexibility. Such individuals will be hard-pressed to change their behavior patterns that have served them well in the past.

9. *Reluctance to expend the energy needed to remove barriers.*

Many people in the organization will be burned out. They won't want to get involved in the mammoth effort that is needed to break down barriers. They may feel abused by the company and don't think the payoff is enough. These employees may try to "ride out" the new methods by acting like they accept the new philosophy but not really changing. They may think that this is another fad that will pass if they wait long enough.

10. *Emphasis on specialization in business schools.*

Business schools offer majors in the functional areas, i.e., marketing, finance, management, etc. Students that follow a course of study in one of these areas tend to view organizations myopically. There is very little integration of information from all areas, which leads to a lack of insight into the overall picture. It also encourages communication with only those who speak the same language and see the world in the same way. This can be very dangerous to individuals, groups, and organizations because it fosters an isolationist attitude that destroys teamwork and reduces information sharing.

10

Replacing Numerical Goals, Posters, and Slogans with Never-Ending Improvement

ELIMINATE ARBITRARY NUMERICAL GOALS, POSTERS, AND SLOGANS FOR THE WORKFORCE WHICH SEEK NEW LEVELS OF PRODUCTIVITY WITHOUT PROVIDING METHODS.

DISCUSSION OF POINT TEN

We have all been convinced that goals are "good things," especially if we quantify them and spell them out clearly for people. This is a philosophy espoused in business schools and in organizations throughout the country. How can people achieve anything unless they are constantly being motivated to reach a goal? Consider the following example.

John and Mary reviewed their daughter Penny's report card and were not pleased. "Penny, we know you can do better than this. Your average is a 75," said John. Mary said, "Yes, Penny, by next term we expect you to raise your average to 85. You'll just have to try harder." "Okay, Mom and Dad," said Penny, "I'll try." The next day when Penny got home from school, she tried to do her work, but she needed help with her math and her parents weren't around. Besides, a neighbor was playing his stereo so loud she couldn't concentrate, and her little brother kept bothering her. When her parents came home from work, she asked if they could help her, but they said they were too tired. The next day Penny asked her teacher for extra help. The teacher said she would be glad to help her, after school. But Penny had to go home after school to babysit for her brother. She wondered, "How can I ever do better in school?"

Poor Penny! She's a victim in this situation. Her parents think they are helping her by setting a goal for her, but it is an irrational plea. They have done nothing to change the system to help Penny achieve the goal. She would like to do better in school and get an 85 average, but what has changed to allow her to do that? Nothing! If Penny's parents are serious about her improvement in school, they should talk with Penny about the problems that are getting in the way of her improvement and should help her work on alleviating those problems. Penny should be involved in the process because she can tell her parents what the barriers are. For example, several problems need to be addressed before Penny can improve.

First, her parents need to be willing to help her or get her the help that is available. Next, if help is only available after school, then alternative babysitting arrangements have to be made. And finally, John or Mary should talk to the neighbor so that Mary can study in a quiet environment.

This is an example of a "system" problem, and the parents (management) have to take responsibility to help solve it. John and Mary should accept this responsibility because Penny cannot do anything about these barriers. She would like to succeed in meeting the goal her parents have set, but she is stuck in an impossible situation that will inevitably lead to depression, frustration, stress, anger, and worsening of her performance.

The Effects of Arbitrary Numerical Goals

If we empathize with Penny in this situation, then we should feel the same way about people working in organizations that set arbitrary numerical goals. However, setting numerical goals has become such common practice that we accept it as a positive way to motivate employees and to improve performance. In fact, it has quite the opposite effect. Dr. Deming states that

> goals are necessary for you and me, but numerical goals set for other people, without provision for a road map to reach the goal, have effects opposite to the effects sought. They generate frustration and resentment. The message that they carry to everyone is that the management is dumping their responsibilities on to the work force.[1]

Slogans, posters, and numerical goals are hollow exhortations because the employee is handicapped by the system and can do nothing to satisfy the slogan. For example, some companies institute "Zero Defect Days." Employees and vendors are assembled and told that as of January 1, the company will no longer accept defective parts. That's a terrific thought, but totally farcical unless management provides the methods and means to achieve it. Other examples of slogans, posters, and numerical goals are:

Do it right the first time.
Our job is quality.
Safety is job one.
Be careful.
Increase return on net assets 3 percent next year.

[1]W. Edwards Deming, *Quality, Productivity, and Competitive Position* (Cambridge, Mass.: M.I.T., Center for Advanced Engineering Studies, 1982), p. 40.

Increase sales 10 percent next year.

Increase patients 5 percent next year.

Decrease costs 10 percent next year.

Cut the work force 5 percent next year.

Nothing is wrong with these goals except people have no way of meeting them—unless changes are made in the system. As long as the process is stable, it will continue to produce the same amount of defectives. Putting up a poster that says "Zero Defects" won't change the process's capability, except maybe to lower it because of the workers' frustration over their inability to meet the new demands.

The kinds of goals listed above do not represent action statements for the workers or help them do a better job. They really articulate management's wishes for a desired result. Saying that you want to decrease costs by 10 percent next year, without providing the methods or tools, is an absurd statement. If you can cut costs by 10 percent next year, why didn't you do it this year? You won't be able to do it next year either, without extensive organizational damage, unless management makes changes in the system. You might as well set the goal as "Cut costs by 90 percent!"

Setting arbitrary numerical goals has negative effects on employees. Surpassing the goals one week (one point on the "good" side of average) is viewed as a success, while one point on the "bad" side of average sends employees scurrying for explanations and excuses. Also, a numerical goal, once reached, is usually raised. This convinces workers that management does not appreciate their work and will never be satisfied. Employees are forever expected to work harder and produce more, without new tools or methods. In extreme cases, workers may be forced to lie and/or cheat to meet a numerical goal.

A particularly horrible example of this occurred in a social service agency that mandated a certain number of contacts with clients for each social worker. A potential client called the office one day to request services from the agency. When the secretary checked the files, she found that the woman was already a client. A social worker had a record on her, indicating that he had seen her weekly for several months. The woman insisted that she never heard of the social worker, and when he was confronted by his supervisor, he admitted that he had falsified the record to meet his number of contacts. He was seriously chastised for his actions and deserved punishment because nothing could justify what he had done. But the management that had created that system and set that arbitrary goal was also responsible for the result.

When workers are measured against goals that they do not understand how to achieve and are judged by management that will discipline them for not achieving the desired results, they become filled with tension, fear, and resentment. Consequently they perform their tasks by rote, unsure of their purpose in the organization or what their jobs are.

A Better Way

If management wants to hang up posters, the emphasis should be on the progress that management is making in never-ending improvement. Control charts that demonstrate this are appropriate mechanisms for communicating management's commitment to the new philosophy. Workers' morale will be improved through such posters, as opposed to being lowered by the slogans and posters that now exist. The first goal a company should have is never-ending improvement. This can be made specific for each particular department, area, and worker, so that everyone knows his or her particular "job" in relation to the never-ending improvement of quality. The company's goals must represent an unshakeable, steady guide toward its mission into the future. Once the workers understand and believe in these goals, they will respond with dedication, confidence, commitment, and cooperation to bring about a new era of increased quality, productivity, and profitability for the company.

HOW POINT TEN RELATES TO THE OVERALL PHILOSOPHY

Eliminating numerical goals for the work force is a strong statement that signals management's commitment to the never-ending improvement of quality. Management must demonstrate a long-term perspective and a constancy of purpose by unifying the entire organization around this larger goal. Everyone is aware of management's desire to stay in business and to compete on the basis of quality improvement, as opposed to pushing the workers on quantity. Therefore, the new goals will now be set in the quality context, instead of arbitrarily targeting some "magic" number as a goal to reach. The new attitude will be graphically shown to workers when posters and slogans are removed from the workplace. Management's credibility will soar as workers see that management is not just paying "lip service" to the new philosophy but is acting congruently with it.

Replacing arbitrary goals with the use of statistical methods, particularly control charts, will also aid in strengthening management's credibility. Workers will begin to believe that they are not being pushed to produce, penalized for variation, or expected to bear the burden of management for taking responsibility for the system.

Arbitrary numerical goals, slogans, and posters will be unnecessary in a "Deming company." The training and ongoing supervision that will be provided will be so thorough and comprehensive that the use of a poster or slogan will seem ludicrous. Upper-level management relies on arbitrary numerical goals when it doesn't trust the lower-level managers and supervisors. This is top management's way of pushing productivity in the absence of being in touch with what is going on in the organization. Supervisory relationships that are developed over time, allowing trust, support, and guidance to replace fear and insecurity, will motivate employees far more than a numerical goal or poster ever could. Fear will slowly dissolve in the corporate atmosphere as workers reflect a more positive, less-pressured demeanor. Barriers will be easier to break down as everyone is truly united around the goal of never-ending improvement of quality and accepts this larger goal as the organizational, departmental, and personal goal for which to strive.

Eliminating numerical goals will also affect other entities in the extended process. Stockholders and boards of directors will have to give up their addiction to goals like "Raise quarterly dividends $1.00 per share" and become comfortable with the more generalized goal of never-ending improvement of quality. In the long run, if they can support the company through its transformation stage, they can expect much larger payoffs: improved quality, increased productivity, lower costs, increased profitability, higher market share, and a competitive edge that will ensure the survival of the organization.

Within the extended process, vendors and customers will likewise be affected by the elimination of numerical goals. No longer will vendors have to meet the goal of "Acceptable quality levels at 90 percent" or purchasing agents have a goal like "Reduce material costs by 5 percent." Virtually the entire system can benefit from an organization's elimination of arbitrary numerical goals if other companies in the process see the transforming company as a model and emulate its actions.

IDEAS FOR ACTION

Eliminating numerical goals and quotas can be a very concrete step that demonstrates management's commitment to the new philosophy. Asking yourself the following questions will help you analyze your organization's current policies regarding numerical goals and quotas.

Questions for Self-Examination

1. Does your organization stress numerical goals as opposed to pushing on quality?

2. When you walk through your company, do you see posters that carry slogans like "Do it right the first time" or "Zero Defects"?

3. Do these posters help anyone do a better job?

4. Do employees in the organization understand its goals and how their work relates to them?

5. Are managers using an MBO (Management by Objective) system to set goals?

6. What happens when people don't meet their objectives?

7. Do your company's goals contain meaningful action statements?

8. Is management involved in helping workers meet their goals?

9. Does management state production goals without providing tools and methods to reach these goals?

We hope that pondering these questions has led you to the conclusion that an unwaivering commitment to eliminate slogans, posters, and, arbitrary numerical goals is necessary. The following section will assist you in establishing new, meaningful goals for the work force.

Remove Meaningless Posters and Slogans

The first step in eliminating arbitrary numerical goals should be removing posters and slogans from offices, hallways, production sites, etc. This should be done with some degree of fanfare and employee involvement because it will be greeted jubilantly and will clearly demonstrate management's commitment to the new philosophy. People probably stopped looking at the posters long ago because they were of no value, but they will take notice of their removal as a symbol of management's new mission. If management feels the need to replace the posters, it should put up control charts, explanations of how to do a job, or reports on management's progress toward never-ending improvement. These will be meaningful and will help people do their jobs and will raise morale.

Establish Meaningful Goals

One of management's responsibilities will be the establishment of meaningful goals. This will have been started in the development of the mission statement and should be followed through and refined so that every employee in the organization knows how his or her job relates to the overall goals of the company. The following is an example of a goal that emanates from a mission statement:

"Strive to continually provide our customers with higher quality products at an attractive price that will meet their needs."

Each department, each manager, and all employees can find meaning and a starting point for action in the adaptation of this goal to their own goals. For example, each worker in the Production Department can understand how the goal of learning statistical process control will contribute to the company's overall goal in satisfying the customer with high-quality products. Those in Purchasing can set a goal of working with vendors to help them improve their processes, thereby reducing defectives purchased and improving the quality of the product. The Marketing Department can look at the overall goal statement and set out to improve methods of obtaining customer feedback and sharing it with the Design Department to better meet customer needs.

Once goals are established, employees need to be educated as to both the overall and the more specific goals and be assisted in their endeavors to meet the goals. Management, supervision, and training must be geared toward support and guidance in meeting goals, as opposed to punishment for not meeting them. In the new system, the end result will be achieved by concentrating all efforts on the real goal of the organization: better and better quality through never-ending improvement of the process.

Get Rid of Management by Objectives (MBO)

"Management by Objectives," which has been embraced by corporations, governments, hospitals and other service providers, and educational institutions in this country, is just a sophisticated method to legitimize arbitrary numerical goals. Using MBO, managers systematically break down the "grand plan" into smaller and smaller subsections, which are then assigned to an individual or group to achieve. This is considered fair because the subsection goals emerge out of negotiation between supervisor and supervisee. For example, an employee may negotiate a 3 percent increase in output instead of $3\frac{1}{2}$ percent, as long as the subsection's goals equal those of the "master plan." It is important to note that the employee is not being given any new tools, resources, or methods to achieve the 3 percent increase, so he or she must scavenge from the existing system to meet the goals. It is also important to note that the request from management to increase 3 percent is totally arbitrary. Why not increase 20 percent or 50 percent? The expectation of increases is absurd unless management makes changes in the system.

Introduce Bottom-Up Financial Planning Based on Processes in Control

Current Financial Planning Systems (FPS) are a subset of MBO goals that deal exclusively with budgetary and financial issues. FPS's are generally constructed to work from top → down, bottom → up, or some combination of both. Regardless of their structure, they are just another form of arbitrary numerical goals. The numerical goals come from the top down, as next quarter's or next year's dogma, or from the bottom up, as watered-down feasibility statements, such as sales projections from the sales force or production projections from the shop foremen.

Top-down planning is usually based on the CEO's (chief executive officer) wish for future results, without any consideration of the system's capability to meet those goals. Consequently, financial officers down the line will simply manufacture the numbers top management wants to hear. Everyone excitedly vows to meet the new goals. They have met the CEO's needs and can relax for awhile. All are happy but totally ignorant. They have absolutely no idea of how the company is or will be functioning. Obviously, this is a futile waste of time and must be stopped.

Bottom-up planning that relies on the knowledge of people further down in the organization to supply their best experiential guess on next quarter's or year's output is equally disastrous. This sounds great except that these employees may tell management only what they think it wants to hear because they fear retribution in their performance appraisals that are connected with MBO. Or, they can only offer a guess because the processes that they supervise are in chaos. They know that they are probably wrong, and that they will be held accountable for their errors.

The only rational alternative to the above two disasters is bottom-up planning based on processes that are in statistical control. In this situation, the center line on the control chart can provide management with predictable numbers on which plans can be based. If management is dissatisfied with the output from a given area, then it has a rational mechanism for allocating resources to reach a desired goal.

POSSIBLE PITFALLS

Removing posters and slogans from the workplace and replacing them with meaningful goals, eliminating arbitrary numerical goals and their derivatives (MBO and FPS), and introducing planning based on statistical process control are all key action points. Potential pitfalls include:

1. *Management's inability to trust the "new" goals.*

   Management traditionally has relied heavily upon numerical goals because it holds the erroneous notions that these: (a) let individuals clearly know what is expected of them, (b) improve communication between supervisors and subordinates, and (c) are needed as motivators to keep people "on track." Since management believes that numerical goals accomplish all these "good" things, they use numerical goals extensively. Replacing numerical goals with meaningful goals will be difficult because management will have a hard time trusting that the "new" goals will work.

2. *Using numerical goals for evaluation.*

   A common belief is that numerical goals make the evaluation process more equitable by focusing on specific accomplishments and by letting subordinates know how they are doing in relation to the organization's goals. The problem is that not all accomplishments can be quantified and not all accomplishments (or their lack) are due to the employees' efforts. The system may be responsible.

3. *Continued reliance on posters and slogans.*

   There is an overwhelming urge for management to unite everyone to "rally round the flag" using posters and slogans. Even in companies that are in the process of changing to "Deming companies," posters and slogans are difficult to remove. They are so engrained in the system that they seem to creep back in without anyone realizing it. Management has to be aware of this and must make sure that posters and slogans are truly eliminated.

11

Replacing Management by Numbers with Never-Ending Improvement

DISCUSSION OF POINT ELEVEN

The Devastating Effects of Quotas

Work standards, measured day work, and piece work are names given to a practice in American industry that is contributing greatly to the demise of our quality, productivity, and competitive position. A work standard is a specified level of performance determined by someone other than the worker who is actually performing the task. Dr. Deming says, "The loss to American industry from work standards, rates, and piece work must be appalling."[1] Work standards and quotas consider only quantity, not quality, so they are totally at odds with the new philosophy. Dr. Deming sees work standards as a "fortress against improvement of quality and productivity."[2] Examples of the effects of quotas and work standards follow.

The authors were visiting a cardboard box plant. During the tour being given by the General Manager, we saw an operation in which a wax coating was being rolled onto the inside of the boxes. These boxes would eventually contain wet material like meat, fruits, and vegetables, so they needed to be waxed/water-proofed.

As the first box came out of the waxing operation, the General Manager leaned over and said, "It's easy to tell a defective box. If the box doesn't shine all over the inside, then the wax isn't on correctly." We asked him if he realized that almost every box coming from the machine was defective. He shrugged and said he knew all about it and had known for years. He said, "All the worker has to do is feed in the cardboard sheets

[1]W. Edwards Deming, *Quality, Productivity, and Competitive Position* (Cambridge Mass.; M.I.T., Center for Advanced Engineering Studies, 1982), p. 42.

[2]Ibid., p. 40.

at an angle, and the wax would adhere much better. That would solve the problem."

We looked at each other, then at the General Manager, and asked simultaneously, "Why don't you tell the worker to do the job right?" He explained that this was impossible because the union negotiated a system whereby workers get paid on piece work over the quota. The contract doesn't specify how the sheets must be fed into the machine, only that the worker has to meet a quota. Since it takes him slightly longer to do it right and he gets paid on quantity, not quality, he goes for the numbers. "If I make him do it right, he has to slow down and he'll lose pay. He would file a grievance and win. So, why bother?"

The above example is a good illustration of the negative effects of generally setting quotas. There are additional devastating effects when quotas are set too low or too high, as described below.

> "One will see any day in hundreds of factories, men and women standing around the last hour or two of the day, waiting for the whistle to blow. They have completed their quotas for the day; they may do no more work, and they cannot go home. Is this good for the competitive position of American industry? Those people are unhappy doing nothing. They would rather work.[3]

Think of the effect of low quotas on those workers' morale, motivation, and attitudes about their job. They certainly realize the stupidity of the situation and cannot have a great deal of respect for the management that perpetuates it.

The pressure on workers to meet a too-high quota is exemplified in this statement: "The job is to make 155 pieces per day. I can't come near this figure . . . and we all have the problem . . . without turning out a lot of defective items.[4] If employees want to produce quality goods, they are hampered by a system that encourages the making of defectives. That doesn't do much for the employee's self-esteem, morale, or pride of workmanship. Again, the worker understands the situation and cannot respect management for creating and fostering it.

Piece work, which is a derivative of work standards, is a cruel form of management. Workers get no assistance in getting above the standard or in increasing their output—hence there is no way to increase their pay. When their output goes up, the piece rate is raised. In essence, the worker is a slave and never gains.

[3]Ibid., p. 41.
[4]Ibid.

Why Work Standards and Quotas Have to Go

Work standards and quotas can have dire effects on the company, management, employees, and, of course, customers. Quotas and work standards don't provide a road map for improvement, and they prohibit good supervision and training. Also they don't help anyone do a better job or separate common and special variation as a basis for taking action to improve the process. In a quota system, workers are blamed for problems of the system that are beyond their control. Meeting quotas is actually a daily lottery because of common variation. No one knows what the system is capable of if it is in chaos, so setting a quota is ludicrous. The process will fluctuate until management deals with the variation in the system. But, the worker is expected to produce a specified amount, bearing the brunt of the system's problems and maintaining a positive attitude all the while.

Work standards and quotas focus on quantity, not quality, so workers are encouraged to produce defectives to meet their quota. This is built into the system and is expected by management. The absurdity of this way of thinking is hard to fathom! Encouraging the production of defectives is tantamount to stealing one's pride of workmanship. Employees want to produce quality goods and to feel positively about themselves and their jobs, but management won't let them. In some companies, it is far worse. Employees are docked pay for defectives which are the fault of the system. This is unfair, cruel, and can only result in worker burnout.

> Work standards are psychologically self-limiting. If the standard is 500 parts per shift, 501 will almost never be reported. If more than 500 are produced, the foreman "bands" the extras in his locker for a rainy day. A new operator who produces more than the standard is quickly educated by his peers not to produce too much.[5]

Workers may deliberately perform below standard because they know that once they achieve it, it will be raised to something they may not be able to meet. Also, they know how variable the system is, and that they are dependent on things like how their machines are functioning on a particular day to make their quota.

Work standards are the subject of union negotiation and have nothing to do with the process's capability. Since they are established through negotiation, rather than through an analysis of the process, they are fre-

---

[5]David R. Schwinn, "Work Standards—Aid or Impediment to Productivity," *Annual Industrial Engineering Conference Proceedings*, 1984.

quently inaccurate. At a General Motors division, a one-year study of machine capacity data demonstrated that twelve out of seventeen operations studied had work standards that were off by more than 10 percent.[6] Since changes in the process's capability are not incorporated into work standards, they remain fixed and do not reflect the potential of the current system. So, basing work standards on union negotiations is not in the best interests of management or employees.

Using work standards for budgeting, planning, and scheduling only provides management with more incorrect information. Such standards don't reflect the process's capability and only provide an arbitrary quota that has usually emerged from union negotiations. A better way to plan, budget, and schedule would be to use a center line from a stable control chart as a measure of process capability.

Work standards and quotas must be eliminated because they are totally counter to the new philosophy of never-ending improvement of quality. They destroy employee morale, motivation, and pride of workmanship, and they are a poor substitute for management's taking responsibility for the system.

HOW POINT ELEVEN RELATES TO THE OVERALL PHILOSOPHY

Management demonstrates its short-term perspective by establishing work standards and quotas. Both of these are set at a particular point in time and often fail to take into account changes in the process over time. Eliminating work standards and replacing them with control charts that can analyze, monitor, and change the process will signal the commitment to a long-term perspective.

Using work standards and quotas is managing for failure. They offer no road map for improvement of quality, and they encourage the production of defective goods. Workers' pride is diminished because they know they are not turning out quality items, and the general atmosphere is clouded with negativity and failure. Workers are either underworked or overworked but certainly not happy and fulfilled.

On the other hand, employing control charts is managing for success because it allows management to see what exists, not some arbitrary figure that it desires. Everyone is involved with actions that can improve quality. The environment undergoes a transformation and becomes a positive, successful, quality-oriented place to work.

---

[6] Ibid.

Management's reliance on work standards and quotas implies a lack of proper supervision and training. Supervisory relationships are hampered because of employees' fears of not reaching quotas, and barriers are created between managers, supervisors, employees, and unions because standards don't encourage meaningful communication. If employees can be supervised and trained using control charts as a common ground for communication, fear and barriers would diminish, the quality of work would improve, and there would be no need for quotas.

Within the extended process, work standards and quotas only serve to raise prices to customers because more defectives are being produced. These defects either are reworked, reducing productivity and raising costs, or they are left defective; either way, the customer suffers. But *you* are the customer also, and quotas and work standards are being used by your vendors. Therefore, it is incumbent upon you to work with vendors to stop the absurd dependence on quotas and work standards.

IDEAS FOR ACTION

Eliminating quotas and work standards requires a real change in management's thinking and behavior. The following questions should assist you in assessing how you think and feel about work standards and quotas.

Questions for Self-Examination

1. Do you use work standards or quotas to motivate your employees, and/or for budgeting and planning purposes?
2. How were those standards and quotas set?
3. How does management decide to raise existing quotas and standards?
4. What happens to the employees if they don't meet the quota or standard?
5. What happens to employees if they surpass the standard?
6. Does management take into account the rate of defectives being produced when quotas and standards are set?
7. Are those defects due to the workers or the system?
8. What is management doing to help employees do a better job?

Now that you have an idea where you stand on quotas and work standards, the following actions can help you successfully remove them from your organization.

Replace Quotas and Work Standards
with Statistical Methods

Removing work standards and quotas must be a priority if the organization is to improve its quality. They have to be replaced with leadership and training that results in the organization-wide use of control charts and other statistical methods. Production people should learn and use statistical methods to bring employees toward their maximum potential, while keeping people happy and fulfilled, and remaining in line with economic constraints. Statistical methods will help everyone in an organization improve in an efficient manner. Employing statistical methods, as described in Chapter 5, will provide an automatic tool for supervision that makes quotas and work standards obsolete. Working with employees is facilitated because the control chart provides factual information that the employee and supervisor can examine. This can significantly reduce the possibility of favoritism or prejudice, and it provides management with information on where problems lie.

Provide a Road Map
for Never-Ending Improvement

Eliminating work standards and relying on statistical methods helps to identify process improvement or deterioration. Management has to be responsible for stabilizing the process and for using the process average from control charts to budget, plan, and schedule. Workers will feel much more secure when they believe that management knows what it is doing. By focusing on quality through the use of statistical methods, management provides a road map for never-ending improvement.

Change the Negotiation Process with Unions
to Reflect the New Policies

Union officials and members have to be educated to the advantages of eliminating quotas and work standards. Since these have always been a mainstay of negotiations, union people may be fearful of change and may resist it, even though it is in everyone's best interest. If management eliminates quotas and work standards, union officials may worry that they will become useless. They have to be trained in the new philosophy and worked with to determine what their roles will be under the new system. (Labor's role will be discussed further in Chapter 15.) No longer can management and unions use quotas and work standards as items for negotiation. Improving the process has to become the most important thing for everyone if the company is to survive, and union people have to support management in its efforts toward never-ending improvement.

POSSIBLE PITFALLS

Getting rid of work standards and quotas will be difficult because they are so much a part of many organizations. Transformation cannot take place, though, unless they are eliminated. Potential pitfalls include:

1. *Clinging to a short-term view.*

   One of the pitfalls management can succumb to is not realizing the long-run process improvement potential of eliminating standards and quotas. Maintaining a short-term view, rather than a "process view," will cause the further decline of American productivity, quality and competitive position.

2. *Eliminating standards and quotas at the wrong time.*

   Timing is critical. As important as eliminating quotas and standards is, it must be done when attitudes have been changed, products and services have been operationally defined, and people have been trained in the use of control charts. Workers, supervisors, and lower-level managers have to have developed some trust in the new system and must have learned basic statistical methods. This may take at least two years, perhaps more. Trying to eliminate standards and introduce process control too fast may scare everyone and backfire. Most management will not know what to do without numerical quotas. Later attempts may be sabotaged if initial ones fail, so it is necessary to work closely with the statistical consultant to avoid problems.

3. *Accepting current work standards as the "Best We Can Do."*

   Often, the present work standard is rationalized as a technological limit of performance for the process. This reduces hopes for long-term process improvements because people feel that there is no possibility to get better. Management has to refuse to "buy into" this line of reasoning and must continue to stress never-ending improvement. Pilot projects that succeed in process improvement have to be a priority, and their results should be communicated to everyone in the organization to inspire further improvements.

12

Promoting Pride of Workmanship

*REMOVE BARRIERS THAT ROB
EMPLOYEES OF THEIR PRIDE OF
WORKMANSHIP.*

DISCUSSION OF POINT TWELVE

Referring to the United States as an underdeveloped nation sounds absurd, stupid, and absolutely ridiculous. However, in the area of using workers to their fullest potential, we could be considered just that. Organizations have systematically robbed workers of their inherent right to have pride in their work. For example, *Inc.* magazine's July 1985 issue told the story of 39-year-old Francis "Skip" Carroll, who left a job with a messenger service to become a courier with Federal Express. He said,

> I'd gotten to a point with my other job where the money was not enough to justify staying there. Not only was there no future, there was no pride. There was no thrill of doing something you had never done before, overcoming the downs that arise every day.
>
> Ever since coming to Federal Express, I've had no doubts in my mind that it was the right move. It's a very important job. . . . It's not the benefits and salary that are the incentive, it's the responsibility. You are given a task to do, and when you leave the building you are not being overseen. There's nobody there to say, "Go faster. Do this. Do that." The payoff is in all the compliments you get.
>
> I am so envious of the people who lived through the early days of the company. . . . I wish I could have been there with them in the trenches. Not to win some sort of badge for people to see, but to win that inner glow, to know that I was involved with it, and it worked.
>
> "Skip" goes on to talk about how important Federal Express is to his family's life and ends up relating his premonition that he will meet Fred Smith (head of Federal Express) and say: "Fred Smith, my name is Skip Carroll. I just wanted to tell you that I'm proud to be working with you.[1]

[1]*Inc.*, July 1985, p. 78.

"Skip" Carroll was lucky. He was able to change his job so that he could work for a company that allows him to feel pride in his work. How unfortunate for the company that lost him, through their denial of his pride of workmanship. Sadly, this company and most others continue to rob employees of their pride.

Loss of pride isn't confined to hourly workers, either. Managerial, hourly, and clerical workers have experienced a decline in loyalty and favorable ratings of their companies over the last fifteen years. For example, the vice president of a major American company stated, "I would have walked on hot coals for this company." Today, he says, "It doesn't seem to matter. It's almost as though I'm reporting to a machine."[2] His company was taken over by another eight years ago, causing his loyalty and devotion to wane.

Today many employees and managers alike share the belief that loyalty to a company is misplaced and that their energies should be devoted exclusively to their families, communities, and personal priorities. The loss of pride and loyalty is an obstacle to achieving competitive advantage. Pride and loyalty provide the impetus to perform better and to create better quality for the worker's self-esteem, for the company, and ultimately, for the customer. People enjoy taking pride in their work, but very few are able to do so because of poor management. Dr. Deming feels that workers' birthrights are robbed in a system that "abuses, misuses, and underuses" their skills and knowledge.[3]

Reasons for Loss of Pride

Organizations have seriously erred in their treatment of employees. Workers and managers are regarded as commodities and are treated accordingly. Not enough attention is paid to people and their problems; management doesn't want to deal with these issues. Consequently, employees become disenfranchised, instead of being involved and utilized to their maximum potential.

There are several factors that contribute to the loss of pride of workmanship. For example, if employees don't understand the company's mission and what is expected from them to achieve that mission, then they will be confused and unable to identify with the organization. This will lead to a loss of pride, as will requiring employees to act as automatons, not able to think or use their knowledge and skills. Being blamed for the problems of the system can also contribute to a loss of pride. For example,

---

[2]*The Wall Street Journal* (New York), July 11, 1985, Sec. 2, p. 27.
[3]Personal conversation with Dr. Deming.

giving an employee a below-average performance appraisal when, in fact, the system was at fault is terribly unfair and will result in anger, disloyalty, and loss of pride.

Hastily designing a product, along with inadequate testing of prototypes, translates into production of low-quality merchandise. Everyone in the organization suffers a loss of pride because everyone is associated with the making of "junk." Inadequate training and supervision send a clear message to the employee that management doesn't really care how the job is done and further prohibit pride of workmanship by creating fear of incompetence. Supervisors who treat employees as children who need discipline, rather than as team members who need "coaching," are responsible for loss of pride, as well as those who provide useless job descriptions and specifications. Supervising through quotas lessens pride of workmanship because usually the worker must produce defectives to meet the quotas. How can anyone maintain pride and self-respect knowing that his or her time is spent making defectives? Given a choice, employees would surely opt to produce "good" items in order to maintain their pride of workmanship.

Faulty equipment, materials, tools, methods, and techniques get in the way of workers doing their jobs properly and feeling good about their performance. This also leads to fears about their own and others' safety, which further lessens positive feelings about the company and their work. Anxiety about salary and job security impedes loyalty and pride because it leads people to believe that no matter what they do, they have no control over what happens to them.

No matter what factors have caused the loss of pride of workmanship, it is obvious that if we are to regain our competitive position, we all have to feel that we are doing the best job possible, in an atmosphere of never-ending improvement of quality.

Benefits of Prideful Employees

Reclamation of work as a source of pride and personal fulfillment will bring tremendous positive elements to an organization, as well as to individuals, families, and communities. The organization will reap the benefits of maximizing the potential of its work force, creating loyalty, excitement, interest, and team spirit. Removing the barriers that rob employees of their pride of workmanship will enable the firm to drop decision making down to its lowest possible level because workers will be able to accept their new responsibilities. Workers will become ambassadors for the organization, captivating the community at large with their positive feelings about their work and the company.

Individuals will benefit because they will realize their potential and will rid themselves of the frustration inherent in not being utilized to their maximum ability. They will be able to grow within the context of their jobs, which is necessary if people are to be fulfilled, happy human beings. Family relationships will improve as workers feel better about themselves and about the work that they are doing. They will experience less stress, which should improve their physical and emotional health and will reduce the need to abuse each other, drugs, and/or alcohol. And if the parents believe that they are doing a good job, and reaching their potential, then they will encourage their children to do the same.

Communities will also eventually benefit from the reclamation of pride of workmanship as people's sense of togetherness and shared identity are rekindled, in a new spirit of cooperation to achieve common goals. Restoring pride of workmanship could provide the impetus to return America to its former position of greatness.

HOW POINT TWELVE RELATES TO THE OVERALL PHILOSOPHY

Restoring pride of workmanship necessitates a long-term perspective on management's part. Employees must be viewed as the most valuable resource of the company and their pride as essential to the company's existence in the long run. Ignoring the needs of the work force is extremely shortsighted because it ignores the benefits of having healthy, motivated workers. Creating a system in which employees can be proud of what they do will contribute to the company's existence in the long run. Workers who are not frustrated about barriers to the performance of their jobs will put forth their best efforts for the good of the company.

Establishing constancy of purpose, developing a mission statement, and socializing employees to the mission will aid in developing the workers' identification with the goals of the company and pride in being part of an organization that has as its mission never-ending improvement of quality.

In contrast, managing for failure, accepting poor quality as a way of life, and handicapping employees with problems in the system—all rob workers of their right to pride of workmanship. Removal of the impediments of the system by management creates an atmosphere in which productivity and quality can improve and employees can feel proud of their work. Management must provide workers with defect-free materials, must use statistical methods to analyze and act on causes of variation, and must provide proper supervision and training to do this. Managing for success involves a positive approach to problem solving, communication between and within departments, and elimination of fear, all of which will contribute to pride of workmanship.

IDEAS FOR ACTION

The degree to which pride of workmanship has degenerated is staggering. To reclaim it will be a monumental process that should begin with an analysis of your current feelings about pride of workmanship.

Questions for Self-Examination

1. Does everyone in the organization feel that he or she is an important part of it?
2. Do employees feel that they are doing their jobs well, in an environment that supports their efforts?
3. Has the company provided training that helps people do a better job?
4. Is the work environment safe?
5. Are people utilized to their fullest potential by the company?
6. Does management work at improving the quality of incoming materials?
7. Is there a mechanism for reporting on problems, and does management act on them once reported?
8. Do people in the organization fear mergers, takeovers, layoffs, and wage cutbacks?

The above questions should provide management with some indications of the problems that give rise to loss of pride of workmanship. Management's task is to act to remove these barriers in a systematic manner that demonstrates to employees its commitment to the new philosophy.

What To Do

If management decides to change the philosophy, goals, and methods of its organization to that of a "Deming company," it will have to engage the services of a consultant trained in Dr. Deming's methods. One of the first things that the consultant should do is to meet with hourly workers, ask them what barriers exist to their taking pride in their work, and videotape their discussion for management to view later. The tape will show hourly employees talking about barriers to their pride of workmanship. When the consultant shows the tape to management, most of the managers will be shocked, some to the point of paralysis. They will be overcome by the problems that exist because they have managed to divorce themselves from their employees and to isolate themselves from their real responsibilities. When they are made aware of the problems, they will realize the monumental task ahead of them. Dr. Deming says,

> Most companies, once the management sees videotapes or listens to audiotapes of meetings with hourly workers, and becomes aware of the problem, will require three to five years, even when the management is shocked and determined. Some companies will require ten years.[4]

The following sections suggest actions that can assist management in its systematic removal of barriers that rob employees of pride of workmanship.

Operationally Define Job Descriptions

Employees need to know what their job is and how it should be performed. Operational definitions are the only meaningful statements of jobs because they are specific and enhance communication, so that all employees with the same job can perform it in the same way. Operationally defining job descriptions will improve quality of performance (assuming proper training), and increased pride of workmanship will be an outgrowth. Employees' input in this process is critical to gather the necessary information and to demonstrate management's commitment to workers' involvement. This procedure will further aid in increasing pride and reducing resistance to change because workers will have a stake in the outcome for which they will be held accountable.

Involve Employees at All Levels in the Process of Improvement

All employees should be trained and supervised to use control charts to monitor their job performance in relation to the operationally defined job description. This will result in decreasing special and common variation and in increasing the improvement of quality. Definitive procedures should be established so that employees are encouraged to report any problems in the system because they know that management will act on their suggestions. If a mechanism is in place and management responds, workers will certainly come up with ways to improve. Mazda's 26,147 employees produced about 1,800,000, suggestions in one year, and management used 930,000, or about 35 per employee, to improve quality.[5] How many suggestions would Mazda have received if there had been no formal

---

[4]W. Edwards Deming, *Quality, Productivity, and Competitive Position* (Cambridge, Mass.: M.I.T., Center for Advanced Engineering Studies, 1982), p. 45.

[5]Charles Kepner, "Focus '84," *Kepner-Tregoe Journal*, December 1983.

procedure and if management had a history of not responding to employees' ideas?

Frequent employee surveys should be conducted so that management can keep in touch with workers' attitudes, needs, and efforts to improve quality. These surveys should be comprehensive and easily understood by all. Employees need to believe that management cares about what they are thinking and feeling. Timely, sincere action on management's part will go a long way in restoring pride of workmanship. Including employees in the research and design of products and organizing quality control circles will further solidify workers' involvement in the process of never-ending improvement. Worker quality circles should be organized after the organization has made substantial progress in the transformation process.

Supply Workers with the Proper Tools, Materials, and Methods

Management must provide a working environment that ensures regular maintenance schedules for all equipment, including preventive maintenance. Workers' reports of problems with tools and equipment should be responded to immediately if management wants to convey the message that it cares. If reports are not heeded, workers will adopt a "so what" attitude because they will assume management has no desire to produce quality goods.

Materials should be purchased from a single-source vendor who can provide statistical evidence of quality. Workers cannot be expected to produce quality goods if they are provided with defective material. Proper training in statistical methods and the "job" will teach the workers how to do their jobs in the most quality-oriented manner.

Stress the Workers' Understanding of Their Importance in the Extended Process

Worker's pride will increase if they understand the extended process and the importance of their roles in it. Management should provide concrete opportunities for this to happen. Rotation of job tasks should be instituted where possible to expose employees to the various aspects of the firm. This will also foster pride of workmanship by breaking up repetitive tasks and the inherent boredom. In this way, management will also demonstrate its concern for employee job satisfaction. To do this, training has to be provided in multiple areas, and policies and procedures have to be thoroughly documented and available.

Periodically, workers should visit suppliers and customers to see the extended process at work. This should include in-company interaction between those in the same department and in different departments. Everyone in the organization should know not only his or her own job but also what the functions of the other employees are, as well as the roles of vendors, customers, community, and the Board of Directors. Providing experiences that stress the worker's importance in the extended process will encourage identification with the organization as a positive entity and make the employee proud to be a part of it.

Meet Basic Work-Related Needs of Employees

Management must consider the basic needs of workers on the job. First and foremost, it has to maintain safe working conditions. The employee is entitled to work in an environment that is as safe as that of management. Job security should be stressed so workers know that they are a valuable asset to the organization. Improvement of quality will make job security possible because it will facilitate sustained corporate growth, assuming management is committed to its employees and their job security.

Once workers feel safe and secure, management must concentrate on their fulfillment and growth. The systems of the organization have to be developed so that they allow workers to see and appreciate the results of their work. Seminars and continued training should be provided and scheduled so that employees can take advantage of them. Management should post job opportunities and should encourage employees who want to change jobs to more fully meet their needs and goals. Looking at employees as total human beings and, if practical, providing alternatives such as flex time and shared jobs so they can meet family obligations is important. Employees who are treated with care and consideration are highly likely to feel that they are valuable to the organization and will pour those positive feelings back into their work.

POSSIBLE PITFALLS

Removing barriers to pride of workmanship is an ongoing process that requires constant attention to details and sincere concern for employees. Failure to act on this point "may be the single most important contribution of management to poor quality and loss of market, save for failure to act on Point 1."[6] The following are some of the possible pitfalls that could impede management's efforts to restore pride of workmanship:

[6]W. Edwards Deming, *Quality, Productivity, and Competitive Position*, p. 66.

1. *Top management's isolation from employees.*

    Top management is protected by an absorbing layer of middle management, whose job often is to make top management think everything is fine. So, top management views the organization through rose-colored glasses, believing that the employees can take pride in their work. Management doesn't realize the degree to which employees fear physical harm, have to work with defective materials, are not properly trained and supervised, etc., so consequently it doesn't realize that things need to be changed. Even if management is aware that changes are needed, it often denies and avoids the issues because of the magnitude of the task.

2. *Trying to instill pride by inappropriate methods.*

    Many people believe that slogans and posters can be used as a rallying point to instill pride in workers, or that fear and discipline can instill pride. As discussed earlier, these are methods that are completely misguided and inappropriate and will not achieve the desired results. The belief that attainment of a numerical goal or quota is a source of pride is yet another delusion because it really is a lottery dependent on common variation. Workers know these methods are futile. Now management has to learn this and has to develop meaningful plans to deal with the problems.

3. *Establishing a Quality Control Department.*

    Setting up one department as responsible for quality sends the message to everyone else that quality is not their concern. Management has to help everyone incorporate never-ending improvement of quality into their every action. Otherwise, there is a loss of pride because management is seen as not really caring about the individual employee's level of quality.

4. *Failure to follow through on employees' suggestions.*

    Very few things can anger and disenfranchise an employee as much as being ignored. Being unresponsive to workers by not following through, or failing to give feedback on why something can't be done or why there are delays is unconscionable. Putting up a suggestion box is worse than useless if no one gives feedback on the employees' ideas. It will only serve as a symbol of management's inability to relate to employees and of its reluctance to deal with problems.

13

Educating and Retraining Everyone

DISCUSSION OF POINT THIRTEEN

Living the Deming philosophy and integrating it into every aspect of an organization will result in changes for everyone involved. Education and training will be necessary to teach people their new jobs and responsibilities, to ready employees for the jobs of tomorrow, and to prevent burnout. Dr. Deming states,

> Improvement in productivity means that fewer people will be needed for some lines of work. At the same time, however, more people will be needed in other lines. Education and training will fit people into new jobs and new responsibilities.[1]

Training and retraining should develop employees for changes in their current jobs, in respect to procedures, materials, machines, techniques, quality characteristics, and operational definitions. Everyone's job will be changing to incorporate the use of statistical methods, from management to hourly workers. Education must be provided so that the transformation process can occur smoothly. Training in the employees' "Deming type" jobs should alleviate anxiety about job security and job performance under the new system. The purpose of education and training should be to fit people to jobs and to responsibilities for which they are well suited.

Management has to look toward the future, develop new products and services, and put resources into research, training, and education. As products and services are continually improved, the organization must look for new and innovative ways to meet customers' needs. Appropriate job retraining will have to be instituted to qualify employees for the new job

---

[1]W. Edwards Deming, *Quality, Productivity, and Competitive Position* (Cambridge, Mass.: M.I.T., Center for Advanced Engineering Studies, 1982), p. 47.

opportunities that will be created. Retraining involves teaching employees new skills so that they can keep up with technological advances.

Education and training can prevent employee burnout because employees are exposed to new information and are provided with a forum to discuss problems. This can be very valuable because it stimulates interest in the job and encourages involvement in problem solving. Training in new jobs and methods can also rekindle the desire to participate on the part of employees who have written off their jobs as a source of fulfillment.

Type of Training Needed

The first type of training to institute is training in the new philosophy as it relates to the organization's mission and goals. Initially, it should involve top and middle managers, and eventually everyone in the company. Next, education in basic statistical techniques is needed. Dr. Deming states,

> Education in simple but powerful statistical techniques is required of all people in management, all engineers and scientists, inspectors, quality control managers, management in the service organizations of the company, such as accounting, payroll, purchase, safety, legal department, consumer service, consumer research. Engineers and scientists need rudiments of experimental design . . . Five days [of statistical training for the above persons] under a competent teacher will suffice as a base.[2]

Statistical training for everyone else in the organization is also necessary to prepare for the implementation of the new methods. "A few hours under a competent teacher is usually sufficient as a start for hourly workers and foremen that wish to learn and adopt the method."[3] If management commits to the new philosophy and inspires the rest of the organization with its new attitude, then people will be motivated to overcome their anxieties and to learn the new techniques.

Other areas that education and training could cover include basic skills such as math, reading, and verbal and written communication; job-related subjects such as chemistry or electronics; and personal improvement topics such as substance-abuse education or stress reduction. The reason for providing training in these areas is often because public education has not met the needs adequately. The organization must attend to its employees' educational needs if it wants to utilize them to their fullest potential and to promote job satisfaction.

[2]Ibid., pp. 47–48.
[3]Ibid., p. 49.

HOW POINT THIRTEEN RELATES TO THE OVERALL PHILOSOPHY

Management has to change its perspective to a long-term one that is supported by constancy of purpose if the company adopts the Deming philosophy. Education and retraining are very dependent on a long-term perspective. They will only be implemented if management alters its view and becomes more aware of the employees' contribution to the long-term survival of the company. As workers acquire new skills, they can be moved within the organization to meet its changing demands and needs. Training will keep employees current with the state of the art, which will ensure the company's longevity. Education in statistical methods will enable both management and workers to communicate through control charts that strengthen their commitment to a long-term perspective. Failure to educate and train employees results in a tremendous loss of resources to an organization in the long run.

Education and retraining are critical components of managing for success. Improving quality and increasing productivity can be achieved through educating management and the work force in Dr. Deming's Fourteen Points. Providing an organization with this road map to achieve its goals instills everyone with a positive attitude and a sense that all can work together, under a management that knows what to do to succeed. Being responsive to customers' needs is also an important part of never-ending improvement of quality. If an organization does not retrain employees in state-of-the-art methods, there is no way customers' needs will be met. Management that doesn't recognize this will invariably fail in its efforts.

IDEAS FOR ACTION

Retraining and education require commitment and allocation of company resources. Therefore, management should carefuly consider how it feels and has acted in respect to training. The following questions should aid in this process.

Questions for Self-Examination

1. Do you have a competent statistician in your company? If not, what are you doing about employing one?
2. Has the statistician been used to educate managers, engineers, foremen, purchasing agents, personnel people, etc., in basic statistical methods?

3. Have you gathered information in respect to the future needs of your customers?

4. What type of training will current employees need to fulfill their new job requirements in respect to those customer needs?

5. Are you planning to allocate the resources necessary to provide employees with the opportunity to advance and stay current in their fields?

Now that you have examined your current status in regard to retraining and education, we will present some ideas on how to organize retraining efforts.

Retraining to Become a "Deming Company"

The organization that commits to the transformation process will be involved in a large retraining and education effort. Several training courses that will be needed and the suggested participants are listed in Table 13–1. Following the table is a detailed description of each of the courses. A Mission and Philosophy course must be a prerequisite for all employees (see Tables 13–2, 13–3, and 13–4). The Basic Statistical Methods course develops the participants' skills in statistical process control and in tools and methods for process improvement. (See Table 13–5.) This course should be included as a part of every employee's job training. Examples and ap-

TABLE 13-1   Training Courses

Suggested Participants	Mission and Philosophy			Basic Statistical Methods	Statistical Applications Seminar
	4 day	2 day	2 day (Union)		
Top management	X			X	
Middle management	X			X	If appropriate
Supervisors and foremen		X		X	If appropriate
Technical personnel (engineers, chemists, etc.)		X		X	X
All other employees (unionized)			X	X	
(nonunionized)		X		X	
Suppliers				X	If appropriate

TABLE 13-2   Company Philosophy—4 Days

Title: Company Name Philosophy—4 days

Description: The purpose of this seminar is to explain the company's mission statement and operating philosophy to top and middle management.

Prerequisites: None.

Texts:

W. E. Deming, *Out of the Crisis* (Cambridge, Mass.: M.I.T., Center for Advanced Engineering Studies, 1986).
H. Gitlow and S. Gitlow, *The Deming Guide to Quality and Competitive Position* (Englewood Cliffs, N.J.: Prentice-Hall, Inc., 1987).

Topics:

Company History with Quality Improvement
The Extended Process and Quality
Types of Variation in the Extended Process
Management and Workers' Responsibility
The Company's Mission Statement and Operating Philosophy
Deming's Fourteen Points for Management
How to Begin Organizing for the Quality Effort

Who Should Attend: All top and middle managers.

---

plications should be provided from all areas of the firm: research, development, testing, manufacturing, clerical, management, legal, marketing and sales, purchasing, etc. The tendency is to use production examples, which makes people from other areas think that the training is not relevant to them.

TABLE 13-3   Company Philosophy—2 Days

Title: Company Name Philosophy—2 Days

Description: The purpose of this seminar is to explain the company's mission statement and operating philosophy to all non-union employees, except top and middle management. This seminar is an abbreviated version of "*Company Name* Philosophy—4 days" shown in Table 13–2.

Text: H. Gitlow and S. Gitlow, *The Deming Guide to Quality and Competitive Position* (Englewood Cliffs, N.J.: Prentice-Hall, Inc., 1987).

Topics:

Company History with Quality Improvement
The Extended Process and Quality
Types of Variation in the Extended Process
Management and Workers' Responsibility
The Company's Mission Statement and Operating Philosophy
Deming's Fourteen Points for Management
How to Begin Organizing for the Quality Effort

Who Should Attend: All employees—new and existing, supervisors, foremen, and technical personnel (chemists, biologists, engineers, etc.). This seminar is not open to top and middle management.

TABLE 13-4   Company Philosophy and Unionism—2 Days

Title: Company Name Philosophy and Unionism—2 days

Description: The purpose of this seminar is twofold: first, to explain the *Company Name* mission statement and operating philosophy to all unionized employees; and second, to explain the mutual benefits achievable by union and management cooperation in respect to the *Company Name* philosophy.

Text: H. Gitlow and S. Gitlow, *The Deming Guide to Quality and Competitive Position* (Englewood Cliffs, N.J.: Prentice-Hall, Inc., 1987).

Topics:
  Company History with Unions
  Company History with Quality Improvement
  The Extended Process and Quality
  Types of Variation in the Extended Process
  Management and Workers' Responsibility
  The Company's Mission Statement and Operating Philosophy
  The Sacrosanct Union Contract
  Deming's Fourteen Points for Management
  The Union's Obligations
  How to Begin Organizing for the Quality Effort

Who Should Attend: All new and current unionized employees.

The Statistical Applications Seminar (see Table 13-6), which should be based on the organization's needs that develop, should be offered to those employees whom it would benefit. It should improve the participants' statistical abilities with hands-on experience. Each participant is required to bring data to class so that everyone can learn to help himself or herself and each other. Possible topics for a course outline include "Design of Experiments," "Methods to Shorten Quality of Redesign Studies," and "Sampling Plans." The statistician's direction is critical in assessing organizational needs for further training. This course is only one possible forum for continued statistical training. Other advanced courses can be developed as they are needed. People can be sent to outside seminars; consultants or teachers can be brought in for special topics, or the company and its vendors can create shared experiences for statistical education. In conjunction with this, a statistical hotline should be established so that all employees and vendors can call for statistical assistance. The telephone number should be widely publicized, and people should be encouraged to use it.

Other Types of Education and Retraining

Training in fields related to the employee's current job, personal improvement, and retraining for the jobs of the future must also be provided. Employees have to be given the necessary tools to work productively in

TABLE 13-5 Basic Statistical Methods—4 Days

Title: Basic Statistical Methods—4 days

Description: The purpose of this seminar is to explain tools and methods to all employees and vendors which will enhance their ability to pursue the *Company Name* mission and operating philosophy.

Prerequisite:
  Company Name Philosophy—4 days
  　　　　　or
  Company Name Philosophy—2 days
  　　　　　or
  Company Name Philosophy and Unionism—2 days

Texts:
  Ford Motor Company, *Continuing Process Control and Process Capability Improvement*, Statistical Methods Office, Dearborn, Michigan, February 1984.
  　　　　　or
  IBM Corporation, *Process Control, Capability, and Improvement*, IBM, The Quality Institute, Southbury, Conn., Second Printing, May 1985.

Topics: Introduction
  Company History in Respect to Quality
  Company Mission Statement and Operating Philosophy

Basics:
  Process, Extended Process, and Quality
  Defining a Process (flow charts and operational definitions)
  Process Variation

Basic Statistics
  Types of Data (attribute, variable)
  Frequency Distributions and Histograms
  Mean, Proportion
  Range, Standard Deviation
  Shape
  Run Chart

Control Charts
  General Theory of Control Charts
  Attribute Charts (p, np, c, u)
  Variables Charts ($\bar{x}$ and r, $\bar{x}$ and s, individuals)
  Out-of-Control Patterns

Specifications and Process Capability Studies
  Specifications
  Process Capability

Tools and Methods for Process Improvement
  Brainstorming
  Cause and Effect Diagrams
  Check Sheets
  Pareto Diagrams

Who Should Attend: All employees and vendors.

TABLE 13–6   Statistical Applications Seminar—4 Days

Title: Statistical Applications Seminar — 4 days
(To be determined based on organizational requirements)

the organization of tomorrow. Each organization will have to consider the needs of its own employees, customers, community, vendors, etc., when developing programs and courses.

POSSIBLE PITFALLS

Several pitfalls in relation to training have been discussed in Chapter 6. However, retraining to transform to a "Deming company" involves some other potential problem areas. Consider the following issues for discussion when you are planning your retraining efforts.

1. *Management's reluctance to get involved in the training.*
     Sometimes top management feels that it really doesn't have to be trained in the statistical methods because on a day-to-day basis, "It's for my people, not me." Managers think that they are too busy to get involved with technical and statistical details. Anyone who believes this has completely missed the point. Managers have to comprehend statistical thinking to know when and how to react in order to avoid erratic, thoughtless adjustment of the system. Reluctance to get involved in training also takes another form. At some point in the organization's transformation process, management should be involved in training others in the philosophy, and, in some cases, in statistical methods. The tendency is to rely on the consultant to do all the training, instead of the managers taking responsibility for it. Without management's involvement on both of these levels, the training effort has little chance of succeeding.[4]

2. *Management's misconceptions about the length of time necessary for retraining.*
     Managers often believe that because they desire something to be so, it will magically become that way. They fail to take into account the process that must occur to allow the change to take place. Some people think that one or two days with a statistical consultant will solve the organization's quality and productivity problems. An-

[4]W. W. Scherkenbach, "How to Train Employees in Statistical Techniques," speech given to the ASQC 24th Annual Quality Clinic, Knoxville, Tennessee, March 10, 1985, p. 1-4-d.

other myth is that "by next month 100 percent of my people will be trained." This thinking fails to consider quality of training, and training as a continual process. Retraining is a time-consuming affair that will require commitment and dedication over a several-year period.[5]

3. *Service departments' belief that never-ending improvement of quality applies only to manufacturing areas.*

    This is a common misconception, usually brought about by the use of only production examples in training. All efforts should be made to develop service examples, as the tools and methods are equally applicable to those areas.[6]

4. *Employees' resistance to getting involved with statistical methods.*

    This attitude can derive from several possible sources. Some employees see quality as the purview of the Quality Control Department as opposed to everyone's responsibility. Others may feel that, "It's the same old statistical process control again," when, in fact, statistical process control is only a part of the overall philosophy and methodology. Another resistance takes the form of "We already did statistical process control in the fifties." The difference between what was practiced then and the current way is that now there is an awareness that getting a process into control is just a starting point for never-ending improvement.[7]

5. *Lack of adequate internal resources for training.*

    Very few companies employ statisticians who are trained in Dr. Deming's philosophy because they are few and far between. Consequently, organizations that want to transform into a "Deming company" have to establish relationships with competent consultants, and with colleges and universities that have statistics departments. Besides Dr. Deming, there are only a handful of other consultants qualified to consult in the Deming philosophy. Considering the tremendous time commitment a consultant must make to each organization, it is obvious that more people need to be trained in statistical methods and in the new philosophy. An assessment of internal personnel may uncover people who are interested and have the ability to undertake this type of training. The company should examine all alternatives, internal and external, to facilitate the implementation of Dr. Deming's philosophy.

[5]Ibid.
[6]Ibid., p. 1-4-e.
[7]Ibid., p. 1-4-d.

14

Structuring
for Never-Ending
Improvement

*CREATE A STRUCTURE WHICH WILL
PUSH THE PRIOR THIRTEEN POINTS
EVERY DAY.*

DISCUSSION OF POINT FOURTEEN

The transformation required to become a "Deming company" is a never-ending process. People who attend Dr. Deming's seminar and are exposed to his ideas usually get very excited and want to begin the journey to quality. If that person is the CEO of an organization, then the wheels can be set in motion, a consultant can be brought in, or an internal statistician can be utilized, and training can begin in the Deming philosophy. Generally, though, this isn't how it happens. Many CEOs and other top managers frequently don't attend seminars; most often, middle managers are the ones who are supposed to improve their managerial skills. Top managers feel that they know all that they need to know. They believe that their time would be wasted in a seminar. Top managers cling to the notion that "those who know, know." Unfortunately, what they know may be ineffective, dangerous, and ignorant management. These managers are unwilling to expose themselves in a learning environment that could reveal them as the proverbial "emperors with no clothes."

The middle managers who attend Dr. Deming's (or others') seminars on "Quality, Productivity, and Competitive Position" are the ones who are exposed to this important material. Some of them are excited by it and are frustrated when they are told that they must have a commitment from their CEO to begin. They know that it will be impossible, either because they can't reach the CEO to present the ideas, or because they know there is no way the CEO will "buy into" the philosophy. Other middle managers resist the philosophy, fearing that it will erode their company's power structure as the workers' stature is raised. They are threatened by the ideas and nervous about what would happen to them if their company is transformed. Still others are not able to grasp the concepts because they are either not intelligent enough or haven't been trained to think abstractly.

Top Management's Desire To Change

A middle manager who is convinced that the Fourteen Points are what's needed in his or her organization must persuade top management to commit to the philosophy. Otherwise, there can be no hope for change. This can be a difficult and painful process. Dr. Deming, in a letter to one of the authors, stated,

> Top management must feel pain and dissatisfaction with past performance and must have the courage to change. They must break out of line, even to the point of exile among their peers. There must be a burning desire to transform their style of management.[1]

Top management has to seek help; it can't be imposed.

Just like someone who is physically ill or has emotional problems, the CEO has to be ready to accept the problems and be willing to change to alleviate them. CEOs have to take responsibility for the problems in their organizations and have to realize that they have the power to initiate the organizational transformation required to help everybody: managers, workers, customers, vendors, and community, etc. Not all CEOs will be capable of implementation of the philosophy, even if they accept it and want to transform their organizations. Some lack the sensitivity, depth, intelligence, strength of conviction, and/or ability to carry out the Fourteen Points.

Top management has to begin by creating a critical mass of people in the company who understand the philosophy and want to change the corporate culture. It will take several years of struggling to absorb the Fourteen Points and to develop a mission and operating philosophy before the company is transformed and begins to realize the major benefits of Dr. Deming's methods. There will be obstacles along the way. People will resist truly integrating the philosophy into their day-to-day behavior. Gradually, though, acts will signal that people are changing, for example, two managers from different departments who never got along begin to work on a project together, or some union officials advocate the philosophy, or workers seem more interested in what's happening. Sometimes it's not even something tangible, just a feeling that people are happier, more involved, open to communication, and excited about the changes. Once things start to happen, people get caught up in the success, and a cycle of "positives" ensues. Buoyed by success, people have more positive energy to expend, which leads to more success, and so on. Top management has a choice:

---

[1]Letter to author from Dr. W. Edwards Deming.

(a) It can remain insulated and isolated from the people it manages, or (b) it can descend from its cloistered offices and get involved in transforming American industry, government, and service organizations.

HOW POINT FOURTEEN RELATES TO THE OVERALL PHILOSOPHY

Point Fourteen is the embodiment of the philosophy itself. Its major thrust is that top management has to accept the responsibility for the never-ending improvement of quality in organizations and has to create a structure conducive to the implementation of this philosophy. Without top management's realization that it is in deep trouble and that it must make a commitment to change, frustration at the lower levels is inevitable, and workers will labor in an atmosphere full of inconsistencies, inequities, needless competition, and fear. This will wear down and burn out middle management and employees. Top management's ignorance of the need to transform can only be considered abusive, and in some cases, criminal.

Changing the structure of an organization necessitates a long-term perspective because the short-term effects may be somewhat chaotic and unsettling. Until top management has trained a substantial number of people in the new philosophy, confusion, distrust, and miscommunication may exist. Management can only undertake these organizational changes if it is prepared to allow enough time for people to adapt to the new structure and methods. "Knee-jerk" reactions by management, in response to discontent stimulated by the new structure, are not the answer. Patience and an understanding of the process of change will enable management to see the company through its metamorphosis.

Pushing the Fourteen Points means absorbing them and living them in a manner that integrates statistical methods, an understanding of systems and a concern for everyone in the organization. This holistic approach is a proven way to improve quality, increase productivity, and gain competitive advantage.

IDEAS FOR ACTION

Creating a structure that will support the implementation of Dr. Deming's methods requires a new way of looking at the organizational titles and roles in relation to quality. The following questions may assist you in your analysis of the firm.

Questions for Self-Examination

1. Do your organization's mission statement and operating philosophy provide a structure conducive to never-ending improvement of quality?
2. Does your organization employ a competent statistician?
3. Who is responsible for quality in your company?
4. Does your firm have a Quality Control Department?
5. Will your Board of Directors support the Fourteen Points?
6. Can everyone in your organization "buy into" the Fourteen Points and accept them as the firm's operating philosophy?

Organizing for quality involves setting up a structure that incorporates statistical methods and never-ending improvement into every aspect of the organization. Let's examine the structure of a "Deming company" to see what is necessary for a successful transformation.

Organizing the "Quality Company"

Dr. Myron Tribus, Director of the Center for Advanced Engineering Study at M.I.T., visited six Japanese companies that had won the "Deming prize."[2] He conducted interviews on how closely these companies actually adhered to the Fourteen Points, and how they implemented them.[3] Figure 14–1 shows the organizational structure of a "quality company." Dr. Tribus reported on how these companies are structured, starting from the top level, the Board of Directors.

A Board of Directors typically has several subcommittees, such as Finance, Personnel, Capital Investments, Research and Development, etc. In the "Deming prize" companies, the Board has a Company-Wide Quality Committee (CWQC). The CWQC has the responsibility of evaluating the quality effort throughout the company and guiding management in this area. People on the Board must understand and support the Fourteen Points. They have to grasp the concept that increasing quality leads to lower costs and higher productivity, eliminating the need for any Board committees on Productivity or Cost Reduction. These quality committees or quality circles should start at the Board level to ensure an atmosphere that fosters the transformation to a "quality company."

[2]The Deming prizes are annual awards. One prize is given to an individual for theoretical developments in statistical theory or its application. The other prize is given to a company for advancement of precision and dependability of product.

[3]Myron Tribus, "Reducing Deming's 14 Points to Practice," October 1983, p. 3.

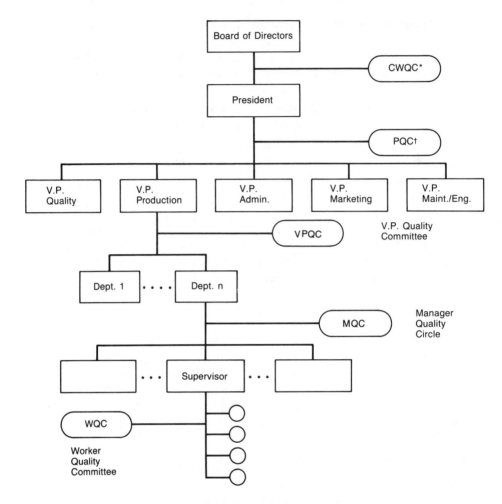

Figure 14–1   Organizational structure of a "Quality Company."

Examing Figure 14–1, one notes the Presidential Quality Committee (PQC). This is one of many committees the President organizes to get input from the Vice Presidents. Other committees might include Long-Range Planning, Personnel, or Capital Expenditures. The PQC's function is planning for never-ending improvement of quality throughout the organization. Again, there are no Productivity or Cost-Reduction committees because the PQC handles these issues, along with the CWQC and lower-level quality committees. The Vice President for Quality has an important role that will be discussed in the next section. Continuing on down the organizational chart (Figure 14–1), one sees the Manager's Quality Com-

mittee (MQC) and the Worker's Quality Circles (WQC). These committees or circles work on never-ending improvement within their areas and
between their areas and the rest of the extended process.

Quality committees or circles have to start at the top and filter down
to the worker level. Employee quality circles should be the last to be organized. Cross-department quality committees can also be effective if the
departments share common concerns or if input from various disciplines
would aid in problem solving. These committees could include hiring
teams, purchasing teams, or project teams, etc.

The job of all the quality committees or circles is to pass information
concerning never-ending improvement and quality up and down the organization, through the quality structure. Plans to improve quality rely
on information flowing upward in the organization from lower-level quality groups. The upward flow of information forms the base for short- and
long-range plans for action. In turn, these plans flow back down the quality structure creating a never-ending cycle of improvement.

Organizing for Statistical Work

A "quality company" requires massive statistical work. This is the
function of the Vice President of Quality. Figure 14-2 depicts a structure
for statistical work that is viable in any organization or industry.

Figure 14-2 includes dotted-line relationships to indicate that the
statisticians (S_1 and S_2) report to several superiors—the Vice President of
Quality and the appropriate departmental heads. This multiple responsibility for reporting should present no problems as it is a common practice
in industry. For example, a mill's local comptroller reports to both the mill
manager and to the corporate CFO (chief financial officer).

The statistician assigned to a department or division must be acceptable to that department/division head. However, his or her promotion
also depends on the quality of statistical work, continual improvement,
and effective application of statistical methods, as judged by the Vice President of Quality. The Vice President of Quality's staff consists of several
theoretical statisticians and other people who provide administra-
tive/secretarial services to the CWQC, PQC, and VPQCs. These statisticians also monitor the activities of the MQCs and WQCs and consolidate
reports at each level to provide managers with the total picture.

The Vice President of Quality must be capable of providing un-
questioned statistical leadership. He or she should have the educational
background and ability to improve the statistical skills and awareness of
his or her subordinates and everyone in the organization. The job, in respect to quality, is similar to that of the Vice President of Finance's job in
respect to financial reporting. The structure outlined ensures that every-

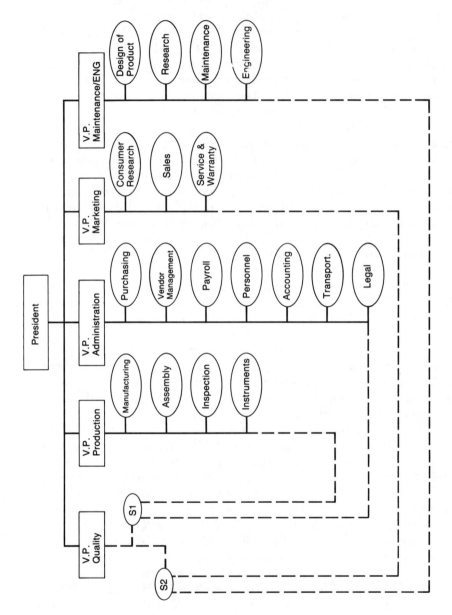

Figure 14-2 Organizational structure for statistical work.

one engaged in statistical work will continually improve through competent guidance. The Vice President of Quality has the following functions:

1. Internal coordination of statistical training, projects, personnel, committees, and reporting, etc.,
2. Provision of staff support to area leaders in quality improvement efforts,
3. Statistical consultation and coordination for suppliers,
4. Statistical consultation and coordination for customers,
5. Assessment of areas to receive prizes and awards for never-ending improvement, and
6. Creation of publicity and ceremonies to emphasize never-ending improvement.

The selection of the Vice President of Quality is a critical decision, as he or she will be involved with the entire organization, as well as with the suppliers and customers in the extended process. The Vice President of Quality should have the statistical expertise and ability to communicate well with all types of people: workers, vendors, Board members, etc. A hiring committee should provide input to the President if a candidate for the Vice President of Quality is brought into the company. If someone is promoted from within, the CEO must take the candidates' statistical ability and communication skills into consideration. The appropriate person *must* have both of these qualities, or failure will result.

POSSIBLE PITFALLS

Point Fourteen brings us to the moment of truth. Are you actually going to embark on the arduous journey that we have outlined? If you decide that your organization has the strengths necessary to begin the process, then creating the structure to push the prior Thirteen Points is something you must consider very carefully.

The following are potential pitfalls that can make or break your efforts at effecting change.

1. *Insulation surrounding top management.*
    If top management persists in remaining insulated and isolated from the problems of the company, there can be no hope for change. The CEO who spends his time wooing Board members and relating

only to high-level managers in the organization will inevitably lose touch with what's really important. Dr. Deming states,

I have no formula on how to reach top management. If the top management do not know that the company is in trouble, and that there is a plan available for top management, there is little that anyone can do for them. In my own practice, I observe the rule to work with a company only on invitation of the top management, and only on a long-term basis, and only if they will engage a competent consultant to work with me and carry on.[4]

All too often, the top managers who need to change most are the ones who least realize it. This is unfortunate because it portends a rather bleak future for American businesses, government, and service agencies.

2. *Lack of constancy of purpose.*
   When an organization shifts goals frequently, due to changes in top management, takeovers, mergers, or new technology, it is impossible to organize a structure conducive to the implementation of the Fourteen Points. Unless the company maintains a sense of purpose for a significant amount of time (10–15 years) attempts to transform the organization will be fruitless. Mobility of top management contributes greatly to this problem because people lose out on the chance of learning how to work together over time. Relationships that encourage growth and synergistic accomplishments take time to develop. The more frequently top management changes in an organization, the more difficult it will be for employees to trust and develop relationships with the new management.

3. *Expecting immediate results.*
   A common pitfall is the desire for speedy transformation and the consequent frustration over the length of time necessary to effect the change process. This leads to pushing people and not allowing them to deal with their reactions and resistances to change. Creating a structure conducive to the Fourteen Points is important, but that's just what it is, a structure. People have to understand their roles within that structure and have to develop the skills necessary to work effectively in it. This will take several years, and it is vitally important that top management allows the time necessary for this process to take place.

---

[4]W. Edwards Deming, *Quality, Productivity, and Competitive Position* (Cambridge, Mass.: M.I.T., Center for Advanced Engineering Studies, 1982), p. 63.

4. *Creating a structure without a competent statistician.*

Trying to implement the Fourteen Points without the guidance of a statistician trained in Dr. Deming's methods is futile. Before top management changes the structure of an organization, it must secure the commitment of such a statistician to work with the company for several years.

The consultant must spend two or three days per month with the organization. Until the company has incorporated the philosophy and methods into its everyday operations and has a critical mass of people who can train others, the statistician's direction will be necessary.

5. *Basing managerial decision-making only on visible figures.*

Business decisions such as how much to pay a vendor or an employee have to be made on the basis of visible numbers. But there are other decisions that have to be based on figures that are "unknown or unknowable."[5] The costs of an unhappy customer, the costs related to an angry or frustrated employee, and the costs of barriers between departments are examples of "unknown and unknowable" figures. They constitute a large portion of costs that have to be understood so management can act. Management must learn to incorporate its philosophical perspective (the organization's mission) and empirical data (visible figures) into its actions.

---

[5]Term coined by Dr. Lloyd S. Nelson of the Nashua Corporation.

15

Working Toward Cooperative Labor-Management Relations

The relationship between labor and management is critical to the implementation of the Fourteen Points. A climate of cooperation and quality consciousness is the only atmosphere that is conducive to transforming to a "Deming company." The current adversarial relationship between labor and management is futile because in the end it serves no one. It must be changed to provide a forum for understanding, resolving conflicts, and working as a team toward never-ending improvement of quality. In the long run, this is the only way that organizations will survive, provide secure jobs, and compete with foreign industry. The following story illustrates the unfortunate state of labor-management relations, a story that is full of misunderstanding, self-interest, and short-sightedness.

One of the authors was speaking to a group of managers and local union officials at a mill which is part of a Fortune 500 company. At the conclusion of the seminar which discussed the Deming philosophy, the attendees were asked what they thought of the material.

The mill manager said: "The material is great, but you don't understand the problems I have with unions." He was asked, "What problems?" and he replied,

> All the union cares about are job territories, work rules, and seniority! I can't turn a profit for the company with these rules. Let me tell you how bad it is. There's a maintenance man who makes $85,000 a year; that's more than I make and I'm the mill manager."

When he was asked how can that be, he said,

This chapter is adapated from Abraham Gitlow and Howard Gitlow, "Union-Management Relations: An Important Piece of the Quality Puzzle," *International Review of Economics and Business* (Milano, Italy), August, 1986.

It all goes back to the job territories and work rules. The union contract says if we call a maintenance man out during his off hours to do an emergency job, regardless of how long it takes, the man is guaranteed 4 hours of work at time and a half. Further, if the job only takes 15 minutes, we can't ask him to do some other work. If we do, we must guarantee him a minimum of 4 hours at time and a half. That's how a maintenance man earns $85,000 a year. The damn union is killing us.

Next the speaker talked with a 26-year-old local union president who was described by his fellow union people as "full of vinegar and ready to fight." The local president said, "The material is great, but you don't understand the problems I have with company management." He was asked what those problems were. He replied,

All management cares about are profits. To hell with the rank and file. The only thing that gives us any security around this place is our contract language which states our job territories, work rules, and seniority. This management is unbelievable; listen to this story. An older worker died of a heart attack, his position opened up, and management wanted to break up his job and give his work to other people. They actually expected the seventeen people in the job bumping line to give up the chance to make $2.25 an hour more, for the rest of their lives. They're crazy. You can't trust a manager who would hurt people like that.

It's an old story—management and union at each other's throats. The dilemma exists and is caused by two dramatically opposing, yet rational, points of view. The conflict generated by the interaction of these two points of view is devastating to a firm's quality consciousness. Yet, it doesn't have to be that way.

CURRENT PLANS FOR IMPROVING UNION-
MANAGEMENT RELATIONS

Several plans which attempt to directly or indirectly improve union-management relations are currently being employed in the United States with varying success: Scanlon Plans, Rucker Plans, Improshare Plans, Quality Circles, Quality of Work Life Plans, and Labor-Management Committees, among others. Reactions to these types of plans have been mixed among the ranks of management and union officials. None of the plans directly addresses and attempts to alter the adversarial nature of collective bargaining.

Mr. Thomas Donahue, Secretary-Treasurer of the AFL-CIO, demonstrated in a January 1982 speech to a QWL (Quality of Work Life) conference that his approach to QWL is one of cautious skepticism:

> American employers have embraced worker participation most recently during times of economic adversity as part of their efforts to regain a stronger competitive position. Other employers are using employee involvement strategies to keep unions out of their organizations. These two facts are consistent with employer behavior at earlier points in American labor history—labor and management have banded together to cooperate during periods of economic or military crisis only to return to more open periods of conflict when the crisis eased. Thus, collective bargaining is viewed as a more flexible and appropriate instrument for dealing with American employers; it allows unions to exert an independent voice for employee interests in whatever fashion works most effectively given the existing environment.[1]

Clearly, Mr. Donahue views QWL as an aid, at best, to the adversarial relationship between management and labor. QWL does not present a foundation upon which a new cooperative union-management relationship can be constructed.

Although all the plans involve some form of increased worker participation, only Quality of Work Life projects, Labor-Management committees, and Quality Circles place substantial emphasis on improving labor-management relations.

A new approach will be presented in the next section which will place major emphasis on labor-management cooperation. This new approach is of vital importance because the trade union movement has not been enthusiastic about the plans mentioned above.

A COOPERATIVE APPROACH TO
LABOR-MANAGEMENT RELATIONS

The Deming philosophy provides a framework for cooperation between labor and management. Although it shares some elements with the plans presented above, it is fundamentally different in several major respects.

First, it is a *philosophy*, not a program, with its primary emphasis on quality. This emphasis on quality is shared with Quality Circles, which are natural outgrowths of the Deming philosophy. The gain sharing plans (i.e., Scanlon, Rucker, and Improshare) focus on productivity improvement, or the output/input ratio, without any concern for the quality of

---

[1]T. A. Kochan, H. C. Katz, and N. Mower, *Worker Participation and American Unions*, W. E. Upjohn Institute, For Employment Research, 300 South Westnedge Avenue, Kalamazoo, Michigan, 49007, 1984, p. 156.

the output. The nongain sharing plans (QWL and Labor-Management committees) depend primarily on the sense of satisfaction the worker derives from the job to improve relations between labor and management.

All of these plans lack a methodology to improve quality, enhance the worker's state of mind, increase productivity, and allow a sharing of the benefits. Only by pursuing the Deming philosophy can an organization achieve all the above goals. The Deming philosophy's objective methodology is based on the application of statistical quality-control concepts and techniques. Although all gain sharing plans employ mathematical and/or statistical techniques for measuring output/input relationships and for arriving at some bonus formula, their techniques do not focus on the output's quality. The Deming philosophy stresses increasing productivity through the improvement of quality.

Second, the Deming philosophy involves the concept of the extended process so that quality control reaches from the individual plant to the source of its inputs, and forward through its channels of distribution, to the customer. Improving quality throughout the extended process increases the efficiency with which deliveries and after-sales service, etc., are handled, extending the scope of productivity improvement and the benefits flowing from that improvement.

The Deming philosophy requires a change in attitudes regarding power over capital. Deming calls on investors, directors, managers, workers, unions, vendors, and the community at large to work together to improve their interconnected processes to meet the consumer's needs, and thereby promote the common good. Investors, through directors and managers, should not insist on sole decision-making power over the use of their capital. Management's traditional view that capital should be exclusively controlled by owners and their agents should be changed because this view compels unions to take a similarly narrow view of seeking their short-term interests, regardless of the long-run common good. The Deming philosophy sees shared decision-making power through cooperation as a superior way to advance everyone's best interests.

LABOR'S COROLLARIES TO THE FOURTEEN POINTS

A firm operating under the Deming philosophy must be guided by Dr. Deming's Fourteen Points for management. The Fourteen Points are the cornerstone of a managerial philosophy which will lead to cooperative labor-management relations, never-ending improvement of quality, and all the resulting benefits.

If implementation of the Deming philosophy is to succeed, labor has to recognize that it has obligations which correspond to those of management. These obligations are summarized in Labor's Corollary. Eleven Points. Labor should pursue the Eleven Points only after management has demonstrated an iron-clad resolve to act in accordance with the Fourteen Points. Labor's Eleven Points are:

1. Absorb and live the company's mission, goals, and operating philosophy.
2. Look toward the long-term good of the firm, not solely toward short-term gains for labor. Consider the needs of investors, directors, management, customers, vendors, and the community through your union.
3. Show genuine concern for the constant improvement of quality. Expand quality consciousness.
4. Communicate ideas to management concerning new products and services, better raw materials, better production methods and training, cost reduction, and reduction of waste. Ideas from labor are essential; however, action is the responsibility of management.
5. Report conditions that rob you of your pride of workmanship to management.
6. Know exactly what your job is and strive for improvement. Embrace "constructive" job-knowledge testing and job-performance measurements as aids to continual improvement.
7. Reject both penalties and payments for defective output due to deficiencies in the system. Consider the long-term effects.
8. Do not demand and create stultifying seniority and work rules. Ignore job boundaries which inhibit helping others.
9. Avoid adversarial and competitive behavior between and within shifts and departments, or with management. Act as part of a team for the common good of all.
10. Request and attend training programs. An elementary grasp of some statistical concepts is very important.
11. Cooperate with management in creating a structure that will push the above points every day.

THE ROAD AHEAD

What needs to be perceived by both management and labor is the importance of their "partnership in quality." This is the critical requirement for implementing the Deming philosophy. Its acceptance and adoption will advance economic good and will enhance the public welfare. Its rejection will generate the opposite dire consequences.

The conflict between management and labor can be reduced by adopting the Deming philosophy. The Fourteen Points for management and the corollary Eleven Points for labor together outline what is required to achieve truly great benefits. However, if management and labor do not cooperate, the future is bleak. Table 15-1 compares several points of conflict between management goals and labor goals, and how they can be transformed when recast by the Deming philosophy.

Several questions are important in determining if labor will wholeheartedly participate with management in applying the Deming philosophy. *First*, can labor's fears and misunderstandings be dispelled, and can labor's attitudes and practices be changed? For example: Can labor realistically adopt the corollary obligations even if it has a strong commitment by top management? Suppose all the members of top management of a firm are killed in a plane crash, or some other catastrophe occurs—then what? How would a new management team behave? Would the mission and philosophy of the company change?

Second, what institutional barriers exist in unions that could block a Deming-type effort? What would the role of the union be in a "Deming company"?

Third, would the specific details of training, retraining, and monitoring programs required by the Deming philosophy be absorbed into labor's consciousness? Labor has to see the Deming philosophy as beneficial to its welfare and must believe that mutual interests are served by the philosophy. Similar concerns and questions exist on management's side of the matter and must be discussed and debated. If American industry and labor embark on the journey to quality, they have a long, hard road to travel. We hope that it will be a road taken.

TABLE 15-1 Comparison of Current Management Goals, Labor Goals, and "Deming" Management Goals

Management Goals	Union Goals*	Deming Goals
Treatment of wages as variable in response to market conditions.	Treatment of wages as nonvariable in the face of the market.	Increase wages and sharing through increased competitive position and profits.
Treatment of labor as a variable input.	Treatment of labor as a nonvariable input, i.e., stability in the employment relationship.	Long-term commitment between the company and workers (not by featherbedding, make-work rules, or stultifying seniority).
Use of new bankruptcy laws to overcome contractual limitations to the variability of labor.	Use of contractual limitations to maintain the employment relationship.	Expansion or stability of employment due to improved quality and productivity.
Treatment of workers as one of several inputs needed for the production process.	Recognition of the worker's status as a human being needing recognition and a sense of improvement.	Recognition of the worker's status as a valuable long-term resource.
Blaming workers for the majority of the failures of the production process.	Blaming management for the majority of failures of the production process.	Proper assignment of responsibility for improvement.
Little or no worker participation in production decisions.	Worker participation in production and other decisions.	Worker participation in attainment of quality, improvement of all areas, and ideas for the company's future.

*For example, the automotive, steel, and construction industries.

16

Selecting the Right Statistician

The word *statistician* conjures up an image for most people. They picture someone carrying a slide rule, calculator, or computer, spouting off formulas in an attempt to explain things that are incomprehensible to a "normal person." Statistics scares many people. It is a subject that is clouded by people's anxieties about math, in general, and is greeted with fear and loathing. Overcoming this negative association is difficult but very important if the Deming philosophy is to transform an organization. Statistics is applied in more fields than any other technical discipline, so the role of the statistician takes on a broad perspective. The statistician's task is to assist others in solving their problems. The following sections will provide information about what qualifications and characteristics to look for in a statistician and what you can expect from him or her.

TYPES OF STATISTICIANS

There are three types of statisticians: mathematical, theoretical, and practical. Mathematical statisticians focus on advancing statistical theory, working generally in mathematics departments of universities or "think tanks." Theoretical statisticians use statistical theory to understand the assumptions and limitations of the methods they apply in practice. They are found in industry, demography, biology, methodological research, etc. Practical statisticians use statistical methods without understanding their underlying assumptions and limitations. They are "cookbook statisticians" and are the bane of the profession. To implement the Deming philosophy, an organization needs a theoretical statistician who understands the philosophy and can assist top management in putting it into action.

CHARACTERISTICS OF AN EFFECTIVE
INDUSTRIAL STATISTICIAN

Selecting the right statistician to guide your organization is vital to the transformation process. The American Statistical Association has developed a list of the characteristics of an effective industrial statistician that can help you in your search for a statistician. This individual:

1. Is trained in the theory and practice of statistics,
2. Can effectively solve problems,
3. Has good oral and written communication skills,
4. Works within the constraints of the real world,
5. Understands the statistical literature,
6. Understands the realities of statistical practice,
7. Has a pleasant personality and is able to work with others,
8. Gets highly involved in the solution of company problems,
9. Is able to extend and develop statistical methodology
10. Adapts quickly to new problems and challenges, and
11. Produces high-quality work in a timely fashion.

In addition, the statistician should be a motivated person with a high energy level. He or she should be someone who can relate well to people at all levels of the organization. The statistician should be able to work on several problems simultaneously and perform well under pressure. The statistician should be confident, outgoing, optimistic, enthusiastic, tactful, organized, creative, inquiring, resourceful, skeptical, and willing to listen.

A statistician who is going to guide an organization in the implementation of the Deming philosophy must also have a good understanding of human behavior, group dynamics, organizational behavior, and the process of change. This is necessary because much of the initial work is behavioral and requires environmental change that may take several years before the organization is ready for the statistical work. If the statistician does not come with this background, he or she can be trained within the organization, through outside courses, or by working with an organizational development specialist in the company.

Statisticians should be able to communicate well with top management, union officials, workers, vendors, customers, Board members, etc. Statisticians must act in a professional manner that encourages confidence in their ability to lead the pursuit of never-ending improvement of quality.

They should follow the Code of Ethics[1] for Statisticians. They should be respected by everyone in the organization and should be trusted to follow tasks through to their completion. Sincerity, honesty, and empathy regarding the problems that inhibit the transformation process are also required. Statisticians must have patience to allow for the proper timing of implementation. Even though they may want to put statistical methods into play, waiting for the atmosphere to be ready is crucial.

PARTIAL LISTING OF HOW TO FIND AN INDUSTRIAL STATISTICIAN

(No responsibility is taken for the completeness of this list.)

1. Interview graduates of university programs with course work in the Deming philosophy. Try the School of Business as a first attempt to find graduates. Next, try the Mathematics Department of the College of Arts and Sciences.

2. Interview graduates of university programs with majors in statistics, with emphasis on statistical quality control. Try the School of Business as a first attempt to find graduates. Next, try the Mathematics Department of the College of Arts and Sciences. (See Table 16–1 at the end of this section.)

3. Look for statisticians seeking employment in:

   (a) *Amstat News*
       Employment Ads
       Applicants Section
       806 15th Street, N.W.
       Suite 640
       Washington, D.C. 20005

   (b) Statistics conference applicant listings; for example, contact:
       The American Statistical Association

---

[1]Deming, W. E., "Code of Professional Conduct," *International Statistical Review*, Vol. 40, No. 2, 1972, pp. 215–219.

Deming, W. E., "Principles of Professional Statistical Practice," *The Annals of Mathematical Statistics*, Vol. 36, No. 6, December 1965, pp. 1883–1900.

Ad Hoc Committee on Professional Ethics, American Statistical Association (C. T. Ireland, L. Hayek, T. Dalenius, S. Hollander, C. Mann, E. S. Marks, J. S. Pierce, F. J. Scheuren, and W. Seltzer), "Ethical Guidelines for Statistical Practice: Report of the Ad Hoc Committee on Professional Ethics," *The American Statistician*, February 1983, Vol. 37, No. 1, pp. 5–6.

806 15th Street, N.W.
Washington, D.C. 20005
(202) 393-3253
Attn: Doris Moss, Executive Secretary
      Conference Employment Services

or

The American Society for Quality Control
230 West Wells Street
Milwaukee, Wisconsin 53203
(414) 272-8575
Attn: Shirley Halladay, Manager
Conferences and Exhibits

to determine when and where their conferences will take place.

(c) Personnel Listing Service
American Society for Quality Control
230 West Wells Street
Milwaukee, Wisconsin 53203
Attn: Pam Siegmund
      Membership Departments

(d) *Quality Progress Magazine*
Classified Advertising
230 West Wells Street
Milwaukee, Wisconsin 53203
Attn: Sue Gregg, Advertising Coordinator

4. Advertise for statisticians in:

(a) *Amstat News*
Employment Ads
Vacancies Section
806 15th Street, N.W.
Suite 640
Washington, D.C. 20005

(b) Statistics conference vacancies listing; for example, contact:
The American Statistical Association
806 15th Street, N.W.
Washington, D.C. 20005
Attn: Doris Moss, Executive Secretary
      Conference Employment Service

or

The American Society for Quality Control
230 West Wells Street

Milwaukee, Wisconsin 53203
(414) 272-8575
Attn: Shirley Halladay, Manager
Conferences and Exhibits

to determine when and where their conferences will take place.

(c) *The Wall Street Journal*

(d) *The New York Times*

(e) Local major city newspapers

(f) Personnel Listing Service
American Society for Quality Control
230 West Wells Street
Milwaukee, Wisconsin 53203
Attn: Pam Siegmund
Membership Department

(g) *Quality Progress Magazine*
Classified Advertising
230 West Wells Street
Milwaukee, Wisconsin 53203
Attn: Sue Gregg, Advertising Coordinator

5. Write or call American Society for Quality Control chapter chairmen for aid in locating an industrial statistician. The list of ASQC chapter chairmen and their addresses can be obtained from the:
American Society for Quality Control
230 West Wells Street
Milwaukee, Wisconsin 53203

TABLE 16-1   U.S. and Canadian Schools Offering Degrees in Statistics
(and Departments with Statistics Concentration)

The listings below provide information as of September 1985 supplied by the individual schools. Any school that offers a degree in statistics or has departments with an emphasis in statistics but does not appear on this list is invited to send information to the American Statistical Association, 806 15th Street, N.W., Washington, DC 20005. Schools that did not respond to this year's questionnaire are listed with last year's information. Users may reproduce this list without requesting permission from the Association. Departments shown with an asterisk are Institutional Members of the American Statistical Association.

ALABAMA

Auburn University
School of Arts and Sciences, Dept. of Math.: M.S. in Prob. and Stat., Ph.D. in Math. (emphasis in Prob.)
No. of Degrees Awarded in Statistics 1984–85: Master 1, Ph.D. 1
Contact: W.N. Hudson, Dept. of Math., Auburn U., Auburn, AL 36849. Phone (205) 826-4290

University of Alabama at Birmingham
Schools of Medicine and Dentistry, Dept. of Biostat. and Biomath.: M.S. and Ph.D. in Stat., Biostat., and Biomath.
No. of Degrees Awarded in Statistics 1984–85: Master 1, Ph.D. 2
Contact: Alfred A. Bartolucci, Ph.D., Prof. and Ch., Dept. of Biostat. and Biomath., Univ. Station, Rust #100, U. of Alabama at Birmingham, Birmingham, AL 35294. Phone (205) 934-4905 or (205) 934-4340

University of Alabama, Tuscaloosa
Graduate School, Program in Statistics: M.S., Ph.D. in Applied Stat., M.S., Ph.D. in Math. with emphasis in Prob. and Stat.; B.A., M.A., Ph.D. in Bus. Admin. with emphasis in Stat.
No. of Degrees Awarded in Statistics 1984–85: Bachelor 3, Master 4, Ph.D. 2
Contact: Jean D. Gibbons, Prof. and Ch., Applied Stat., U. of Alabama, Box J, University, AL 35486. Phone (205) 348-6085

University of South Alabama
College of Arts and Sciences, Dept. of Math. and Stat.: B.S. in Math. (Stat. option), M.S. in Applied Math. (Stat. option), Program in Applied Stat. (minor option)
No. of Degrees Awarded in Statistics 1984–85: Bachelor 2, Master 1
Contact: Alvin P. Rainosek, Prof. and Ch., Comm. on Stat., Dept. of Math. and Stat.,

U. of South Alabama, Mobile, AL 36688. Phone (205) 460-6266

ARIZONA

Arizona State University
College of Business, Dept. of Decision and Infor. Syst.: B.S., Masters, Ph.D. in Business with emphasis in Stat.
No. of Degrees Awarded in Statistics 1984–85: Bachelor 12, Master 3
Contact: Richard K. Burdick, Assoc. Prof., Dept. of Decision and Infor. Syst., College of Business, Arizona State U., Tempe, AZ 85287. Phone (602) 965-5439 or 6350
College of Education, Quant. Methods Section, Dept. of Educ. Psych.: M.A. in Educ., Educ. Psych.; Ph.D. in Educ. Psych., Quant. Methods Specialization
No. of Degrees Awarded in Statistics 1984–85: Master 4, Ph.D. 2
Contact: David J. Krus, Prof., Educ. Psych., 302 Payne Hall, Arizona State U., Tempe, AZ 85287. Phone (602) 965-6859
*College of Liberal Arts, Dept. of Math.: B.S. and M.S. (option of Prob. Stat., O.R.), Ph.D. in Math. with emphasis in Stat.
No. of Degrees Awarded in Statistics 1984–85: Master 2
Contact: Dennis L. Young, Prof., Dept. of Math., Arizona State U., Tempe, AZ 85287. Phone (602) 965-5003.

Northern Arizona University
College of Arts and Sciences, Dept. of Math.: B.S. in Math. and Stat. (joint major), M.S. with emphasis in Stat.
No. of Degrees Awarded in Statistics 1984–85: Bachelor 4, Master 2
Contact: Graydon Bell, Assoc. Prof. of Stat., Dept. of Math., Northern Arizona U., Box 5717, Flagstaff, AZ 86011

University of Arizona
College of Arts & Sciences, Faculty of Sciences, Dept. of Stat.: M.S. in Stat., Ph.D. minor in Stat.
No. of Degrees Awarded in Statistics 1984–85: Master 4
Contact: Prof. Jean Weber, Head, Dept. of Stat., U. of Arizona, 317 Economics Bldg., Tucson, AZ 85721. Phone (602) 621-4158

ARKANSAS

University of Arkansas
J. William Fulbright College of Arts and Sciences, Dept. of Math. Sci., Stat. Div.: B.S. in Math. with emphasis in Stat., M.S. in Stat., and Ph.D. in Math. with emphasis in Prob. and Stat.
No. of Degrees Awarded in Statistics 1984–85: Master 2
Contact: James E. Dunn, Ch., Dept. of Math. Sci., Stat. Div., SE 301, U. of Arkansas, Fayetteville, AR 72701. Phone (501) 575-3351

CALIFORNIA

California Polytechnic State University
School of Science and Mathematics, Dept. of Stat: B.S. in Stat.
No. of Degrees Awarded in Statistics 1984–85: Bachelor 6
Contact: James C. Daly, Ch., Stat. Dept., Cal. Poly. State U., San Luis Obispo, CA 93407. Phone (805) 546-2709

California State University, Chico
School of Natural Sciences, Dept. of Math.: B.S. in Math. (General, Applied, Stat. options)
No. of Degrees Awarded in Statistics 1984–85: Bachelor 15
Contact: Tom McCready, Ch., Dept. of Math., Cal. State U., Chico, CA 95929. Phone (916) 895-6111

California State University, Hayward
*School of Science,** Dept. of Stat.: B.S., M.S. in Stat.
No. of Degrees Awarded in Statistics 1984–85: Bachelor 35, Master 35
Contact: Michael Orkin, Prof. and Ch., Dept. of Stat., Cal. State U., Hayward, CA 94542. Phone (415) 881-3435

California State University, Los Angeles
School of Business and Economics, Dept. of Econ. and Stat.: B.S., B.A., M.A., M.S.
No. of Degrees Awarded in Statistics 1983–84: Bachelor 145, Master 30
Contact: Dr. John Tomaske, Ch., Dept. of Econ. and Stat., Simpson Tower F917, Cal. State U., Los Angeles, CA 90032. Phone (213) 224-3884

Claremont University
Claremont Graduate School, Dept. of Math.: M.A. and M.S. in Math. with emphasis in O.R. and Stat., Ph.D. in Math.
No. of Degrees Awarded in Statistics 1983–84: Master 2, Ph.D. 1
Contact: Prof. Robert Williamson, Prof. and Ch., Dept. of Math., Claremont Grad. School, Claremont, CA 91711. Phone (714) 621-8080

Loma Linda University
School of Health, Dept. of Biostat. and Epidem.: M.P.H., M.S.P.H. in Biostat., M.S.P.H. with emphasis in Epidem. and Computer Sci.
No. of Degrees Awarded in Statistics 1984–85: Master 3
Contact: Jan W. Kuzma, Prof. and Ch., Dept. of Biostat. and Epidem., School of Health, Loma Linda U., Loma Linda, CA 92350. Phone (714) 824-4590

Pomona College
Dept. of Math.: B.S. in Math. with emphasis in Stat./Prob.
No. of Degrees Awarded in Statistics 1984–85: Bachelor 2
Contact: Donald L. Bentley, Prof., Dept. of Math., Pomona College, Claremont, CA 91711. Phone (714) 621-8000 X2941

San Diego State University
College of Sciences, Dept. of Math. Sci.: B.S. in Math. with emphasis in Stat., M.S. in Stat.
Contact: C.B. Bell, Prof., Dept. of Math. Sci., San Diego State U., San Diego, CA 92182. Phone (619) 265-6191

Stanford University
School of Humanities and Sciences, Dept. of Stat.: M.S. in Stat., M.S. in Data Anal. and Stat. Computing, Ph.D. in Stat.
No. of Degrees Awarded in Statistics 1984–85: Master 38, Ph.D. 9
Contact: Herbert Solomon, Ch., Dept. of Stat., Sequoia Hall, Stanford U., Stanford, CA 94305. Phone (415) 497-2625

University of California, Berkeley

School of Public Health, Graduate Div., Biostat. Dept.: M.A., Ph.D. in Biostat., M.P.H., with emphasis in Biostat.

No. of Degrees Awarded in Statistics 1984–85: Master 5, M.P.H. 2, Ph.D. 2

Contact: C.L. Chiang, Prof. and Co-Ch., Group in Biostat., School of Public Health, 101 Haviland, U. of Cal., Berkeley, CA 94720. Phone (415) 642-1593; or Elizabeth L. Scott, Prof. and Co-Ch., Group in Biostat., Stat. Dept., 419 Evans Hall, U. of Cal., Berkeley, CA 94720. Phone (415) 642-2777

College of Letters and Science and Graduate Div., Dept. of Stat.: A.B., M.A., Ph.D. in Stat.

No. of Degrees Awarded in Statistics 1984–85: Bachelor 32, Master 11, Ph.D. 7

Contact: David A. Freedman, Prof. and Ch., Dept. of Stat., 367 Evans Hall, U. of Cal., Berkeley, CA 94720. Phone (415) 642-2781

University of California, Davis

College of Letters and Science, Intercollege Div. of Stat.: B.A., B.S., M.S., and Ph.D. in Stat.

No. of Degrees Awarded in Statistics 1984–85: Bachelor 9, Master 4, Ph.D. 1

Contact: Robert H. Shumway, Graduate Advisor, Div. of Stat., 469 Kerr Hall, U. of Cal., Davis, CA 95616. Phone (916) 752-6475 or (916) 752-2361

University of California, Los Angeles

College of Letters and Science, Dept. of Math.: M.A. in Math. with emphasis in Stat.; Ph.D. in Math. with emphasis in Prob. or Stat.

No. of Degrees Awarded in Statistics 1984–85: Ph.D. 2

Contact: Graduate Advisor, Dept. of Math., UCLA, Los Angeles, CA 90024. Phone (213) 825-4971

School of Medicine, Dept. of Biomath.: M.S., Ph.D. in Biomath.

No. of Degrees Awarded in Statistics 1984–85: Ph.D. 3

Contact: Avis Williams or Dr. Kenneth Lang, Prof. and Ch., Dept. of Biomath., School of Medicine, UCLA, Los Angeles, CA 90024. Phone (213) 825-5018

*School of Public Health, Div. of Biostat.: M.P.H. with concentration in Biostat.; M.S. in Biostat.; Dr.P.H. with specialty in Biostat.; Ph.D. in Biostat.

*No. of Degrees Awarded in Statistics 1984–85: Master 14, Ph.D. 3

Contact: William G. Cumberland, Ph.D., Div.

Head, Biostat. Div., School of Public Health, UCLA, Los Angeles, CA 90024. Phone (213) 825-5250

Graduate School of Management, Dept. of Mgmt.: M.S., Ph.D. in Mgmt. with emphasis in Stat.

Contact: Arthur Geoffrion, Prof., Grad. School of Mgmt., UCLA, Los Angeles, CA 90024. Phone (213) 825-1581

University of California, Riverside

College of Natural and Agricultural Sciences, Dept. of Stat.: A.B., B.S., ·M.S. in Stat.; Ph.D. in Applied Stat.; B.S. in Stat. Computing

No. of Degrees Awarded in Statistics 1984–85: Bachelor 3, Master 5, Ph.D. 3

Contact: Barbara McNitt, Dept. of Stat., U. of Cal., Riverside, CA 92521. Phone (714) 787-3776

University of California, Santa Barbara

College of Letters & Science, Dept. of Math.: B.S. in Math. with emphasis in Stat.; M.A. and Ph.D. in Stat.

No. of Degrees Awarded in Statistics 1984–85: Bachelor 48, Master 8, Ph.D. 2

Contact: Prof. S. Rao Jammalamadaka, Dept. of Math., U. of Cal., Santa Barbara, CA 93106. Phone (805) 961-3119

University of Southern California

School of Medicine, Dept. of Preventive Medicine: M.S., Ph.D. in Biometry with emphasis in Health Sciences Research for individuals with strong quantitative background; M.S. in Applied Biometry for individuals with a liberal arts/clinical background.

No. of Degrees Awarded in Statistics 1984–85: Master 5, Ph.D. 1

Contact: Stanley P. Azen, Prof., Dept. of Preventive Med., PMB B-101, 1420 San Pablo St., U. of Southern Cal., Los Angeles, CA 90033. Phone (213) 224-7204

COLORADO

Colorado State University

*College of Natural Sciences, Dept. of Stat.: B.S., M.S., Ph.D. in Stat.

No. of Degrees Awarded in Statistics 1984–85: Bachelor 4, Master 2, Ph.D. 3

Contact: Dr. Duane C. Boes, Ch., Dept. of Stat., Colorado State U., Fort Collins, CO 80523. Phone (303) 491-5269

University of Colorado Health Sciences Center
School of Medicine, Dept. of Preventive Med.
and Biometrics: M.S., Ph.D. in Biometrics
No. of Degrees Awarded in Statistics 1984–85:
Master 2
Contact: Richard H. Jones, Dir. Grad. Prog. in
Biometrics, Dept. of Prev. Med. and Bio-
metrics, U. of Colorado, 4200 E. 9th Ave.,
Box B-119, Denver, CO 80262. Phone (303)
394-7605

University of Denver
College of Business Administration, Dept. of
Stat. & Operations Research: B.S. in Decision
Sciences
Contact: Thomas E. Obremski, Ch., Dept. of
Stat. & O.R., U. of Denver, Denver, CO
80208. Phone (303) 871-3346

University of Northern Colorado
College of Arts and Sciences, Dept. of Math.
and Applied Stat.: B.A. and M.A. in Math.;
M.S. and Ph.D. in Applied Stat. and Research
Methods
No. of Degrees Awarded in Statistics 1984–85:
Master 5, Ph.D. 9
Contact: Sam Houston, Prof., Dept. of Math.
and Applied Stat., U. of Northern Colorado,
Greeley, CO 80639. Phone (303) 351-2235 or
(303) 351-2820

CONNECTICUT

Central Connecticut State University
School of Arts and Sciences, Dept. of Math.
and Computer Science: B.A., M.A., both
with emphasis in Stat.
No. of Degrees Awarded in Statistics 1984–85:
Bachelor 2, Master 2
Contact: Daniel S. Miller, Area Coord., Dept.
of Math. and Comp. Sci., Central Connecticut State U., New Britain, CT 06050. Phone
(203) 827-7344

University of Connecticut
College of Liberal Arts and Sciences, Dept. of
Stat.: B.A., B.S., M.S., Ph.D., in Stat.
No. of Degrees Awarded in Statistics 1984–85:
Bachelor 15, Master 7, Ph.D. 1
Contact: Timothy J. Killeen, Prof., Stat. Dept.,
Box U-120, 196 Auditorium Rd., U. of Con-
necticut, Storrs, CT 06268. Phone (203) 486-
4192

Yale University
Graduate School, Dept. of Stat.: M.A., M.Phil.,
Ph.D. in Stat.

No. of Degrees Awarded in Statistics 1984–85:
M.Phil. 1, Ph.D. 2
Contact: I. Richard Savage, Ch., Dept. of Stat.,
Yale U., Box 2179-Yale Sta., New Haven, CT
06520. Phone (203) 436-0792
School of Medicine, Dept. of Epidem. and
Public Health: M.P.H. in Biostat., M.Phil.,
Ph.D., Dr.P.H.
No. of Degrees Awarded in Statistics 1984–85:
Master 3
Contact: Dr. T. Holford, Assoc. Prof., Dept. of
Epidemiology and Public Health, Yale U.
School of Medicine, P.O. Box 3333, 60 Col-
lege St., New Haven, CT 06510. Phone (203)
785-2838

DELAWARE

University of Delaware
*College of Arts and Sciences, Dept. of Math.
Sci.: B.S., M.S., Ph.D. in Stat.
No. of Degrees Awarded in Statistics 1984–85:
Bachelor 10, Master 3, Ph.D. 1
Contact: James S. Wolfe, Assoc. Prof., Dept.
of Math. Sci., U. of Delaware, Newark, DE
19716. Phone (302) 451-2653

DISTRICT OF COLUMBIA

American University
College of Arts and Sciences, Dept. of Math.,
Stat. and Computer Sci.: B.S., M.A., Ph.D.
in Stat.
No. of Degrees Awarded in Statistics 1984–85:
Bachelor 2, Master 2, Ph.D. 2
Contact: Austin Barron, Ch., Dept. of Math.,
Stat. & Comp. Sci., Clark Hall, American U.,
Washington, DC 20016. Phone (202) 885-3120

Georgetown University
School of Medicine, Div. of Biostat. and Epi-
dem.: M.S. in Biostat.
No. of Degrees Awarded in Statistics 1984–85:
Master 3
Contact: Leonard Chiazze, Jr., Dir., Div. of
Biostat. and Epidem., Dept. of Community
and Family Med., Georgetown U., 3750
Reservoir Rd., N.W., Rm. 410 Kober Cogan
Bldg., Washington, DC 20007. Phone (202)
625-7772

George Washington University
Columbian College and Graduate School of
Arts and Sciences, Dept. of Stat./Comp. &
Info. Systems: B.A. in Stat. with Computer

Sci. option; B.A., M.A., Ph.D. in Math. Stat.; B.S. and M.S. in Applied Stat.; B.S. in Comp. and Info. Systems, M.S. concentration in Applied Stat., Biostat., Sampling & Survey Research, Computer Science

No. of Degrees Awarded in Statistics 1984–85: Bachelor 12, Master 5, Ph.D. 5

Contact: A.D. Kirsch, Ch., Dept. of Stat., George Washington U., Washington, DC 20052. Phone (202) 676-6356

FLORIDA

Florida International University
College of Arts and Sciences, Dept. of Math. Sci.: B.S. in Stat., M.S. in Math. Sci.

No. of Degrees Awarded in Statistics 1984–85: Bachelor 2, Master 1

Contact: Samuel S. Shapiro, Prof., Dept. of Math. Sci., Florida International U., Tamiami Trail, Miami, FL 33199. Phone (305) 554-2741

Florida State University
*College of Arts and Sciences, Dept. of Stat.: B.S., M.S., Ph.D. in Stat.

No. of Degrees Awarded in Statistics 1984–85: Bachelor 4, Master 14, Ph.D. 3

Contact: Frederick Leysieffer, Prof. and Ch., Dept. of Stat., Florida State U., Tallahassee, FL 32306-3033. Phone (904) 644-3218

University of Central Florida
College of Arts and Sciences, Dept. of Stat.: B.S. in Stat., M.S. in Stat. Comp.

No. of Degrees Awarded in Statistics 1984–85: Bachelor 4, Master 1

Contact: Dr. Linda C. Malone, Ch., Dept. of Stat., U. of Central Florida, Orlando, FL 32816. Phone (305) 275-2289

University of Florida
*College of Liberal Arts and Sciences, Dept. of Stat.: M.S. and Ph.D. in Stat.

No. of Degrees Awarded in Statistics 1984–85: Bachelor 15, Master 11, Ph.D. 6

Contact: Richard L. Scheaffer, Prof. and Ch., Dept. of Stat., 524 Nuclear Science Center, U. of Florida, Gainesville, FL 32611. Phone (904) 392-1941

University of Miami
*School of Business Administration, Dept. of Mgmt. Sci.: M.S. in Stat. (from Mgmt. Sci.), Interdepartmental M.S. in Stat. (from Mgmt. Sci. and Math.)

No. of Degrees Awarded in Statistics 1984–85: Master 10, Ph.D. 1

Contact: Howard S. Gitlow, Prof., Dept. of Mgmt. Sci., School of Bus. Admin., U. of Miami, Coral Gables, FL 33124. Phone (305) 284-6595

University of North Florida
College of Arts and Sciences, Dept. of Math. Sci.: B.A., B.S., M.A. in Math Sci. with emphasis in Stat.

No. of Degrees Awarded in Statistics 1984–85: Bachelor 1, Master 4

Contact: William J. Wilson, Grad, Dir., Dept. of Math. Sci., U. of North Florida, Jacksonville, FL 32216. Phone (904) 646-2653

University of West Florida
College of Arts and Sciences, Dept. of Math. and Stat.: M.S. in Math. with emphasis in Stat.

No. of Degrees Awarded in Statistics 1984–85: Master 1

Contact: David L. Sherry, Ch., Dept. of Math./Stat., U. of West Florida, Pensacola, FL 32514. Phone (904) 474-2288

GEORGIA

Emory University
*Graduate School of Arts and Sciences and School of Medicine, Dept. of Stat. and Biometry: M.S., Ph.D. in Stat. and Biometry (combined)

No. of Degrees Awarded in Statistics 1984–85: Master 2

Contact: Elmer C. Hall, Ch., Dept. of Stat. and Biometry, Uppergate House, Emory U., Atlanta, GA 30322. Phone (404) 329-7692

Georgia Institute of Technology
College of Engineering, Science and Liberal Studies, and Management, Schools of Industrial and Systems Engineering and Math., and College of Management (Joint Program): M.S. in Stat., Ph.D. with emphasis in Stat.

No. of Degrees Awarded in Statistics 1984–85: Master 6, Ph.D. 2

Contact: Harrison M. Wadsworth, Stat. Program Admin., School of Industrial & Systems Engrg., Georgia Inst. of Tech., Atlanta, GA 30332. Phone (404) 894-2332

Georgia State University
School of Arts and Sciences, Dept. of Math. and Computer Science: M.S. with emphasis in Stat.

No. of Degrees Awarded in Statistics 1984–85: Master 5

Contact: Fred A. Massey, Ch., Dept. of Math. and Computer Science, 900 Lawyers Title Bldg., U. Plaza, Georgia State U., Atlanta, GA 30303. Phone (404) 658-2253

College of Business Administration, Dept. of Decision Sciences: M.D.S., M.S., D.S. in Stat.

No. of Degrees Awarded in Statistics 1984–85: Master 8

Contact: Dr. Bikramjit S. Garcha, Prof., Dept. of Decision Sci., U. Plaza, Georgia State U., Atlanta, GA 30303. Phone (404) 658-4000

University of Georgia
Franklin College of Arts and Sciences, Dept. of Stat.: B.A., B.S., M.S., Ph.D. in Stat.; M.A.M.S. (Master of Applied Math. Sci.)

No. of Degrees Awarded in Statistics 1984–85: Bachelor 15, M.A.M.S. 2, Ph.D. 2

Contact: Lynne Billard, Prof. & Head, Dept. of Stat., U. of Georgia, Athens, GA 30602. Phone (404) 542-5232

HAWAII

University of Hawaii-Manoa
School of Public Health, Dept. of Public Health Sci. (Biostat. Unit): M.S., M.P.H. with emphasis in Biostat., Ph.D. in Biomed. Sci. (Biostat.-Epidem.)

No. of Degrees Awarded in Statistics 1984–85: Master 6, Ph.D. 2

Contact: C.S. Chung, Prof. & Ch., Dept. of Public Health Sci., School of Public Health, U. of Hawaii-Manoa, 1960 East-West Rd., Honolulu, HI 96822. Phone (808) 948-8577

IDAHO

University of Idaho
*College of Letters and Sciences, Dept. of Math. and Applied Stat.: M.S. in Applied Stat.

No. of Degrees Awarded in Statistics 1984–85: Master 4

Contact: James Calvert, Ch., Dept. of Math. and Applied Stat., U. of Idaho, Moscow, ID 83843. Phone (208) 885-8742

ILLINOIS

Northeastern Illinois University
*College of Arts and Sciences, Dept. of Math.: B.S., M.S. in Math. with emphasis in Stat.

No. of Degrees Awarded in Statistics 1984–85: Bachelor 10, Master 6

Contact: Dr. J. Koo, Assoc. Prof., Dept. of Math., Northeastern Illinois U., 5500 N. St. Louis Ave., Chicago, IL 60625. Phone (312) 583-4050, X726

Northern Illinois University
*College of Liberal Arts and Sciences, Dept. of Math. Sci.: B.S. in Math. Sci. with emphasis in Prob. and Stat., M.S. in Applied Prob. and Stat.

No. of Degrees Awarded in Statistics 1984–85: Bachelor 10, Master 10

Contact: Stanley M. Trail, Asst. Ch. and Assoc. Prof., Dept. of Math. Sci., Northern Illinois U., DeKalb, IL 60115-2888. Phone (815) 753-0566

Sangamon State University
College of Arts and Sciences, Dept. of Math. Systems: B.A. in Comp. Sci., B.A., M.A. in Math. Systems (with emphasis in Stat. and Operations Research or M.A. in Comp. Sci.)

No. of Degrees Awarded in Statistics 1984–85: Bachelor 3

Contact: M.K. Yntema, Prof., Dept. of Math. Systems, Sangamon State University, Springfield, IL 62708. Phone (217) 786-6770

Southern Illinois University at Carbondale
College of Education, Dept. of Educ. Psych.: Ph.D. in Educ. with emphasis in Stat. and Measurement

No. of Degrees Awarded in Statistics 1984–85: Ph.D. 3

Contact: Patricia B. Elmore, Ph.D., Prof. and Coordinator, Stat. and Measurement, Dept. of Educ. Psych., Wham Bldg., Room 223H, Southern Illinois U. at Carbondale, Carbondale, IL 62901. Phone (618) 536-7763

College of Science, Dept. of Math.: M.S. in Stat., Ph.D. in Math. with emphasis in Prob. and Stat.

No. of Degrees Awarded in Statistics 1984–85: Master 4

Contact: S.W. Dharmadhikari, Prof., Dept. of Math., Southern Illinois U., Carbondale, IL 62901. Phone (618) 453-5302

University of Chicago
Physical Sci. Div., Dept. of Stat.: M.S., Ph.D. in Stat.

No. of Degrees Awarded in Statistics 1984–85: Ph.D. 1

Contact: Paul Meier, Ch., Dept. of Stat., U. of Chicago, 5734 University Ave., Chicago, IL 60637. Phone (312) 962-8333

University of Illinois at Urbana-Champaign
*College of Liberal Arts and Sciences, Div. of

Stat., Dept. of Math.: M.S., A.M., Ph.D. in Stat.; Ph.D. in Math. with emphasis in Prob.
No. of Degrees Awarded in Statistics 1984–85: Bachelor 5, Master 8, Ph.D. 1
Contact: Jerome Sacks, Ch., Div. of Stat., Dept. of Math., U. of Illinois, 1409 W. Green St., Urbana, IL 61801. Phone (217) 333-2167

University of Illinois at Chicago
College of Business Administration, Dept. Information and Decision Sciences: B.S. in Bus. Admin. with major in Quant. Methods; M.B.A. with specialization in Mgmt. Info. Systems or Operations Mgmt.; M.A. in Econ. with specialization in Quant. Methods.
No. of Degrees Awarded in Statistics 1984–85: Bachelor 45, Master 50
Contact: Prof. Stanley L. Sclove, Dept. of Information and Decision Sciences, U. of Illinois at Chicago, Box 4348, Chicago, IL 60680. Phone (312) 996-2676
*College of Liberal Arts and Sciences, Dept. of Math., Stat., and Comp. Sci.: B.S. in Stat. and O.R.; M.S. and Ph.D. in Math. with emphasis in Stat. and Prob.
No. of Degrees Awarded in Statistics 1984–85: Bachelor 12, Master 6
Contact: A Samad Hedayat, Prof. and Ch., Comm. on Stat., Dept. of Math., Stat., and Comp. Sci., U. of Illinois at Chicago, P.O. Box 4348, Chicago, IL 60680. Phone (312) 996-4831 or (312) 996-3041
School of Public Health, Dept. of Epidem. and Biometry: M.P.H., M.S., Ph.D. with concentration in Epidem. and Biometry
No. of Degrees Awarded in Statistics 1984–85: Master 6, Ph.D. 3
Contact: Paul S. Levy, Prof. and Dir. Epidem. and Biometry Program, U. of Illinois at Chicago, P.O. Box 6998, Chicago, IL 60680. Phone (312) 996-4731

INDIANA

Ball State University
*College of Sciences and Humanities, Dept. of Math. Sci.: M.S. and B.S.
No. of Degrees Awarded in Statistics 1984–85: Bachelor 3
Contact: Mir Masoom Ali, Prof. of Math. Sci., Ball State U., Muncie, IN 47306. Phone (317) 285-8670

Indiana University
College of Arts and Sciences, Dept. of Math.: M.A., Ph.D. in Math. with special emphasis in Prob. and Stat.

No. of Degrees Awarded in Statistics 1984–85: Master 3, Ph.D. 2
Contact: M.L. Puri, Prof., Dept. of Math., Indiana U., Bloomington, IN 47405. Phone (812) 335-9537
School of Business, Dept. of Decision Sciences: Ph.D. in Applied Stat.
No. of Degrees Awarded in Statistics 1984–85: Ph.D. 1
Contact: A. Victor Cabot, Prof. & Ch., Dept. of Decision Sciences, School of Bus., Indiana U., Bloomington, IN 47405. Phone (812) 335-9703

Purdue University
*School of Science, Dept. of Stat.: M.S., Ph.D. in Stat. and Prob.; M.S. in Applied Stat.; M.S. in Applied Stat. and Computer Sci.; B.S. in Stat.
No. of Degrees Awarded in Statistics 1984–85: Bachelor 8, Master 18, Ph.D. 4
Contact: Shanti S. Gupta, Prof. and Head, Dept. of Stat., Purdue U., West Lafayette, IN 47907. Phone (317) 494-6031

IOWA

Drake University
College of Business Admin., Dept. of Stat.: B.S. in Stat., B.S. in Actuarial Sci.
No. of Degrees Awarded in Statistics 1984–85: Bachelor 13
Contact: Vasanth B. Solomon, Assoc. Prof., Dept. of Stat., Drake U., Des Moines, IA 50311. Phone (515) 271-2132

Iowa State University
*College of Sciences and Humanities, Dept. of Stat.: B.S., M.S., Ph.D. in Stat.; B.S. in Biometry (College of Agriculture)
No. of Degrees Awarded in Statistics 1984–85: Bachelor 8, Master 20, Ph.D. 15
Contact: Dean L. Isaacson, Actg. Dir. and Actg. Head, Stat. Lab. and Dept. of Stat., 102 Snedecor Hall, Iowa State U., Ames, IA 50011. Phone (515) 294-3440

University of Iowa
College of Education, Div. of Psych. and Quantitative Foundations: M.A., Ph.D., both in Educ. Measurement and Stat.
No. of Degrees Awarded in Statistics 1984–85: Master 3, Ph.D. 5
Contact: Leonard S. Feldt, Prof., Div. of Psych. & Quant. Fndtns., 334 Lindquist Center, U. of Iowa, Iowa City, IA 52242. Phone (319) 353-3354

*College of Liberal Arts, Dept. of Stat. and Actuarial Sci.: B.S. in Stat., B.S. in Actuarial Sci., M.S. in Stat., M.S. in Actuarial Sci., Ph.D. in Stat.

No. of Degrees Awarded in Statistics 1984–85: Bachelor 10, Master 23, Ph.D. 5

Contact: John J. Birch, Acting Ch., Dept. of Stat. and Actuarial Sci., 101C MacLean Hall, U. of Iowa, Iowa City, IA 52242. Phone (319) 353-4849

College of Medicine, Dept. of Preventive Med.: M.S., Ph.D. in Preventive Med. with emphasis in Biostat.

No. of Degrees Awarded in Statistics 1984–85: Master 3, Ph.D. 1

Contact: Robert F. Woolson, Prof., Dept. of Prev. Med., U. of Iowa, Iowa City, IA 52242. Phone (319) 353-6751

KANSAS

Kansas State University
*College of Arts and Sciences, Dept. of Stat. and Stat. Lab.: B.A., B.S., M.S., Ph.D. in Stat.

No. of Degrees Awarded in Statistics 1984–85: Bachelor 1, Master 2, Ph.D. 3

Contact: George A. Milliken, Head and Dir., Dept. of Stat., Kansas State U., Manhattan, KS 66506. Phone (913) 532-6883

KENTUCKY

Eastern Kentucky University
College of Natural and Mathematical Sciences, Dept. of Math., Stat., and Comp. Sci.: B.S. in Stat., M.S. in Math. Sci. with emphasis in Stat.

No. of Degrees Awarded in Statistics 1984–85: Bachelor 2, Master 2

Contact: Patricia Costello, Asst. Prof., Dept. of Math., Stat., and Comp. Sci., Wallace 402, Eastern Kentucky U., Richmond, KY 40475-0959. Phone (606) 622-5942

University of Kentucky
College of Arts and Sciences, Dept. of Stat.: M.S. in Stat., Ph.D. in Stat.

No. of Degrees Awarded in Statistics 1984–85: Master 3, Ph.D. 3

Contact: Prof. Constance L. Wood, Dir. of Grad. Studies, Dept. of Stat., 801 Patterson Office Tower, U. of Kentucky, Lexington, KY 40506-0027. Phone (606) 257-5904

LOUISIANA

Louisiana State University
*College of Agriculture, Dept. of Exper. Stat.: M.S. in Applied Stat.

No. of Degrees Awarded in Statistics 1984–85: Master 18

Contact: Kenneth L. Koonce, Hd., Dept. of Exper. Stat., Louisiana State U., Baton Rouge, LA 70803. Phone (504) 388-8305

College of Bus. Admin., Dept. of Quant. Bus. Analysis: M.S. with Major Area of Study in Quant. Bus. Analysis (Stat. option available); Ph.D. in Bus. Admin. with concentration in Quant. Bus. Analysis

No. of Degrees Awarded in Statistics 1984–85: Master 3, Ph.D. 2

Contact: Michael H. Peters, Ch., Dept. of Quant. Bus. Analysis, LSU, 3190 CEBA Bldg., Baton Rouge, LA 70815. Phone (504) 388-2126

Louisiana State University Medical Center
School of Graduate Studies, Dept. of Biometry: M.S. in Biometry

No. of Degrees Awarded in Statistics 1984–85: Master 3

Contact: Robert C. Elston, Prof. and Head, Dept. of Biometry, LSUMC, 1901 Perdido St., New Orleans, LA 70112. Phone (504) 568-6150

McNeese State University
College of Science, Dept. of Math., Comp. Sci., and Stat.: B.S. in Stat., M.S. in Math. Sci. with concentration in Prob. and Stat.

No. of Degrees Awarded in Statistics 1984–85: Bachelor 4, Master 1

Contact: Dr. George F. Mead, Head, Dept. of Math., Comp. Sci., and Stat., McNeese State U., Lake Charles, LA 70609. Phone (318) 477-2520 X425

Tulane University
Graduate School, Dept. of Biostat.: M.Sc., Ph.D. in Biostat.

No. of Degrees Awarded in Statistics 1984–85: Ph.D. 1

Contact: Dr. Frances J. Mather, Assoc. Prof., Dept. of Biostat., Tulane U., Tulane Medical Center, 1430 Tulane Ave., New Orleans, LA 70112. Phone (504) 588-5164

Graduate School, Special Program: M.S. in Applied Stat.

No. of Degrees Awarded in Statistics 1984–85: Master 1

Contact: J.E. Diem, Head, Prog. in Applied Stat., Rm. 424, Gibson Hall, Tulane U., New Orleans, LA 70118. Phone (504) 865-5727

*School of Arts and Sciences, Dept. of Math.: M.S. in Stat.; M.S., Ph.D. in Math. with emphasis in Stat.

No. of Degrees Awarded in Statistics 1984–85: Master 1

Contact: Arnold Levine, Prof., Tulane U., New Orleans, LA 70118. Phone (504) 865-5727

University of New Orleans
*College of Sciences, Dept. of Math.: B.S. and M.S. in Math. with emphasis in Stat.

No. of Degrees Awarded in Statistics in 1984–85: Bachelor 1

Contact: Terry A. Watkins, Ch., Dept. of Math., U. of New Orleans, New Orleans, LA 70148. Phone (504) 286-6331

University of Southwestern Louisiana
*College of Biological, Math., and Physical Sciences, Dept. of Stat.: B.S., M.S., Ph.D. in Stat.

No. of Degrees Awarded in Statistics 1984–85: Bachelor 3, Master 7, Ph.D. 3

Contact: Thomas L. Boullion, Ch., Dept. of Stat., U. of Southwestern Louisiana, Lafayette, LA 70504. Phone (318) 231-6772

MARYLAND

Johns Hopkins University
G.W.C. Whiting School of Engineering, Dept. of Math. Sci.: B.A., B.S., M.A., M.S.E., Ph.D.

No. of Degrees Awarded in Statistics 1984–85: Bachelor 8, Master 4, Ph.D. 1

Contact: Alan F. Karr, Prof. and Ch., Dept. of Math. Sci., Johns Hopkins U., Baltimore, MD 21218. Phone (301) 338-7214

School of Hygiene and Public Health, Dept. of Biostat.: Sc.M., M.H.S., Ph.D. in Biostat.

No. of Degrees Awarded in Statistics 1984–85: Master 3, Ph.D. 1

Contact: Charles A. Rohde, Prof. and Ch., Dept. of Biostat., Johns Hopkins U., 615 N. Wolfe St., Baltimore, MD 21205-2179. Phone (301) 955-3539

Loyola College of Maryland
School of Arts and Sciences, Dept. of Math. Sci.: B.S. in Math. Sci. with emphasis in Stat.

No. of Degrees Awarded in Statistics 1984–85: Bachelor 4

Contact: Richard E. Auer, Asst. Prof., Dept. of Math. Sci., Loyola College of Maryland, 4501 N. Charles St., Baltimore, MD 21210. Phone (301) 323-1010 X2523

Salisbury State College
School of Sciences, Dept. of Math. Sci.: B.S. in Math. Sci. (Stat. option)

No. of Degrees Awarded in Statistics 1984–85: Bachelor 10, Master 1

Contact: Dr. Homer W. Austin, Assoc. Prof., Dept. of Math. Sci., Salisbury State College, Salisbury, MD 21801. Phone (301) 543-6468

University of Baltimore
*Yale Gordon College of Liberal Arts, Dept. of Computer Sci., Math., and Stat.: B.S. in Applied Stat.

No. of Degrees Awarded in Statistics 1984–85: Bachelor 2

Contact: Japobrata Choudhury, Prof., Dept. of Computer Sci., Math., and Stat., U. of Baltimore, Charles at Mt. Royal, Baltimore, MD 21201. Phone (301) 625-3447

University of Maryland-Baltimore County
Dept. of Math.: M.S. and Ph.D. in Stat.; M.S. and Ph.D. in Applied Math.

No. of Degrees Awarded in Statistics 1984–85: Bachelor 50, Master 8, Ph.D. 1

Contact: Nam P. Bhatia, Prof., Dir. of Graduate Prog., Dept. of Math., UMBC, Catonsville, MD 21228. Phone (301) 455-2407

University of Maryland-College Park
Mathematical Statistics Program: M.S., Ph.D.

No. of Degrees Awarded in Statistics 1984–85: Ph.D. 1

Contact: Grace L. Yang, Acting Dir., Math. Stat. Program, Math. Dept., U. of Maryland, College Park, MD 20742. Phone (301) 454-4883

College of Business and Management, Unit of Management Sci. and Stat.: M.S., Ph.D. in Management Sci. and Stat.

No. of Degrees Awarded in Statistics 1984–85: Master 4, Ph.D. 4

Contact: Frank B. Alt, Assoc. Prof., Unit of Management Sci. and Stat., College of Bus. and Mgmt., U. of Maryland, College Park, MD 20742. Phone (301) 454-6315

College of Education, Dept. of Measurement, Stat., and Evaluation: M.A., Ph.D. in Stat. & Eval.

No. of Degrees Awarded in Statistics 1984–85: Master 1, Ph.D. 2

Contact: Dr. Robert W. Lissitz, Prof. and Ch., Dept. of Meas., Stat., and Eval., U. of Maryland, College of Educ., College Park, MD 20742. Phone (301) 454-3747

MASSACHUSETTS

Boston University
College of Liberal Arts/Graduate School, Dept.
of Math.: B.A., M.A., Ph.D. in Math. with
emphasis in Stat.
No. of Degrees Awarded in Statistics 1984–85:
Bachelor 5, Master 6, Ph.D. 1
Contact: Ralph B. D'Agostino, Prof. of Math.
& Stat., Dept. of Math., Boston U., 111 Cum-
mington St., Boston, MA 02215. Phone (617)
353-2767

Harvard University
Faculty of Arts and Sciences, Dept. of Stat.:
A.M., Ph.D.
No. of Degrees Awarded in Statistics 1984–85:
Master 1, Ph.D. 1
Contact: Donald B. Rubin, Ch., Dept. of Stat.,
Sci. Center 609, 1 Oxford St., Harvard U.,
Cambridge, MA 02138. Phone (617) 495-1600
School of Public Health, Dept. of Biostat.:
Master and Doctor of Sci. in Biostat., Master
and Doctor of Public Health with concentra-
tion in Biostatistics
No. of Degrees Awarded in Statistics 1984–85:
Master 6, D.S. 5
Contact: Marvin Zelen, Ch., Dept. of Biostat.,
Harvard U., School of Public Health, 677
Huntington Ave., Boston, MA 02115. Phone
(617) 732-1056

Massachusetts Institute of Technology
School of Science, Stat. Center (Interdepart-
mental Program): M.S., Ph.D. in Stat.
No. of Degrees Awarded in Statistics 1984–85:
Master 4, Ph.D. 2
Contact: Roy E. Welsch, Dir., Stat. Center,
Room E40-129, Mass. Inst. of Tech., Cam-
bridge, MA 02139. Phone (617) 253-8411

University of Lowell
College of Pure & Applied Science, Dept. of
Math.: B.S., M.S. in Math. with emphasis in
Stat.
No. of Degrees Awarded in Statistics in 1984–85:
Bachelor 4, Master 2
Contact: Dr. Shelley Rasmussen, Assoc. Prof.,
Dept. of Math., U. of Lowell, 1 University
Ave., Lowell, MA 01854. Phone (617) 452-
5000 X2520

University of Massachusetts
*College of Arts and Sciences, Dept. of Math.
and Stat.: B.S., M.A., Ph.D. in Math., with
options in Stat.
No. of Degrees Awarded in Statistics 1984–85:
Bachelor 2, Master 1

Contact: J. Horowitz, Prof., Dept. of Math. and
Stat., U. of Massachusetts, Amherst, MA
01003. Phone (413) 545-2807 or 545-1522
School of Health Sciences, Div. of Public
Health, Biostat./Epidem. Program: M.S. and
Ph.D. in Public Health with emphasis in
Biostat.
No. of Degrees Awarded in Statistics 1984–85:
Master 2
Contact: David W. Hosmer, Jr., Assoc. Prof.,
Div. of Public Health, School of Health
Sciences, U. of Massachusetts, Amherst, MA
01003. Phone (413) 545-1319

MICHIGAN

Andrews University
School of Education, Dept. of Educ. and Psych.
Services: M.A. in Res. and Stat. Methodol-
ogy
No. of Degrees Awarded in Statistics 1984–85:
Master 3
Contact: W.G.A. Futcher, Prof., Dept. of Educ.
and Psych. Services, Andrews U., Bell Hall
160, Berrien Springs, MI 49104. Phone (616)
471-3415

Michigan State University
College of Natural Science, Dept. of Stat. &
Prob.: M.S., Ph.D.
No. of Degrees Awarded in Statistics 1984–85:
Bachelor 2, Master 8, Ph.D. 1
Contact: James Hannan, Prof., Dept. of Stat. &
Prob., A424 Wells Hall, Michigan State U.,
East Lansing, MI 48824. Phone (517) 355-9677

Michigan Technological University
School of Sciences and Arts, Dept. of Math.
and Computer Sci.: B.S. and M.S. in Math.
with option in Stat.
No. of Degrees Awarded in Statistics 1984–85:
Bachelor 8, Master 1
Contact: Martyn Smith, Assoc. Prof., Dept. of
Math. and Computer Sci., Michigan Tech.
U., Houghton, MI 49931. Phone (906) 482-
2068

Oakland University
College of Arts and Sciences, Dept. of Math.
Sci.: B.S. in Math. with emphasis in Stat.,
Graduate Certificate Program in Applied
Stat.
No. of Degrees Awarded in Statistics 1984–85:
Bachelor 3, Master 4
Contact: Harvey Arnold, Prof., Dept. of Math.
Sci., Oakland U., Rochester, MI 48063.
Phone (313) 377-3430

University of Michigan
College of Literature, Science, and Arts, Dept. of Stat.: B.A., M.S., Ph.D.
No. of Degrees Awarded in Statistics 1984–85: Bachelor 5, Master 4, Ph.D. 6
Contact: Edward D. Rothman, Ch. and Prof., Dept. of Stat., U. of Mich., 1444 Mason Hall, 419 South State Street, Ann Arbor, MI 48109-1027. Phone (313) 763-3519
Graduate School of Business Administration, Dept. of Stat. and Management Sci.: M.B.A. with emphasis in Operations Res. and Mgmt. Sci.; Ph.D. in Stat./Mgmt. Sci.
Contact: Prof. Roger L. Wright, Assoc. Prof., Dept. of Stat./Mgmt. Sci., U. of Michigan, Grad. School of Bus., Ann Arbor, MI 48109. Phone (313) 764-3128
School of Public Health, Dept. of Biostat.: M.S., M.P.H., Ph.D. in Biostat.
No. of Degrees Awarded in Statistics 1984–85: Master 6, Ph.D. 5
Contact: Morton B. Brown, Ch., Dept. of Biostat., U. of Michigan, 109 Observatory, Ann Arbor, MI 48109. Phone (313) 764-5450

Wayne State University
College of Liberal Arts, Dept. of Math.: M.A. in Math. Stat., Ph.D. in Math. with major in Math. Stat.
No. of Degrees Awarded in Statistics 1983–84: Master 2, Ph.D. 1
Contact: Morris Katz, Assoc. Prof., Dept. of Math., Wayne State U., 697 MacKenzie Hall, Detroit, MI 48202. Phone (313) 577-2479

Western Michigan University
*College of Arts and Sciences, Dept. of Math.: B.A., B.S., M.A., M.S. in Stat.; M.S. in Biostat.; Ph.D. in Math. with emphasis in Prob. or Stat.
No. of Degrees Awarded in Statistics 1984–85: Bachelor 13, Master 10
Contact: Joseph T. Buckley, Ch., Dept. of Math., Western Michigan U., Kalamazoo, MI 49008. Phone (616) 383-6165

MINNESOTA

Carlton College
Dept. of Math.: B.A. in Math. specializing in Prob. & Stat.
No. of Degrees Awarded in Statistics 1984–85: Bachelor 3
Contact: Frank L. Wolf, Prof., Dept. of Math., Carleton College, Northfield, MN 55057. Phone (507) 663-4370

St. Mary's College
Quantitative Div., Dept. of Math. and Stat.: B.A. in Math. with emphasis in Prob. & Stat., B.A. in Applied Stat.
No. of Degrees Awarded in Statistics 1984–85: Bachelor 11
Contact: Dr. Robinson Situmeang, Assoc. Prof., Dept. of Math. and Stat., St. Mary's College, Winona, MN 55987. Phone (507) 452-4430 X1486

St. Olaf College
Dept. of Math.: B.A. in Math. with concentration in Stat.
No. of Degrees Awarded in Statistics 1984–85: Bachelor 11
Contact: Richard S. Kleber, Prof. of Math. and Dir. of Concentration in Stat., St. Olaf College, Northfield, MN 55057. Phone (507) 663-3416

University of Minnesota
College of Liberal Arts, School of Stat.: B.A., B.S., M.S., Ph.D. in Stat.
No. of Degrees Awarded in Statistics 1984–85: Bachelor 15, Master 7, Ph.D. 6
Contact: Christopher Bingham, Dir. of Grad. Studies, Dept. of Applied Stat., U. of Minnesota, 1994 Buford Ave., St. Paul, MN 55108. Phone (612) 373-0988
School of Public Health, Div. of Biometry: B.A., M.P.H. in Biometry; M.S., Ph.D. in Biometry & Health Info. Systems
No. of Degrees Awarded in Statistics 1984–85: Master 15, Ph.D. 4
Contact: Marcus O. Kjelsberg, Prof. & Head, Div. of Biometry, 1226 Mayo, Box 197, U. of Minnesota, Minneapolis, MN 55455. Phone (612) 373-8042
School of Management, Dept. of Mgmt. Sci.: M.B.A. with concentration in Decision Sci.; Ph.D. with major or minor in Applied Stat.
No. of Degrees Awarded in Statistics 1984–85: Master 2, Ph.D. 1
Contact: P. George Benson, Head, Decision Sci. Area., Dept. of Mgmt. Sci., School of Mgmt., U. of Minnesota, Minneapolis, MN 55455. Phone (612) 373-5632

Winona State University
School of Natural and Applied Sciences, Dept. of Math. and Computer Sci.: B.S. in Math. (Stat. option)
No. of Degrees Awarded in Statistics 1983–84: Bachelor 3
Contact: Dr. Frederick M. Olson, Prof. of Math. & Computer Sci., Coordinator Tri-

College Stat. Program, Dept. of Math. & Computer Sci., Winona State U., Winona, MN 55987. Phone (507) 457-5371

MISSISSIPPI

Mississippi State University
College of Business and Industry, Dept. of Bus. Info. Systems and Quantitative Analysis: B.B.A. in BISQA; M.B.A., M.S. (with major in BISQA); D.B.A. (with major or minor in BISQA)
No. of Degrees Awarded in 1984–85: Bachelor 75, Master 5, Ph.D. 5
Contact: E.R. Callahan, Jr., Head, Dept. of Bus. Info. Systems and Quant. Anal., Drawer DB, Mississippi State U., Mississippi State, MS 39762. Phone (601) 325-3812
*College of Arts and Sciences, Dept. of Math. and Stat.: B.S., B.A. in Math.; M.A., M.S. in Stat.; M.A., M.S. in Math.; M.S. in Applied Math.
No. of Degrees Awarded in Statistics 1984–85: Bachelor 9, Master 6
Contact: J.L. Solomon, Prof. and Head, Dept. of Math. and Stat., Mississippi State U., P.O. Drawer MA, Mississippi State, MS 39762. Phone (601) 325-3414

MISSOURI

University of Missouri-Columbia
*College of Arts and Sciences, Dept. of Stat.: B.A., M.A., Ph.D. in Stat.
No. of Degrees Awarded in Statistics 1984–85: Bachelor 2, Master 1, Ph.D. 2
Contact: John E. Hewett, Prof. and Ch., Dept. of Stat., 222 Math. Sci. Bldg., U. of Missouri-Columbia, Columbia, MO 65211. Phone (314) 882-6376
College of Engineering, Dept. of Indust. Eng.: M.S., Ph.D.
No. of Degrees Awarded in Statistics 1984–85: Master 10
Contact: Dir. of Graduate Studies, Dept. of Indust. Eng., U. of Missouri, 113 Electrical Eng. Bldg., Columbia, MO 65211. Phone (314) 882-2691

University of Missouri-Rolla
*College of Arts and Science, Dept. of Math. and Stat.: M.S. in Applied Math.; Ph.D. in Math. with emphasis in Prob. and Stat.
No. of Degrees Awarded in Statistics 1984–85: Master 1

Contact: Louis Grimm, Ch., Dept. of Math. and Stat., U. of Missouri, Rolla, MO 65401. Phone (314) 341-4641

Washington University in St. Louis
Graduate School of Arts and Sciences, Dept. of Math.: M.A., Ph.D. in Stat. or Math.
Contact: Prof. Robert H. McDowell, Dept. of Math., Washington U. in St. Louis, Box 1146, St. Louis, MO 63130. Phone (314) 889-6760

MONTANA

Eastern Montana College
School of Liberal Arts, Dept. of Math.: B.S. in Math. with emphasis in Stat.; Stat. minor
No. of Degrees Awarded in Statistics 1984–85: Bachelor 3
Contact: Dr. Joe Howell, Assoc. Prof., Dept. of Math., Eastern Montana College, Billings, MT 59101. Phone (406) 657-2972

Montana State University
*College of Letters and Sciences, Dept. of Math. Sci.: B.S., M.S., Ph.D. in Stat.
No. of Degrees Awarded in Statistics 1984–85: Bachelor 7, Master 4
Contact: Kenneth J. Tiahrt, Dir. Stat. Center, Montana State U., Bozeman, MT 59715. Phone (406) 994-3601

University of Montana
College of Arts and Sciences, Dept. of Math. Sci.: B.A., M.A., Ph.D. in Math. with emphasis in Stat.
No. of Degrees Awarded in Statistics 1984–85: Bachelor 2, Master 1, Ph.D. 1
Contact: Don O. Loftsgaarden, Prof., Dept. of Math., U. of Montana, Missoula, MT 59812. Phone (406) 243-5311

NEBRASKA

Kearney State College
School of Natural and Social Sciences, Dept. of Math. & Stat.: B.S., M.S. in Math., B.S. in Stat.
No. of Degrees Awarded in Statistics 1984–85: Bachelor 9
Contact: Dr. Richard L. Barlow, Prof. of Math. & Stat., Kearney State College, Kearney, NE 68849. Phone (308) 234-8551

University of Nebraska-Lincoln
*College of Arts and Sciences, Dept. of Math.

and Stat.: M.S., Ph.D. in Stat., M.S. in Applied Stat.

No. of Degrees Awarded in Statistics 1984–85: Master 4, Ph.D. 1

Contact: David Logan, Ch., Dept. of Math. and Stat., U. of Nebraska-Lincoln, Lincoln, NE 68588-0323. Phone (402) 472-3731

*Institute of Agriculture and Natural Resources, Biometrics Center: Substantial course offerings in Biostat.

Contact: Wilfred M. Schutz, Prof. and Head, Biometrics Ctr., 103 Miller Hall, U. of Nebraska, Lincoln, NE 68583. Phone (402) 472-2903

NEW HAMPSHIRE

University of New Hampshire
College of Engineering and Physical Sciences, Dept. of Math.: B.S. in Math. with option in Stat.; M.S., Ph.D. in Math. with emphasis in Prob. and Stat.

No. of Degrees Awarded in Statistics 1984–85: Bachelor 2, Master 1

Contact: Kenneth Constantine, Asst. Prof., Dept. of Math., U. of New Hampshire, Durham, NH 03824. Phone (603) 862-2320

NEW JERSEY

Montclair State College
School of Math. and Natural Sciences, Dept. of Math. and Computer Sci.: M.A. in Math. (Stat. concentration)

No. of Degrees Awarded in Statistics 1984–85: Bachelor 7, Master 1

Contact: Dr. Helen M. Roberts, Grad. Advisor, Dept. of Math. & Computer Sci., Montclair State College, Upper Montclair, NJ 07043. Phone (201) 893-7262

Princeton University
*Dept. of Stat.: Ph.D. in Stat.

No. of Degrees Awarded in Statistics 1984–85: Ph.D. 3

Contact: J. Michael Steele, Dir. of Grad. Studies, Dept. of Stat., Princeton U., Room 206 Fine Hall, Washington Rd., Princeton, NJ 08544. Phone (609) 452-6486

Rutgers-The State University of New Jersey
Graduate School, Faculty of Arts & Sciences, Dept. of Stat.: M.S., Ph.D. in Applied & Math. Stat.; B.S. in Stat. & Math.

No. of Degrees Awarded in Statistics 1984–85: Bachelor 9, Master 22, Ph.D. 2

Contact: Dr. Joseph I. Naus, Ch., Dept. of Stat., Hill Ctr., Busch Campus, Rutgers U., Piscataway, NJ 08854. Phone (201) 932-2693

NEW MEXICO

New Mexico State University
*College of Arts and Sciences, Dept. of Math. Sci.: M.S., Ph.D. in Math. with emphasis in Prob. or Stat.

No. of Degrees Awarded in Statistics 1984–85: Master 2

Contact: Gerald S. Rogers, Prof., Dept. of Math. Sci., New Mexico State U., Las Cruces, NM 88003-0131. Phone (505) 646-2217

University of New Mexico
*College of Arts & Sciences, Dept. of Math. and Stat.: M.A., Ph.D. with emphasis in Appl. Stat.

No. of Degrees Awarded in Statistics 1984–85: Bachelor 5, Master 3, Ph.D. 1

Contact: Clifford Qualls, Prof., Dept. of Math. and Stat., U. of New Mexico, Albuquerque, NM 87131. Phone (505) 277-4619

NEW YORK

City University of New York-Baruch College
School of Business and Public Administration, Dept. of Stat. and Computer Information Systems: B.B.A. in Stat., Operations Research, Stat., and Computer Systems; M.B.A., M.S. in Stat., Operations Research, and Computer Methodology; Ph.D. in Bus. (participating); B.B.A. in Computers and Stat. with specialization in Stat. and Computers.

No. of Degrees Awarded in Statistics and Computers 1984–85: Bachelor (B.B.A.) 210, Master (M.S. and M.B.A.) 45, in computers; Bachelor (B.B.A.) 35, Master (M.S. and M.B.A.) 6, in Stat.

Contact: Manus Rabinowitz, Ch., Stat. & Computer Info. Systems, Baruch College, 17 Lexington Ave., Box 513, New York, NY 10010. Phone (212) 725-3168

City University of New York-Hunter College
School of Arts & Sciences, Dept. of Math. Sci.: B.A., M.A. (combined B.A. and M.A.) in Applied Math.

No. of Degrees Awarded in Statistics 1984–85: Bachelor 2, Master 3

Contact: Assoc. Prof. Ben Binkowski, Dept. of Math. Sci., Hunter College, 695 Park Ave.,

(H.C. Box 64), New York, NY 10021. Phone (212) 772-5300

Columbia University
*School of Public Health, Div. of Biostat.: M.S., Ph.D. in Biostat.; M.P.H., Dr.P.H. with concentration in Biostat.
No. of Degrees Awarded in Statistics 1984–85: Master 10, Dr.P.H. 1
Contact: Joseph L. Fleiss, Prof. & Head., Div. of Biostat., Columbia U., 600 W. 168 St., New York, NY 10032. Phone (212) 694-3936
Arts and Sciences, Dept. of Stat.: B.A. with major in Stat.; M.A. in Stat.; M.A., M.Phil., Ph.D. in Math. Stat.
No. of Degrees Awarded in Statistics 1984–85: Bachelor 1, Master 7, Ph.D. 4
Contact: Prof. John Van Ryzin, Ch., Dept. of Stat., 618 Math. Bldg., Columbia U., New York, NY 10027. Phone (212) 280-3652

Cornell University, Ithaca
Graduate Program, Field of Stat.: M.S. and Ph.D. programs in cooperation with stat. faculty in several depts.: Biometrics Unit, Dept. of Elec. Engr., Ind. Labor Relations, Dept. of Math., School of Op. Res./Ind. Engr.
No. of Degrees Awarded in Statistics 1984–85: M.S. 4, Ph.D. 7
Field of Stat. Info.: T.J. Santner, Grad. Faculty Rep., 364 Upson Hall, Cornell U., Ithaca, NY 14853. Phone (607) 256-4856
Related Graduate Programs:
Field of Biometry: M.S. and Ph.D. in Biometrics
Field Information: George Casella, Grad. Faculty Rep., 320 Warren Hall, Cornell U., Ithaca, NY 14853. Phone (607) 256-5488
Field of Mathematics: M.S. and Ph.D. in Math.
Field Information: Roger Farrell, Grad. Faculty Rep., 235 White Hall, Cornell U., Ithaca, NY 14853. Phone (607) 256-4008
Field of Operations Research: M.S. and Ph.D. in Operations Research
Field Information: David Heath, Grad. Faculty Rep., 318 Upson Hall, Cornell U., Ithaca, NY 14853. Phone (607) 256-4856
Field of Industrial and Labor Relations: M.S. and Ph.D. in Economic and Social Statistics
Field Information: P.J. McCarthy, Grad. Faculty Rep., 358 Ives Hall, Cornell U., Ithaca, NY 14853. Phone (607) 256-4497.
Undergraduate Program: B.S. in Statistics and Biometry
No. of Degrees Awarded in 1984–85: B.S. 7

Further Information: S.J. Schwager, Biometrics Unit, Cornell U., Ithaca, NY 14853. Phone (607) 256-4488

Cornell University, New York City
Graduate School of Medical Sciences, Biostat. Unit: Ph.D. in Biostat.
Contact: Dr. James Godbold, Head, Biostat. Unit, Cornell U., 1275 York Ave., New York, NY 10021. Phone (212) 794-7546

New York Medical College
School of Health Sciences, Dept. of Community and Preventive Medicine (Stat. Track): M.S., M.P.H. in Biostat.
Contact: Dr. Marvin Glasser, Assoc. Prof., Dept. of Community and Preventive Medicine, New York Medical Coll., Valhalla, NY 10595. Phone (914) 993-4255

New York University
Schools of Business (College of Bus. & Public Admin., and Graduate School of Bus. Admin.), Dept. of Stat. and Operations Research: B.A. in Stat., Operations Research, and Actuarial Sci.; M.S., M.B.A., and Ph.D. in Stat. and Operations Research
No. of Degrees Awarded in Statistics 1984–85: Bachelor 12, M.S. 13, M.B.A. 3, Ph.D. 4
Contact: Aaron Tenenbein, Ch., Grad. Sch. of Bus. Admin., Dept. of Stat./O.R. Area., New York U., 100 Trinity Pl., New York, NY 10006. Phone (212) 285-6180

Polytechnic Institute of New York
Division of Arts and Sciences, Dept. of Math.: M.S. in Indust. and Appl. Math.; M.S., Ph.D. in Appl. Stat.
No. of Degrees Awarded in Statistics 1984–85: Master 1
Contact: Andrew J. Terzuoli, Prof. of Math. and Admin. Officer, Polytech. Inst. of N.Y., 333 Jay St., Brooklyn, NY 11201. Phone (212) 643-4104

Rensselaer Polytechnic Institute
Graduate School, Interdisciplinary Program in Oper. Res. and Stat.: M.S., Ph.D. in Oper. Res. and Stat.
No. of Degrees Awarded 1984–85: Master 27, Ph.D. 2
Contact: Prof. Pitu B. Mirchandani, Dept. of Oper. Res. and Stat., Rensselaer Polytech. Inst., Troy, NY 12181. Phone (518) 266-6483
School of Management, Dept. of Stat. Mgmt. and Information Sci.: B.S., M.S., and Ph.D. in Mgmt. with Mgmt. Systems option

Contact: Prof. W.A. Wallace, Dept. of Stat., Mgmt., and Info. Sci., School of Mgmt., RPI, Troy, NY 12180. Phone (518) 266-6405

Rochester Institute of Technology
*College of Continuing Education, Center for Quality & Applied Stat., Dept. of Graduate Stat.: M.S. in Applied and Math. Stat.
No. of Degrees Awarded in Statistics 1984–85: Master 18
Contact: Dr. Edward G. Schilling, Ch., Dept. of Graduate Stat., Rochester Inst. of Tech., College of Cont. Educ., One Lomb Memorial Drive, Rochester, NY 14623. Phone (716) 475-6129
College of Science, Dept. of Math.: B.S. in Applied Stat. and Applied Math.; B.S. in Computational Math.
No. of Degrees Awarded in Statistics 1984–85: B.S. 31
Contact: Dr. George T. Georgantas, Head, Dept. of Math., Rochester Inst. of Tech., Rochester, NY 14623. Phone 716 (475-2498)

State University of New York at Albany
College of Science & Mathematics, Dept. of Math. and Stat.: M.S., Ph.D. in Math. and Math. & Stat.
No. of Degrees Awarded in Statistics 1984–85: Bachelor 76, Master 10, Ph.D. 5
Contact: Lloyd Lininger, Assoc. Prof., Dept. of Math. & Stat., State Univ. of New York at Albany, 1400 Washington Ave., Albany, NY 12222. Phone (518) 442-4606

State University of New York at Binghamton
*College of Arts and Sciences, Dept. of Math. Sci.: M.A., Ph.D. with emphasis in Prob. and Math. Stat. or Appl. Stat. & Comp. Sci.
No. of Degrees Awarded in Statistics 1984–85: Master 3, Ph.D. 1
Contact: David Lee Hanson, Prof. and Ch., Dept. of Math. Sci., SUNY-Binghamton, Binghamton, NY 13901. Phone (607) 798-2450

State University of New York at Buffalo
Faculty of Natural Sciences and Math., Dept. of Stat.: B.A., M.S., Ph.D. in Stat.
No. of Degrees Awarded in Statistics 1984–85: Bachelor 41, Master 7, Ph.D. 2
Contact: Dr. Peter Enis, Ch., Dept. of Stat., SUNY/Buffalo, A1, 4230 Ridge Lea Rd., Amherst, NY 14226. Phone (716) 831-3255

State University of New York at Oneonta
Division of Liberal Arts, Dept. of Math. Sci.: B.S. in Stat.

No. of Degrees Awarded in Statistics 1984–85: Bachelor 6
Contact: Dr. Esmat Nouri, Prof. and Ch. of Stat., Dept. of Math. Sci., SUNY, Oneonta, NY 13820. Phone (607) 431-3229

State University of New York at Stony Brook
School of Engineering and Applied Science, Dept. of Appl. Math. & Stat.: B.S., M.S., Ph.D.
No. of Degrees Awarded in Statistics 1984–85: Bachelor 145, Master 9, Ph.D. 3
Contact: Stephen Finch, Assoc. Prof., Dept. of Appl. Math. & Stat., SUNY, Stony Brook, NY 11794. Phone (516) 246-6773

St. John's University
*College of Business Administration, Dept. of Quant. Anal.: B.S., M.B.A. Quantitative Analysis
No. of Degrees Awarded in Statistics 1984–85: Bachelor 28, Master 40
Contact: Dr. Natalie Calabro, Assoc. Prof., Dept. of Q.A., St. John's University, College of Bus. Admin., Jamaica, Queens, New York, NY 11439. Phone (718) 990-6161 X7239
Notre Dame College, Dept. of Math. and Sci.: B.A., B.S., Applied Stat.
No. of Degrees Awarded in Statistics 1984–85: Bachelor 3
Contact: Michael Capobianco, Prof. of Math., Dept. of Math. and Sci., St. John's U., 300 Howard Ave., Staten Island, NY 10301. Phone (212) 447-4343 X296

Syracuse University
College of Arts and Sciences, Dept. of Math.: M.S. in Math. with emphasis in Stat. and Prob.
No. of Degrees Awarded in Statistics 1984–85: Master 1
Contact: Prof. Edward J. Dudewicz, Ch., University Stat. Council, Dept. of Math., 200 Carnegie, Syracuse U., Syracuse, NY 13210. Phone (315) 423-2889 or 423-2101
School of Education, Arts and Sciences, Dept. of Psych., Stat. & Meas.: M.S., Ph.D. in Psych. or Educ. with emphasis in Stat. & Meas.
No. of Degrees Awarded in Statistics 1984–85: Master 1
Contact: Silas Halperin, Prof. and Program Dir., Dept. of Stat. and Meas., Dept. of Psych., Syracuse U., Syracuse, NY 13210. Phone (315) 423-2705

Union College
Graduate Division, Institute of Admin. and

Mgmt.: M.S. (Appl. Stat./Oper. Research) M.B.A., Ph.D. (Admin. and Engineering Systems)

No. of Degrees Awarded in Statistics 1984–85: Master 4, Ph.D. 2

Contact: Josef Schmee, Prof. & Dir., Institute of Admin. and Mgmt., Union College, Schenectady, NY 12308. Phone (518) 370-6235

University of Rochester
College of Arts and Science, Dept. of Stat.: M.A. and Ph.D. in Stat., M.A. in Medical Stat.

No. of Degrees Awarded in Statistics 1984–85: Bachelor 15, Master 4

Contact: K. Ruben Gabriel, Ch., Dept. of Stat., HY 710, U. of Rochester, Rochester, NY 14627. Phone (716) 275-3645

NORTH CAROLINA

Appalachian State University
College of Arts and Sciences, Dept. of Math. Sci.: B.S. Stat.; M.A. Applied Math.

No. of Degrees Awarded in Statistics 1984–85: Bachelor 3, Master 1

Contact: Gary Kader, Assoc. Prof., Dept. of Math. Sci., Appalachian State U., Boone, NC 28608. Phone (704) 262-3050

Duke University
Graduate School, Dept. of Math.: M.S. in Appl. Stat.; Ph.D. in Math. with specialization in Prob. & Stat.

Contact: Lawrence C. Moore, Jr., Dir. of Grad. Studies, Assoc. Prof., Dept. of Math., Duke U., Durham, NC 27706. Phone (919) 684-2321

North Carolina State University
*School of Physical and Math. Sci., Dept. of Stat.: B.S., M.S., Ph.D. in Stat., Master of Stat., M.S., Ph.D. in Biomath., Master of Biomath.

No. of Degrees Awarded in Statistics 1984–85: Bachelor 7, Master 9, Ph.D. 5

Contact: Daniel L. Solomon, Prof. and Head, Dept. of Stat., North Carolina State U., Box 8203, Raleigh, NC 27695-8203. Phone (919) 737-2528

University of North Carolina at Chapel Hill
*School of Arts and Sciences, Dept. of Stat.: M.S., Ph.D. in Stat.

No. of Degrees Awarded in Statistics 1984–85: Master 3, Ph.D. 5

Contact: Walter L. Smith, Ch., Dept. of Stat., 321 Phillips Hall 039A, U. of NC, Chapel Hill, NC 27514. Phone (919) 962-1047

*School of Public Health, Dept. of Biostat.: B.S.P.H., M.P.H., M.S., Ph.D., Dr.P.H. in Biostat.

No. of Degrees Awarded in Statistics 1984–85: Bachelor 6, M.P.H. 5, M.S. 13, Ph.D. 9, Dr.PH 3

Contact: Dr. James E. Grizzle, Ch., Dept. of Biostat., School of Pub. Health, 400 Rosenau Hall, 201H, U. of NC, Chapel Hill, NC 27514. Phone (919) 966-1107

University of North Carolina at Greensboro
College of Arts and Sciences, Dept. of Math.: B.A., M.A. in Math. with concentration in Stat.

No. of Degrees Awarded in Statistics 1984–85: Bachelor 3, Master 3

Contact: David G. Herr, Assoc. Prof., Dept. of Math., U. of NC, Greensboro, NC 27412. Phone (919) 379-5891

NORTH DAKOTA

North Dakota State University
College of Science and Mathematics, Division of Math. Sci., Dept. of Stat.: M.S. in Applied Stat.

No. of Degrees Awarded in Statistics 1984–85: Master 3

Contact: Doris Hertsgaard, Prof., Dept. of Math. Sci., 300 Minard Hall, North Dakota State U., Fargo, ND 58105. Phone (701) 237-8191

OHIO

Bowling Green State University
*College of Arts and Sciences, Dept. of Math. and Stat.: B.S. with major in Stat.: M.A., Ph.D. in Math. with concentration in Prob. and Stat., M.S. in Appl. Stat.

No. of Degrees Awarded in Statistics 1984–85: Bachelor 9, Master 5, Ph.D. 1

Contact: Arjun K. Gupta, Prof. and Ch., Dept. of Math. & Stat., Bowling Green State U., Bowling Green, OH 43403. Phone (419) 372-2636

College of Business Administration, Dept. of Appl. Stat. & O.R.: M.S. in Appl. Stat.

No. of Degrees Awarded in Statistics 1984–85: Bachelor 6, Master 9

Contact: James A. Sullivan, Prof. and Ch., Dept. of Appl. Stat. & O.R., Bowling Green State U., Bowling Green, OH 43403. Phone (419) 372-2363

Case Western Reserve University
Case Institute of Technology, Dept. of Math.
and Stat.: B.A., B.S., M.S. in Math.; B.A., B.S.,
in Stat.; M.S. in Applied Math., Math. Stat.,
and Applied Stat.; Ph.D. in Math. and Stat.
No. of Degrees Awarded in Statistics 1984–85:
Bachelor 10, Master 5, Ph.D. 2
Contact: Baldeo Taneja, Asst. Prof., Dept. of
Math. and Stat., Case Western Reserve U.,
Cleveland, OH 44106. Phone (216) 368-2880
School of Medicine, Dept. of Epidemiology:
M.S., Ph.D. in Biostat., M.D./Ph.D. in Biostat.,
M.S., Ph.D. in Comp. Appl. in Health Sci.,
M.S., Ph.D. in Epidemiology
No. of Degrees Awarded in Statistics 1984–85:
Master 3, Ph.D. 1
Contact: Sara M. Debanne, Ph.D., Dept. of Epi-
demiology, 2119 Abington Road, Case West-
ern Reserve U., Cleveland, OH 44106. Phone
(216) 368-3195

Miami University
*College of Arts and Sciences, Dept. of Math.
& Stat.: B.A., B.S., M.A., M.S. with emphasis
in Prob. & Stat., M.S. in Stat.
No. of Degrees Awarded in Statistics 1984–85:
Bachelor 18, Master 8
Contact: John H. Skillings, Asst. Ch., Dept. of
Math. & Stat., Miami U., Oxford, OH 45056.
Phone (513) 529-3539

Ohio State University
College of Administrative Sciences: B.S./B.A.
in Business Admin. with a specialty in Stat.,
Ph.D. in Quantitative Methods (a combined
Stat./Operations Research degree)
No. of Degrees Awarded in Statistics 1984–85:
Bachelor 4, Ph.D. 1
B.S./B.A. Contact: Dean Robert Georges, Col-
lege of Admin. Sci., 1775 College Rd., Colum-
bus, OH 43210
No. of Degrees Awarded in Statistics 1984–85:
Bachelor 4, Ph.D. 1
Ph.D. Contact: Glenn W. Milligan, Assoc.
Prof./Dean, Faculty of Management Sci.,
1775 College Rd., Columbus, OH 43210.
Phone (614) 422-6318
*College of Math. and Physical Sciences, Dept.
of Stat.: M.S., M.A.S. in Stat.; Ph.D. in Stat.
and Biostat.
No. of Degrees Awarded in Statistics 1984–85:
Bachelor 1, Master 10, Ph.D. 3
Contact: Jagdish S. Rustagi, Ch., Dept. of Stat.,
Ohio State U., 1958 Neil Ave., Columbus,
OH 43210. Phone (614) 422-2866

University of Akron
Buchtel College of Arts & Sciences, Dept. of

Math. Sci.: B.S. in Math., Applied Math.,
Stat., and Computer Sci.; M.S. in Math.,
Applied Math., and Stat.
No. of Degrees Awarded in Statistics 1984–85:
Bachelor 3, Master 2
Contact: W.H. Beyer, Head, Dept. of Math.
Sci., U. of Akron, Akron, OH 44325. Phone
(216) 375-7401

University of Cincinnati
*College of Arts and Sciences, Dept. of Math.
Sci.: M.S., Ph.D. in Stat. and in Prob. & Stat.
No. of Degrees Awarded in Statistics 1984–85:
Bachelor 10, Master 6, Ph.D. 1
Contact: C.W. Groetsch, Head, Dept. of Math.
Sci., Mail #025, U. of Cincinnati, Cincinnati,
OH 45221. Phone (513) 475-3352

*College of Medicine, Dept. of Biostat. and
Epidem.: M.S., Ph.D. in Biostat.
No. of Degrees Awarded in Statistics 1984–85:
Master 3
Contact: C.R. Buncher, Dir., Dept. of Biostat.
and Epidem., U. of Cincinnati Med. Center,
Mail #183, Cincinnati, OH 45267. Phone
(513) 872-5631

University of Toledo
*College of Arts and Sciences, Dept. of Math.:
B.S. in Math., M.S. in Stat.
No. of Degrees Awarded in Statistics 1984–85:
Master 3
Contact: H. Wolfe, Ch., Dept. of Math., U. of
Toledo, Toledo, OH 43606. Phone (419)
537-2568
College of Engineering, Dept. of Indust. Engr.:
B.S., M.S. in Indust. Engr. or Engr. Sci.; Ph.D.
Systems Engr.
No. of Degrees Awarded in Indust. Engr.
1984–85: Bachelor 32, Master 5.
Contact: James Daschbach, Ph.D., Ch., Dept.
of Indust. Engr., 2801 W. Bancroft St., U. of
Toledo, Toledo, OH 43606. Phone (419)
537-2412
College of Education and Allied Professions,
Dept. of Educ. Psychology, Research, and
Social Foundations
No. of Degrees Awarded in Statistics 1984–85:
Master 2
Contact: Reemt Baumann, Prof., Dept. of Educ.
Psych., Research, and Social Foundations, U.
of Toledo, Toledo, OH 43606. Phone (419)
537-4337

Wright State University
College of Business and Admin., Dept. of
Mgmt.: B.S. in Bus. with Applied Stat. con-
centration

No. of Degrees Awarded in Statistics 1984–85:
Bachelor 5, Master 5

Contact: Dr. Michael J. Cleary, Prof., Dept. of
Management, College of Business, Wright
State U., Dayton, OH 45435. Phone (513)
873-2290

*College of Science and Engineering, Dept. of
Math. and Stat.: M.S. in Math. with emphasis in Stat., B.S. in Math. with Stat. concentration

No. of Degrees Awarded in Statistics 1984–85:
Bachelor 1, Master 6

Contact: Won J. Park, Prof., Dept. of Math.
and Stat., Wright State U., Dayton, OH 45435.
Phone (513) 873-2837

Youngstown State University
College of Arts and Sciences, Dept. of Math.
and Comp. Sci.: A.B., B.S., M.S. in Math.,
concentration in Prob. and Stat. avail.

No. of Degrees Awarded in Statistics 1983–84:
Bachelor 54, Master 4

Contact: Richard L. Burden, Ch., Dept. of
Math. and Computer Sci., Youngstown State
U., Youngstown, OH 44555. Phone (216)
742-3302

OKLAHOMA

Oklahoma State University
*College of Arts and Sciences, Dept. of Stat.:
B.S., M.S., Ph.D. in Stat.

No. of Degrees Awarded in Statistics 1984–85:
Bachelor 4, Master 2, Ph.D. 4

Contact: J. Leroy Folks, Head., Dept. of Stat.,
Oklahoma State U., Stillwater, OK 74078.
Phone (405) 624-5684

University of Oklahoma Health Sciences Center
College of Public Health, Dept. of Biostat. and
Epidem.: M.P.H., M.S., Ph.D., and Dr.P.H.
in both Biostat. and Epidem.

No. of Degrees Awarded in Statistics 1984–85:
M.P.H.—2 Biostat., 6 Epidem.; Masters—1
Biostat., 1 Epidem.; Ph.D.—1 Biostat., 2
Epidem.

Contact: Stanley L. Silberg, Ph.D., Prof. and
Acting Ch., Dept. of Biostat. and Epidem.,
U. of Oklahoma, P.O. Box 26901, Oklahoma
City, OK 73190. Phone (405) 271-2229

OREGON

Oregon State University
*College of Science, Dept. of Stat.: M.S., Ph.D.
in Stat. and O.R.

No. of Degrees Awarded in Statistics 1984–85:
Master 5, Ph.D. 3

Contact: Justus F. Seely, Dir. of Grad. Studies,
Dept. of Stat., Oregon State U., Corvallis, OR
97331. Phone (503) 754-3366

University of Oregon
College of Arts and Sciences, Dept. of Math.:
B.S., M.S., Ph.D. in Math. with emphasis in
Prob. and Stat.

No. of Degrees Awarded in Statistics 1983–84:
Bachelor 2, Master 1

Contact: Donald R. Truax, Prof., Dept. of
Math., U. of Oregon, Eugene, OR 97403.
Phone (503) 686-4732

College of Business: B.S., M.S., Ph.D. in Stat.

No. of Degrees Awarded in Statistics 1983–84:
Master 2, Ph.D. 1

Contact: Larry E. Richards, Ch., Dept. of Decision Sciences, College of Bus. Admin., U. of
Oregon, Eugene, OR 97403. Phone (503)
686-3315

PENNSYLVANIA

Carnegie-Mellon University
School of Humanities and Social Science, Dept.
of Stat.: B.S., M.S., Ph.D. in Stat.

No. of Degrees Awarded in Statistics 1984–85:
Master 8, Ph.D. 7

Contact: John Lehoczky, Head, Dept. of Stat.,
Carnegie-Mellon U., Pittsburgh, PA 15213.
Phone (412) 578-8725

Lehigh University
College of Arts and Science, Dept. of Math.:
B.S. in Stat., M.S. and Ph.D. in Math. with
emphasis in Prob. or Stat.

No. of Degrees Awarded in Statistics 1984–85:
Bachelor 2, Master 1

Contact: E.P. Salathé, Prof. and Ch., Dept. of
Math., Lehigh U., Bethlehem, PA 18015.
Phone (215) 861-3730

Pennsylvania State University
College of Business Administration, Dept. of
Mgmt. Sci.: B.S. in Quant. Bus. Anal.; M.S.,
Ph.D. in Mgmt. Sci.

No. of Degrees Awarded in Statistics 1984–85:
Bachelor 110, Master 2, Ph.D. 4

Contact: G. Heitmann, Prof. and Ch., Dept. of
Mgmt. Sci., Pennsylvania State U., 310 Bus.
Admin. Bldg., University Park, PA 16802.
Phone (814) 865-0073

*College of Science, Dept. of Stat.: M.A., M.S.,
Ph.D. in Stat.; Dual M.A., M.S., Ph.D. in Stat.
and Operations Research

No. of Degrees Awarded in Statistics 1984–85: Master 8, Ph.D. 3

Contact: W.L. Harkness, Prof. and Head, Dept. of Stat., Pennsylvania State U., 218 Pond Laboratory, University Park, PA 16802. Phone (814) 865-1348

Capitol Campus, Dept. of Math. Sci.: B.S. in Math. Sci.

No. of Degrees Awarded in Statistics 1984–85: Bachelor 19

Contact: V.N. Murty, Prof. of Math. and Stat., Dept. of Math. Sci., Pennsylvania State U., Capitol Campus, Rm. E258, Middletown, PA 17057. Phone (717) 948-6085

Temple University
*School of Business Administration, Dept. of Stat.: M.S./Ph.D. in Stat.; Bachelor, M.S., Ph.D. in Bus. Admin. with major in Stat.; M.B.A. with major in Stat.

No. of Degrees Awarded in Statistics 1984–85: Bachelor 2, Master 8, Ph.D. 3

Contact: Richard M. Heiberger, Assoc. Prof., Dept. of Stat., Temple U., Philadelphia, PA 19122. Phone (215) 787-6879

College of Arts and Sciences, Dept. of Math.: M.S., Ph.D. in Math. with emphasis in Prob. and Stat.

No. of Degrees Awarded in Statistics 1984–85: Master 5, Ph.D. 2

Contact: R. Srinivasan, Prof., Dept. of Math., Temple U., Broad & Montgomery, Philadelphia, PA 19122. Phone (215) 787-7841

University of Pennsylvania
*The Wharton School, Dept. of Stat.: M.A., Ph.D. in Stat., secondary concentration in Stat. in M.B.A. Program

No. of Degrees Awarded in Statistics 1984–85: Master 2

Contact: Paul Shaman, Prof., Dept. of Stat., The Wharton School, U. of Pennsylvania, Philadelphia, PA 19104. Phone (215) 898-8749

University of Pittsburgh
Graduate School of Public Health, Dept. of Biostat.: M.S. in Biostat.; M.P.H. in Public Health Stat.; Ph.D. in Biostat.

No. of Degrees Awarded in Statistics 1984–85: Master 3, Ph.D. 3

Contact: Dr. Carol K. Redmond, Act. Ch., Dept. of Biostat., 318 Parran Hall, Grad. School of Public Health, U. of Pittsburgh, Pittsburgh, PA 15261. Phone (412) 624-3027

*Faculty of Arts and Science, Dept. of Math. and Stat.: M.A., M.S., and Ph.D.

No. of Degrees Awarded in Statistics 1984–85: Master 9, Ph.D. 3

Contact: P.R. Krishnaiah, Prof., Dept. of Math. Stat., 913 Schenley Hall, U. of Pittsburgh, Pittsburgh, PA 15260. Phone (412) 624-5814

School of Education, Dept. of Educational Research Methodology: M.A., M.Ed., Ph.D. with emphasis in Applied Stat., Design, Measurement, and Evaluation

No. of Degrees Awarded in Statistics 1984–85: Master 7, Ph.D. 5

Contact: Charles E. Stegman, Ch., Dept. of Educ. Research, 5C32 Forbes Quadrangle, U. of Pittsburgh, Pittsburgh, PA 15260. Phone (412) 624-4106

Villanova University
*School of Arts and Sciences, Dept. of Math. Sci.: M.S. in Appl. Stat.

No. of Degrees Awarded in Statistics 1984–85: Master 9

Contact: Michael L. Levitan, Assoc. Prof., Dept. of Math. Sci., Villanova U., Villanova, PA 19085. Phone (215) 645-4850

PUERTO RICO

University of Puerto Rico
College of Business Administration, Dept. of Stat.: B.B.A. in Stat.

No. of Degrees Awarded in Statistics 1984–85: Bachelor 3

Contact: Josuc Guzman, Assoc. Prof., U. of Puerto Rico, Dept. of Stat., P.O. Box 21877, UPR Station, Rio Piedras, PR 00931. Phone (809) 764-0000 X3146

RHODE ISLAND

University of Rhode Island
*College of Arts and Sciences, Dept. of Comp. Sci. and Stat.: M.S. in Stat., Ph.D. in Applied Math. Sci. (emphasis in Stat., Applied Prob., Applied Math., Operations Research and Computer Sci.)

No. of Degrees Awarded in Statistics 1984–85: Master 1

Contact: James F. Heltshe, Prof., Dept. of Computer Sci. and Stat., U. of Rhode Island, Kingston, RI 02879. Phone (401) 792-2701

College of Business Administration, Dept. of Mgmt. Sci.: Ph.D. in Applied Math. with emphasis in Stat., M.B.A. with emphasis in Stat. and O.R.

No. of Degrees Awarded in Applied Mathematics 1984–85: Bachelor 15, Master 5

Contact: Jeffrey Jarrett, Ch., Dept. of Mgmt. Sci., U. of Rhode Island, Kingston, RI 02881. Phone (401) 792-2089

SOUTH CAROLINA

Clemson University
College of Agricultural Sciences, Dept. of Experimental Stat.
Contact: Wilbert P. Byrd, Ch., Dept. of Exper. Stat., F-148, P & AS Bldg., Clemson U., Clemson, SC 29631. Phone (803) 656-3028
***College of Sciences,** Dept. of Math. Sci.: B.S., M.S., Ph.D. in Math. Sci. with concentration in Stat.
No. of Degrees Awarded in Statistics 1984–85: Bachelor 7, Master 3, Ph.D. 4
Contact: T.G. Proctor, Dir. of Grad. Studies., Dept. of Math. Sci., Clemson U., Clemson, SC 29631. Phone (803) 656-3434

Medical University of South Carolina
***College of Graduate Studies,** Dept. of Biometry: M.S. and Ph.D. in Biometry
No. of Degrees Awarded in Statistics 1983–84: Master 3, Ph.D. 4
Contact: Hurshell H. Hunt, Grad. Prog. Coordinator, Dept. of Biometry, Medical U. of South Carolina, 171 Ashley Ave., Charleston, SC 29412. Phone (803) 792-2261

University of South Carolina
***College of Science and Mathematics,** Dept. of Stat.: Ph.D., M.S., and B.S. in Stat.
No. of Degrees Awarded in Statistics 1984–85: Bachelor 14, Master 5, Ph.D. 2
Contact: W.J. Padgett, Prof. and Ch., Dept. of Stat., U. of South Carolina, Columbia, SC 29208. Phone (803) 777-5071

TENNESSEE

Memphis State University
College of Arts and Sciences, Dept. of Math. Sci., Div. of Stat.: B.S., M.S., Ph.D. in Applied Stat.
No. of Degrees Awarded in Statistics 1984–85: Bachelor 5, Master 4, Ph.D. 2
Contact: Ch., Dept. of Math. Sci., Memphis State U., Memphis, TN 38152. Phone (901) 454-2482

University of Tennessee-Knoxville
College of Business Administration, Dept. of Stat.: B.A., B.S., M.S. in Stat.
No. of Degrees Awarded in Statistics 1984–85: Bachelor 10, Master 3
Contact: David L. Sylwester, Prof. and Head, Dept. of Stat., College of Business, U. of Tennessee, 332 Stokely Management Center, Knoxville, TN 27996-0532. Phone (615) 974-2556

Vanderbilt University
School of Medicine, Div. of Biostat.
Contact: William K. Vaughn, Dir., Div. of Biostat., Vanderbilt U., Medical School, Nashville, TN 37232. Phone (615) 322-2001

TEXAS

Baylor University
***College of Arts and Sciences,** Dept. of Math.: M.S. in Math. with emphasis in Applied Math. and Stat.
No. of Degrees Awarded in Statistics 1984–85: Master 3
Contact: Danny W. Turner, Grad. Prog. Coordinator, Dept. of Math., Baylor U., Waco, TX 76798. Phone (817) 755-3561
Graduate School, Dept. of Psych. with Dept. of Math. and Dept. of Computer and Eng. Sci.: M.A. (Behavioral Stat.), Ph.D. in Behavioral Stat.
Contact: Roger E. Kirk, Dir. of Behav. Stat. Program, Dept. of Psych., Baylor U., Waco, TX 76798. Phone (817) 755-2961

Rice University
School of Engineering, Dept. of Math. Sci.: B.A., M.A., M.A. Math. Sci., Ph.D.
No. of Degrees Awarded in Statistics 1984–85: Master 2, Ph.D. 1
Contact: James R. Thompson, Prof., Dept. of Math. Sci., Rice U., Box 1892, Houston, TX 77251-1892. Phone (713) 527-4828

Southern Methodist University
***Dedman College,** Dept. of Stat.: M.S., Ph.D. in Stat.
No. of Degrees Awarded in Statistics 1984–85: Master 6, Ph.D. 2
Contact: W.R. Schucany, Ch., Dept. of Stat., Room 144, Heroz Bldg., Southern Methodist U., Dallas, TX 75275. Phone (214) 692-2441

Stephen F. Austin State University
School of Sciences and Math., Dept. of Math. and Stat.: M.S. in Stat.
No. of Degrees Awarded in Statistics 1984–85: Master 2
Contact: Thomas A. Atchison, Ch., Dept. of Math. and Stat., Stephen F. Austin State U., P.O. Box 13040, Nacogdoches, TX 75962. Phone (409) 569-3805

Texas A&M University
College of Education, Dept. of Educ. Psych.: Ph.D. in Educ. Psych. with concentration in Quant. Methods, Measurement, and Educ. Stat.

No. of Degrees Awarded in Statistics 1984–85: Ph.D. 1

Contact: Prof. James F. McNamara, Dept. of Educ. Psych., College of Educ., Texas A&M U., College Station, TX 77843. Phone (713) 845-1831

College of Science, Dept. of Stat.: B.S. in Appl. Math. Sci.; M.S., Ph.D. in Stat.

No. of Degrees Awarded in Statistics 1984–85: Bachelor 12, Master 8, Ph.D. 4

Contact: Dr. W.B. Smith, Head, Dept. of Stat., Texas A&M U., College Station, TX 77843. Phone (409) 845-3141

Texas Tech University

***College of Arts and Sciences,** Dept. of Math.: M.S. in Stat., M.S., Ph.D. in Math. with emphasis in Stat.

No. of Degrees Awarded in Statistics 1984–85: Master 8, Ph.D. 1

Contact: Benjamin S. Duran, Prof., Dept. of Math., Texas Tech. U., Lubbock, TX 79409. Phone (806) 742-2595

College of Business Administration, Area of Info. Systems & Quant. Sci.: M.S., D.B.A. in Bus. Stat.

Contact: W.J. Conover, Area Coord., Info. Systems & Quant. Sci., Texas Tech. U., Coll. of Bus. Admin., Lubbock, TX 79409. Phone (806) 742-1546

University of Houston-University Park

College of Business Admin., Dept. of Quant. Mgmt. Sci.: Ph.D. in Bus. Admin. with emphasis in Applied Stat./Mgmt. Sci.

No. of Degrees Awarded in Statistics 1984–85: Bachelor 3, Master 2, Ph.D. 2

Contact: Edward P.C. Kao, Doctoral Prog. Coord., Dept. of Quant. Mgmt. Sci., U. of Houston-Univ. Park, Houston, TX 77004. Phone (713) 749-3957

College of Engineering, Dept. of Industrial Engnr.: M.S., Ph.D. in Operations Research; B.S., M.S., Ph.D. in Indust. Engr.

No. of Degrees Awarded in Statistics 1984–85: Bachelor 17, Master 12, Ph.D. 2

Contact: Dr. Japhet S. Law, Dir. of O.R., Dept. of Indust. Engnr., E203-D3, U. of Houston, Houston, TX 77004. Phone (713) 749-4800

University of Texas at Arlington

College of Science, Dept. of Math.: B.S. and M.A. in Math. with Stat. option, and Ph.D. in Math. Sci. with concentration in Stat.

No. of Degrees Awarded in Statistics 1984–85: Bachelor 15, Master 3

Contact: Danny Dyer, Prof., Dept. of Math., U. of Texas, P.O. Box 19408, Arlington, TX 76019. Phone (817) 273-3261

University of Texas at Austin

College of Business Administration, Dept. of General Business: B.B.A. in Stat., Ph.D. in General Bus. with emphasis in Stat.

Contact: Thomas W. Sager, Assoc. Prof., Dept. of General Bus., CBA 5.232, University of Texas, Austin, TX 78712. Phone (512) 471-3322

College of Natural Sciences, Graduate College, Dept. of Math.: M.A., M.S., Ph.D. in Math. with emphasis in Stat.

No. of Degrees Awarded in Statistics 1984–85: Master 5, Ph.D. 6

Contact: Peter W.M. John, Prof., Dept. of Math., U. of Texas, Austin, TX 78712. Phone (512) 471-7711

University of Texas at Dallas

School of Natural Sciences and Math., Programs in Mathematical Sciences: B.S., M.S., Ph.D. in Math. Sciences with concentration in Stat.

No. of Degrees Awarded in Statistics 1984–85: Bachelor 2, Master 1, Ph.D. 1

Contact: John W. Van Ness, Program Head, Dept. of Math. Sci., U. of Texas at Dallas, P.O. Box 830688, Richardson, TX 75080. Phone (214) 690-2161

University of Texas at El Paso

College of Science, Dept. of Math. Sci.: M.S. in Stat.

No. of Degrees Awarded in Statistics 1984–85: Master 3

Contact: Eugene F. Schuster, Ch., Dept. of Math. Sci., U. of Texas, El Paso, TX 79968-0514. Phone (915) 747-5761

University of Texas Health Science Center at Houston

School of Public Health, Dept. of Biometry: M.S. and Ph.D. in Biometry

No. of Degrees Awarded in Statistics 1984–85: Master 1, Ph.D. 3

Contact: Dr. Jay Glasser, Assoc. Prof. of Biometry, U. of Texas, School of Public Health, P.O. Box 20186 Astrodome Station, Houston, TX 77225. Phone (713) 792-4372

UTAH

Brigham Young University

***College of Physical and Math. Science,** Dept. of Stat.: M.S. in Stat.

No. of Degrees Awarded in Statistics 1984–85: Bachelor 15, Master 3

Contact: Alvin C. Rencher, Ch., Dept. of Stat., 222 TMCB, Brigham Young U., Provo, UT 84602. Phone (801) 378-4505

Utah State University
  College of Science, Dept. of Applied Stat.: B.S.
    and M.S. in Appl. Stat.
  No. of Degrees Awarded in Statistics 1984–85:
    Bachelor 3, Master 3
  Contact: Dr. Ronald Canfield, Dir. of Grad.
    Prog., Applied Stat., Utah State U., UMC 42,
    Logan, UT 84321. Phone (801) 750-2434

VERMONT

University of Vermont
  College of Eng. and Math., Stat. Prog., Dept.
    of Math.: B.S., M.S. in Stat., M.S. in Biostat.
  No. of Degrees Awarded in Statistics 1984–85:
    Bachelor 5; Master: Stat. 4, Biostat. 2
  Contact: Dr. Takamaru Ashikaga, Dir., Stat.
    Prog., Dept. of Math. and Stat., U. of Ver-
    mont, Given Medical Bldg., Burlington, VT
    05405. Phone (802) 656-2526

VIRGINIA

George Mason University
  ***College of Arts and Sciences,** Dept. of Man-
    agement Sci.: B.S., B.A., M.B.A., Ph.D. in
    Applied Math.
  No. of Degrees Awarded in Mathematics
    1983–84: Bachelor 21, Master 5
  Contact: John Miller, Assoc. Prof., Dept. of
    Math. Sci., George Mason U., 4400 Univer-
    sity Drive, Fairfax, VA 22003. Phone (703)
    323-2733

Hollins College
  School of Arts and Sciences, Dept. of Stat.:
    B.A. in Stat., B.A. in Computational Sci.
  No. of Degrees Awarded in Statistics 1984–85:
    Bachelor 15
  Contact: David Weinman, Prof. and Ch., Dept.
    of Stat., Hollins College, Roanoke, VA 24020.
    Phone (703) 362-6525

James Madison University
  College of Letters and Sciences, Dept. of Math.
    and Computer Sci.: B.S., B.A. in Math. with
    concentration in Stat.; M.S. in Math. with
    emphasis in Prob. and Stat.
  No. of Degrees Awarded in Statistics 1984–85:
    Bachelor 2
  Contact: C.Y. Chiang, Asst. Prof. and Ch., Stat.
    Comm., Dept. of Math. and Computer Sci.,
    James Madison U., Harrisonburg, VA 22807.
    Phone (703) 568-6919 or 568-6184

Old Dominion University
  School of Sciences and Health Professions,
    Dept. of Math. Sci.: B.S., M.S., and Ph.D.
    options in Stat.
  No. of Degrees Awarded in Statistics 1984–85:
    Bachelor 2, Master 2, Ph.D. 1
  Contact: Ram C. Dahiya, Prof. and Stat. Prog.
    Director, Dept. of Stat., Old Dominion U.,
    Norfolk, VA 23508. Phone (804) 440-3904

Radford University
  College of Arts and Sciences, Dept. of Math.
    and Stat.: B.S., B.A.
  No. of Degrees Awarded in Statistics 1984–85:
    Bachelor 12
  Contact: J.S. Milton, Prof. of Stat., Radford U.,
    Box 5837, Radford, VA 24142. Phone (703)
    731-5340

University of Virginia
  ***College of Arts and Sciences,** Dept. of Math.:
    M.S. in Math. with concentration in Stat.;
    Ph.D. in Math. with concentration in Proba-
    bility and Math. Stat.
  No. of Degrees Awarded in Statistics 1984–85:
    Master 2
  Contact: Hamparsum Bozdogan, Asst. Prof.,
    Dept. of Math., Math/Astronomy Bldg., U.
    of Virginia, Charlottesville, VA 22903. Phone
    (804) 924-4922
  School of Engineering and Applied Science,
    Dept. of Applied Math.: M.S., Ph.D. in
    Applied Math. with concentration in Prob.
    and Stat.
  Contact: Prof. William Roberts, Dept. of Ap-
    plied Math., School of Eng. and Applied Sci.,
    U. of Virginia, Charlottesville, VA 22903.
    Phone (804) 924-1038

Virginia Commonwealth University
  ***College of Humanities and Sciences,** Dept.
    of Math. Sci.: B.S., M.S. in Math. Sci./Stat.
  No. of Degrees Awarded in Statistics 1984–85:
    Bachelor 5, Master 2
  Contact: William E. Haver, Ch., Dept. of Math.
    Sci., Virginia Commonwealth U., 1015 W.
    Main St., Richmond, VA 23284. Phone (804)
    257-1319
  **Medical College of Virginia, School of Basic
    Health Sci.,** Dept. of Biostat.: M.S., Ph.D. in
    Biostat.
  No. of Degrees Awarded in Statistics 1984–85:
    Master 1, Ph.D. 4
  Contact: Vernon M. Chinchilli, Grad. Program
    Dir., Dept. of Biostat., Medical College of
    Virginia Commonwealth U., P.O. Box 32,
    MCV Station, Richmond, VA 23298. Phone
    (804) 786-9824

Institute of Statistics
Contact: Paul D. Minton, Dir., Inst. of Stat., Virginia Commonwealth U., 901 W. Franklin St., Richmond, VA 23284. Phone (804) 257-0001

Virginia Polytechnic Institute and State University
*College of Arts and Sciences, Dept. of Stat.: B.S., M.S., Ph.D.
No. of Degrees Awarded in Statistics 1984–85: Bachelor 13, Master 8, Ph.D. 8
Contact: Klaus Hinkelmann, Prof. and Head, Dept. of Stat., Virginia Polytechnic Inst. & State U., Blacksburg, VA 24061. Phone (703) 961-5657

WASHINGTON

University of Washington
*College of Arts and Sciences, Dept. of Stat.: B.S., M.S., Ph.D. in Stat.
No. of Degrees Awarded in Statistics 1984–85: Bachelor 8, Master 3, Ph.D. 1
Contact: Jon A. Wellner, Grad. Adv., Dept. of Stat., U. of Washington, GN-22, Seattle, WA 98195. Phone (206) 543-6207
Graduate School, Biomath. Group: M.S., Ph.D. in Biomath.
No. of Degrees Awarded in Statistics 1984–85: Master 9, Ph.D. 5
Contact for Biomath.: Richard A. Kronmal, Ch., Dept. of Biomath., Biomath. Group SC-32, U. of Washington, Seattle, WA 98195. Phone (206) 543-1044

WEST VIRGINIA

West Virginia University
College of Arts and Sciences, Dept. of Stat. and Comp. Sci.: B.S., M.S. in Stat., Ph.D. in Stat. Genetics
No. of Degrees Awarded in Statistics 1984–85: Bachelor 3, Master 2
Contact: Donald F. Butcher, Prof. and Ch., Dept. of Stat. & Comp. Sci., 311 Knapp Hall, West Virginia U., Morgantown, WV 26506. Phone (304) 293-3607

WISCONSIN

Marquette University
*College of Arts and Sciences, Dept. of Math., Stat., and Computer Sci.: M.S. in Stat., M.S. in Special Prog. for Secondary School Teachers

No. of Degrees Awarded in Statistics 1984–85: Master 3
Contact: G.G. Hamedani, Assoc. Prof., Dept. of Math., Stat., and Computer Sci., Marquette U., Milwaukee, WI 53233. Phone (414) 224-6348

Medical College of Wisconsin
Graduate School, Biostat./Clinical Epidem. Dept.: M.S. in Biostat.
No. of Degrees Awarded in Statistics 1984–85: Master 2
Contact: Alfred A. Rimm, Prof., Biostat./ Clinical Epidem., Medical College of Wisconsin, P.O. Box 26509, Milwaukee, WI 53226. Phone (414) 257-8280

University of Wisconsin, Green Bay
College of Environmental Sciences, Program in Math.: B.S. in Math., Program in Stat.
No. of Degrees Awarded in Statistics 1984–85: Bachelor 3
Contact: Dennis Girard, U. of Wisconsin, Green Bay, WI 54302. Phone (414) 465-2371

University of Wisconsin-LaCrosse
College of Arts, Letters and Sciences, Dept. of Math.: B.S. in Math. with emphasis in Stat.
No. of Degrees Awarded in Statistics 1984–85: Bachelor 3
Contact: David W. Bange, Ch., Dept. of Math., U. of Wisconsin-LaCrosse, LaCrosse, WI 54601. Phone (608) 785-8383

University of Wisconsin-Madison
College of Letters and Science, Dept. of Stat.: B.S., M.S., Ph.D. in Stat.; M.S., Ph.D. in Business-Stat.; M.S., Ph.D. in Stat. with emphasis in Biostat.
No. of Degrees Awarded in Statistics 1984–85: Bachelor 6, Master 12, Ph.D. 10
Contact: G.K. Bhattacharyya, Ch., Dept. of Stat., U. of Wisconsin-Madison, 1210 W. Dayton St., Madison, WI 53706. Phone (608) 262-3720
School of Education, Dept. of Educ. Psych.: M.S., Ph.D. in Educ. Psych. with emphasis in Stat.
No. of Degrees Awarded in Statistics 1984–85: Master 1
Contact: Frank B. Baker, Dir., Lab. of Exper. Design, Educ. Sci. Bldg., U. of Wisconsin, Madison, WI 53705. Phone (608) 262-0841

University of Wisconsin-Milwaukee
College of Letters and Science, Dept. of Math. Sci.: B.S., M.S., Ph.D. in Math. with emphasis in Prob. and Stat.

No. of Degrees Awarded in Statistics 1984–85:
Bachelor 4, Master 3
Contact: Tom O'Bryan, Assoc. Prof., Dept. of
Math. Sci., U. of Wisconsin, Milwaukee, WI
53201. Phone (414) 963-4836

WYOMING

University of Wyoming
College of Commerce and Industry, Dept. of
Stat.: M.S., Ph.D. in Stat., Biostat., Geostat.;
B.S. in Math./Stat., Biostat., Comp. Sci/Stat.,
Stat.
No. of Degrees Awarded in Statistics 1984–85:
Master 1
Contact: Barbara Rouse or Lyman L. McDonald,
Ch., Dept. of Stat., U. of Wyoming, Box 3332,
University Station, Laramie, WY 82071. Phone
(307) 766-4229

CANADA

ALBERTA

University of Alberta
Faculty of Science, Dept. of Stat. and Applied
Prob.: B.Sc. with specialization and Honours
in Stat., M.Sc. in Stat. and Applied Prob.,
Ph.D. in Stat. and Applied Prob.
No. of Degrees Awarded in Statistics 1983–84:
Bachelor 4, Master 1
Contact: Dr. John R. McGregor, Ch., Dept. of
Stat. and Applied Prob., 501 CAB, U. of
Alberta, Edmonton, Alberta T6G 2G1,
CANADA. Phone (403) 432-2052 or (403)
432-4269

University of Calgary
Faculty of Science, Div. of Stat.: B.Sc., M.Sc.,
and Ph.D. in Stat. and B.Sc. in Actuarial Sci.,
M.Sc. in Applied Prob. & Stat.
No. of Degrees Awarded in Statistics 1984–85:
Bachelor 2, Master 1, Ph.D. 1
Contact: Jagannath K. Wani, Ch., Div. of Stat.,
University of Calgary, 2500 University Dr.,
N.W., Calgary, Alberta T2N 1N4, CANADA.
Phone (403) 220-6796

BRITISH COLUMBIA

Simon Fraser University
Faculty of Science, Dept. of Math. and Stat.:
B.Sc., M.Sc., Ph.D., with emphasis in Stat.
No. of Degrees Awarded in Statistics 1984–85:
Bachelor 25, Master 2, Ph.D 1

Contact: M.A. Stephens, Prof., Dept. of Math.
and Stat., Simon Fraser U., Burnaby, B.C.
V5A 1S6, CANADA. Phone (604) 291-3577/
3331

University of British Columbia
*Faculty of Science, Dept. of Stat.: M.Sci.,
Ph.D. in Stat.
No. of Degrees Awarded in Statistics 1984–85:
Master 2
Contact: James V. Zidek, Head, Dept. of Stat.,
U. of British Columbia, 2021 West Mall,
Vancouver, B.C. V6T 1W5, CANADA. Phone
(604) 228-2234

University of Victoria
Faculty of Arts and Science, Dept. of Math.:
B.A., B.Sc., M.A., M.Sc. with emphasis in
Prob. and Stat.
No. of Degrees Awarded in Statistics 1984–85:
Bachelor 3
Contact: W.J. Reed, Assoc. Prof., Dept. of
Math., U. of Victoria, P.O. Box 1700, Victoria,
B.C. V8W 2Y2, CANADA. Phone (604) 721-
7469

MANITOBA

University of Manitoba
Faculty of Science, Dept. of Stat.: M.S., Ph.D.
in Stat.
No. of Degrees Awarded in Statistics 1984–85:
Bachelor 51, Master 6
Contact: Smiley W. Cheng, Prof., Dept. of
Stat., U. of Manitoba, Winnipeg, Manitoba
R3T 2N2, CANADA. Phone (204) 474-9826

NEW BRUNSWICK

University of New Brunswick
Faculty of Arts, Dept. of Math. and Stat.: B.A.,
B.Sc., M.A., Ph.D. in Math. or Stat.
No. of Degrees Awarded in Statistics 1984–85:
Bachelor 4, Master 2
Contact: Dr. S. Rinco, Ch., Dept. of Math. &
Stat., U. of New Brunswick, P.O. Box 4400,
Fredericton, N.B. E3B 5A3, CANADA. Phone
(506) 453-4771

NOVA SCOTIA

Dalhousie University
Faculty of Arts and Science, Dept. of Math.,
Stat., and Comp. Sci.: M.S. and Ph.D. in
Math. with emphasis in Prob. and Stat.

No. of Degrees Awarded in Statistics 1984–85:
Bachelor 4, Master 2

Contact: R.P. Gupta, Prof., Dept. of Math.,
Stat., and Computer Sci., Dalhousie U.,
Halifax, N.S. B3H 4H8, CANADA. Phon
(902) 424-3595

ONTARIO

Carleton University
Faculty of Science, Dept. of Math. and Stat.:
B.Sc., B.A., M.Sc., Ph.D. in Math. with em-
phasis on Prob. and Stat.

No. of Degrees Awarded in Statistics 1984–85:
Bachelor 8, Master 5, Ph.D. 3

Contact: J.N.K. Rao, Prof. of Stat., Dept. of
Math. and Stat., Carleton U., Ottawa, Ontario K1S 5B6, CANADA. Phone (613) 231-
5500

McMaster University
Faculty of Science: B.Sc., M.Sc. in Stat.

No. of Degrees Awarded in Statistics 1984–85:
Bachelor 2, Master 4

Contact: C.W. Dunnett, Prog. Coordinator,
Dept. of Math. Sci., McMaster U., Hamilton,
Ontario L8S 4K1, CANADA. Phone (416)
525-9140 X4688

School of Graduate Studies, Graduate Program
in Statistics

Contact: Dr. C.W. Dunnett as given above.

Queen's University
Faculty of Arts and Science, Dept. of Math. &
Stat.: B.Sc., M.Sc., Ph.D. in Stat.

No. of Degrees Awarded in Statistics 1984–85:
Bachelor 2, Master 6, Ph.D. 2

Contact: H.A. Still, Ch. of Stat., Dept. of Math.
and Stat., Queen's U., Kingston, Ontario K7L
3N6, CANADA. Phone (613) 547-6146

University of Guelph
College of Physical Science, Dept. of Math. &
Stat.: B.Sc. and B.A. in Stat., Math., and Appl.
Math.; M.Sc. with emphasis in Stat. and
Appl. Math.

No. of Degrees Awarded in Statistics 1984–85:
Bachelor 51, Master 7

Contact: W.R. Smith, Ch., Dept. of Math. and
Stat., U. of Guelph, Guelph, Ontario N1G
2W1, CANADA. Phone (519) 824-4120
X2155-56

University of Ottawa
School of Science Engineering, Dept. of Math.:
M.A., M.Sc. in Math. with emphasis in Prob.
or Stat.; Ph.D. in Math. with emphasis in
Prob.

Contact: Dr. M. Alvo, Assoc. Prof., Dept. of
Math., U. of Ottawa, 585 King Edward,
Ottawa, Ontario K1N 9B4, CANADA. Phone
(613) 564-6550

University of Toronto
School of Graduate Studies, Dept. of Stat.:
M.Sc., Ph.D. in Stat., Prob. and Actuarial
Sci.

No. of Degrees Awarded in Statistics 1984–85:
Bachelor 25, Master 7, Ph.D. 2

Contact: David Brenner, Assoc. Prof. and
Grad. Coord., Dept. of Stat., Sidney Smith
Hall, U. of Toronto, 100 St. George St.,
Toronto, Ontario M5S 1A1, CANADA. Phone
(416) 978-6368

Faculty of Medicine, Dept. of Preventive Med.
and Biostat.: M.Sc. (Biostat.), Ph.D. (Biostat.)

No. of Degrees Awarded in Statistics 1984–85:
Master 1

Contact: Prof. D.F. Andrews, Dir. Grad. Pro-
gram Biostat., Dept. of Preventive Med. &
Biostat., U. of Toronto, Toronto, Ontario
M5S 1A8, CANADA. Phone (416) 978-4460

University of Waterloo
*Faculty of Mathematics, Dept. of Stat. and
Actuarial Sci.: B.Math., M.Math., Ph.D.

No. of Degrees Awarded in Statistics 1984–85:
Bachelor 21, Master 12, Ph.D. 4

Contact: J.D. Kalbfleisch, Ch., Dept. of Stat.,
U. of Waterloo, Waterloo, Ontario N2L 3G1,
CANADA. Phone (519) 888-4476

University of Western Ontario
*Faculty of Science, Dept. of Stat. and Actu-
arial Sci.: B.A./B.Sc., B.A.(Hons.), B.Sc.(Hons.),
M.Sc., Ph.D.

No. of Degrees Awarded in Statistics 1984–85:
Bachelor 15, Master 6, Ph.D. 2

Contact: Dr. I.B. MacNeill, Ch., Dept. of Stat.
& Actuarial Sci., U. of Western Ontario,
London, Ontario N6A 5B9, CANADA. Phone
(519) 679-2196

University of Windsor
Faculty of Science and Math., Dept. of Math.
and Stat.: M.Sc., Ph.D. in Stat.

No. of Degrees Awarded in Statistics 1984–85:
Master 3, Ph.D. 1

Contact: D.S. Tracy, Prof., Dept. of Math. and
Stat., U. of Windsor, Windsor, Ontario N9B
3P4, CANADA. Phone (519) 253-4232 X3035

York University
Faculty of Graduate Studies, Dept. of Math.:
M.A. in Math. with emphasis in Stat. and
Applied Prob.

No. of Degrees Awarded in Statistics 1984–85:
Master 13

Contact: G. Tourlakis, Dir., Graduate Programme in Math., York U., 4700 Keele St., North York, Ontario M3J 1P3, CANADA. Phone (416) 667-3920

QUEBEC

Concordia University
Faculty of Arts and Science, Dept. of Math.: B.A., B.Sc. in Stat., M.A. in Math.
No. of Degrees Awarded in Statistics 1983–84: Bachelor 20, Master 4
Contact: Z. Khalil, Ch., Stat. Group., Dept. of Math., Concordia U., 7141 Sherbrooke St., W., Montreal, Quebec H4B 1R6, CANADA. Phone (514) 482-0320 X729

McGill University
Faculty of Science, Dept. of Math. and Stat.: M.Sc. in Applied Stat., M.Sc. in Applied Math., Ph.D. in Math. with emphasis in Stat. & Prob.
No. of Degrees Awarded in Statistics 1984–85: Master 2
Contact: Prof. M. Herschorn, Ch., Dept. of Math. and Stat., McGill U., 805 Sherbrooke St., W., Montreal, Quebec H3A 2K6, CANADA. Phone (514) 392-8286

Universite Laval
*Faculté des Sciences et de Génie, Dept. de Math.: B.Sc. in Stat., M.Sc. in Math., Ph.D. in Math.

No. of Degrees Awarded in Statistics 1984–85:
Bachelor 17, Master 2
Contact: Robert Côté, Prof., Dept. de Math., U. Laval, Quebec, Quebec G1K 7P4, CANADA. Phone (418) 656-2973

Universite de Montréal
*Faculté des Arts et des Sciences, (F.A.S.) Dépt. de mathématiques et de statistique: B.Sc. (orientation in Stat.), M.Sc. (orientation in Stat.), Ph.D. (orientation in Stat.)
No. of Degrees Awarded in Statistics 1984–85: Bachelor 13, Master 8, Ph.D. 3
Contact: Aubert Daigneault, Ch., Dept. de Math. et de Stat., U. de Montreal, C.P. 6128, Succursale "A", Montréal, Québec H3C 3J7, CANADA. Phone (514) 343-6743
Faculté des Arts et des Sciences, Dept. d'Info. et de Recherche Operationalle: B.Sc., M.Sc., Ph.D. in O.R., with emphasis in Stat.
No. of Degrees Awarded in Statistics 1984–85: Bachelor 9, Master 4, Ph.D. 1
Contact: R. Cleroux, Dept. d'Info. et de Recherche Oper., U. de Montreal, C.P. 6128, Montreal, P.Q. H3C 3J7, CANADA. Phone (514) 343-6952

Université de Quebec à Montréal
Famille des Sciences, Dept. de Math. et Computer Sci.: M.S. (Math. Appliquées)
No. of Degrees Awarded in Statistics 1984–85: Bachelor 4, Master 2
Contact: Prof. Mazoor Ahmad, Dept. de Math. et Comp. Sci., C.P. 8888, Station A, Montreal, Quebec H3C 3P8, CANADA. Phone (514) 282-3207

References

ARTICLES

BOARDMAN, T. J. and HAHN, G. J., "The Statistician's Role in Quality Improvement," *Amstat News*, March 1985, pp. 5–8.

DEMING, W. E., "On the Distinctions between Enumerative and Analytic Surveys," *Journal of the American Statistical Association*, 48 (1953), 244–55.

———, "Principles of Professional Statistical Practice," *The Annals of Mathematical Statistics*, 36, no. 6 (December 1965), 1883–1900.

———, *"Code of Professional Conduct,"* 40, no. 2 (1972), 215–19.

———, "Report to Management—Viewpoints," *Quality Progress*, 5 (1972), 41.

———, "Economic Production," *Interfaces*, 5 (August 1975), 1–15.

———, "On Probability as a Basis for Action," *The American Statistician*, 29 (1975), 146–52.

———, "On the Use of Judgment—Samples," *Reports of Statistical Applications*, 23 (March 1976), 25–31.

———, "Improvement of Quality and Productivity Through Action by Management," *National Productivity Review* (Winter 1981–1982), pp. 12–22.

GARVIN, D. A., "Quality On the Line," *Harvard Business Review*, 83, no. 5 (September-October, 1983), 64–75.

GITLOW, A., and H. GITLOW, "Union-Management Relations: An Important Piece of the Quality Puzzle," *International Review of Economics and Business* (Milano, Italy) August, 1986.

GITLOW, H., "Definition of Quality," *Proceedings-Case Studies Seminar-Dr. Deming's Management Methods: How They Are Being Implemented in the U.S. and Abroad*, G.O.A.L., November 6, 1984, Andover, Mass., pp. 4–15.

GITLOW, H., and P. HERTZ, "Product Defects and Productivity," *Harvard Business Review* (September/October 1983), pp. 131–41.

GITLOW, H., and D. WIESNER, "Vendor Management: An Important Piece of the Quality Puzzle," *University of Miami Working Paper Series*, 1985.

JOINER, B., "The Key Role of Statisticians in the Transformation of North American Industry," *The American Statistician*, 39, no. 3 (August 1985), 224–34.

SCHERKENBACK, W. W., *The Process of Never-Ending Improvement*. Director of Statistical Methods, Ford Motor Company, Dearborn, Mich., n.d.

————, *The Transition to Continuing Improvement*. Director of Statistical Methods, Ford Motor Company, Dearborn, Mich., n.d.

————, "Performance Appraisal and Quality: Ford's New Philosophy," *Quality Progress*, April 1985.

American Statistical Association Committee on Training of Statisticians for Industry (T. J. Boardman, G. J. Hahn, W. J. Hill, R. R. Hocking, W. G. Hunter, W. H. Lawton, R. L. Ott, R. D. Snee (Chair), and W. E. Strawderman), "Preparing Statisticians for Careers in Industry: Report of the ASA Section on Statistical Education Committee on Training of Statisticians for Industry," *The American Statistician*, May 1980, Vol. 34, no. 2, pp. 65–75.

TRIBUS, M., *Deming's Way*. Cambridge, Mass.: M.I.T., Center for Advanced Engineering Study, n.d.

————, *Reducing Deming's 14 Points to Practice*. Cambridge, Mass.: M.I.T., Center for Advanced Engineering Study, June 1983.

————, *Creating the Quality Company Through Company-Wide Quality Control*. Cambridge, Mass.: M.I.T., Center for Advanced Engineering Study, October 6–7, 1983.

BOOKS

DEMING, W. E., *Out of the Crisis*. Cambridge, Mass.: M.I.T., Center for Advanced Engineering Study, 1986.

DEMING, W. E., *Quality, Productivity, and Competitive Position*. Cambridge, Mass.: M.I.T., Center for Advanced Engineering Study, 1982.

————, *Some Theory of Sampling*. New York: John Wiley & Sons, 1950. Reprinted 1984, Dover.

JURAN, J. M., *Quality Control Handbook*, 3rd ed. New York: McGraw-Hill Book Company, 1979.

MANN, N. R., *The Keys to Excellence: The Story of the Deming Philosophy*, Los Angeles, Calif.: Prestwick Books, 1985.

OUCHI, W.. *Theory Z*. Reading, Mass.: Addison-Wesley Publishing Company, 1981.

————, *The M-Form Society*. Reading, Mass.: Addison-Wesley Publishing Company, 1984.

SCHERKENBACH, W. W., *The Deming Route to Quality and Productivity: Road Maps and Roadblocks*. Rockville, Md.: Mercury Press/Fairchild Publications, 1986.

TAGUCHI, G., *On-Line Quality Control During Production*. Japanese Standards Association, 1–24, Akasaka 4-chome Minato-ku, Tokyo, 107, Japan, 1981.

TAGUCHI, G., and Y. WU, *Introduction to Off-Line Quality Control*. Central Japan Quality Control Association, 2nd ed., Toyota Bldg. 3F, 4-10-27 Meieki Nakamura-ku, Magaya, Japan, 1979.

VIDEOTAPES AND FILMS

1. *Road Map for Change—The Deming Approach* (29 minutes)

   and

2. *Road Map for Change II—The Deming Legacy* (26 minutes)

   and

3. *Management's Five Deadly Diseases* (16 minutes)
   Encyclopaedia Britannica Educational Corp.
   780 South Lapeer Road
   Lake Orion, Mich. 48035
   (800) 554-6970
   (313)693-4232 (in Michigan)

4. *The Deming Videotapes: What America's Managers Must Do to Improve Quality, Productivity, and Competitive Position* (14 video cassettes)

   and

5. *Action Plans for Implementing Quality and Productivity* (3 video cassettes—30 minutes each)

   and

6. *Chain Reaction: Quality, Productivity, Lower Cost, Capture the Market*

   and

7. *Curing the Deadly and Destructive Diseases of Management*
   Massachusetts Institute of Technology
   77 Massachusetts Avenue, Room 9-234
   Cambridge, Mass. 02139
   (617) 253-7444

8. *Nashua Conference* (30 minutes—*Excerpts from a presentation by William Conway, CEO of Nashua Corporation, to Ford executives.*

   and

9. *The Task Before Us* (10 minutes)—A review of Ford's commitment to the statistical methods of Dr. W. Edwards Deming.

   and

10. *The McCord Story* (30 minutes)—Excerpts from a presentation by the McCord Gasket Division, Ex-Cell-O Corporation, regarding their implementation of the principles advocated by Dr. W. Edwards Deming.

Ford Motor Company
Dearborn, Mich.
(313)322-4618

11. *The Teaching of Statistics in the Industrial Crisis that Confronts the Western World* (60 minutes)—Presentation by W. Edwards Deming, 1981.

and

12. *Deming and Statistics in Industry for Statisticians and for Statistical Education* (60 minutes). W. E. Deming with panel discussants, 1981.

and

13. *If Japan Can, Why Can't We?* (90 minutes)NBC-TV documentary (1981)
American Statistical Association
806 15th Street, N.W.
Washington, D.C. 20005
(202) 393-3253

SEMINARS

Methods for Management of Productivity and Quality, presented by Dr. Deming. For further information contact:
George Washington University
School of Engineering and Applied Science
Continuing Education Program
Washington, D.C. 20052
(202)676–7219
(800)424–9773 (USA)
(800)535–4567 (Canada)

LOCAL DEMING USERS GROUPS

For information on local Deming Users Groups telephone the George Washington University School of Continuing Education at (800)424–9773.